Enabling Engagements

Enabling Engagements

Edmund Spenser and the Poetics of Patronage

JUDITH OWENS

McGill-Queen's University Press
Montreal & Kingston · London · Ithaca

© McGill-Queen's University Press 2002
ISBN 0-7735-2331-6

Legal deposit first quarter 2002
Bibliothèque nationale du Québec

Printed in Canada on acid-free paper that is
100% ancient forest free (100% post-consumer
recycled), processed chlorine free, and printed
with vegetable-based, low VOC inks.

This book has been published with the help of
a grant from the Humanities and Social Sciences
Federation of Canada, using funds provided by
the Social Sciences and Humanities Research
Council of Canada.

McGill-Queen's University Press acknowledges the
financial support of the Government of Canada
through the Book Publishing Industry Development
Program (BPIDP) for its publishing activities. It also
acknowledges the support of the Canada Council
for the Arts for its publishing program.

**National Library of Canada Cataloguing in
Publication Data**

Owens, Judith
 Enabling engagements: Edmund Spenser and the
poetics of patronage
 Includes bibliographical references and index.
 ISBN 0-7735-2331-6
 1. Spenser, Edmund, 1552?–1599 – Criticism and
interpretation. 2. Authors and patrons – England –
History – 16th century. I. Title.
PR2363.094 2002   821'.3   C2001-903331-1

Typeset in Palatino 10.5/13
by Caractéra inc., Quebec City

to Gilbert, Madeleine, and Adriana

Contents

    Preface   ix

    Acknowledgments   xi

1 Contexts   3

2 *The Shepheardes Calender*   40

3 Commendatory Verses   69

4 The Dedicatory Sonnets   88

5 Ralegh in *The Faerie Queene* III   110

6 Conclusion   133

    Notes   143

    Works Cited   163

    Index   177

Preface

This study emerges from my interest in Spenser's laureate ambitions, subject position, nationalism, and Irish tenure, concerns which have been treated individually in recent criticism but not yet brought together. My lens for focusing this cluster of concerns is patronage. My primary texts are *Complaints*, *The Shepheardes Calender*, and the 1590 *Faerie Queene*.

I maintain the related convictions that Spenser grapples intensely with the moral imperatives of fashioning self and nation; that patronal relations figure prominently in such fashioning; and that Spenser exercises a strong sense of agency within the potential restrictions of patronage and courtly culture. I aim to demonstrate that Spenser's engagements with patrons and promoters elicit the whole range of his poetic powers – which is to say that Spenser's poetics is highly attuned to socio-political currents. I focus closely on effects of language and line, image and analogy, voice and theme, in order to provide a scale sufficiently precise to gauge immediately felt pressures of patronage, an aim which to date has not been pursued comprehensively.

Given this nexus of concerns, my study necessarily enters current debates regarding the degrees and kinds of freedoms available to the Elizabethan subject. I contend that Spenser imagines into being, for both private subject and Tudor citizen, and for both poet and hero, positions of strength and independence. My findings thus encourage the supposition that the Elizabethan subject assumed agency within a wide variety of the institutions by which the state incorporated its citizens. My study also invites us to review Elizabethan processes of cultural commodification. Students of early modern culture, literature, and theatre have begun to chart the counter-currents which lead away from the assumption of courtly hegemony, largely by focusing on the resources of "popular" culture. My argument similarly challenges the assumption of courtly hegemony, but by mapping counter-currents in a poet long considered to be pre-eminently courtly. I argue that Spenser thoroughly resists the centripetal pull of the court in fashioning himself, his laureate poetics, and his nationalism. My emphasis on Spenser's Irish tenure in particular allows me to reread Spenser's nationalism as less court-bound than has been customarily supposed. Especially through his close engagement with Ralegh, the foremost patron of the 1590 *Faerie Queene*, Spenser offers a reformist vision of empire which runs athwart official Tudor designs.

That Spenser repeatedly stakes his ground so surely even within the potential confinements of patronage speaks at once to his boldness of enterprise, tenacity of purpose, and amplitude of imagination.

Acknowledgments

To examine patronage is to be pleasantly reminded of the many and salutary ways in which family, friends, and colleagues countenance one's academic work.

I am grateful for the encouragement, support, and advice I have received in writing this book. Myron Turner, whose teaching of Spenser and Sidney first drew me, dazzled, to the sixteenth century, and under whose supervision this study began, returned me repeatedly – and always with new ways of seeing – to the poetry. Judith Weil, whose reading of this study at a crucial early stage encouraged me to consider the wider applications of my approach, has always insisted, by example and precept, that I rethink my positions. Arthur Kinney, who read this study in an early, much different, form, responded – with characteristic generosity – to its possibilities. Alexander Gordon, who also read an early version, posed challenging questions from his vantage point in French studies. I am likewise grateful to the anonymous readers for the press and the Humanities Federation for instructive comments, to John Zucchi for his expeditious handling of the manuscript, to Judy Williams for her sharp and consistent eye, to Joan McGilvray for her unfailing courtesy, to Douglas Brooks for the chance to present a portion of chapter 4 at the Sixteenth Century Conference in Toronto, and to William Oram for encouraging my reading of Spenser's Ralegh.

Robert Finnegan and John Rempel, colleagues at the University of Manitoba, commented generously on portions of what became the final version; beyond that, they have engaged me over the years with many and spirited hallway conversations. Faye McIntyre, the staunchest and most patient of friends, has followed the progress of this study with much greater attention than anyone has the right to ask from someone whose own academic interests lie elsewhere; for this, as for much else in our friendship, I am grateful. Faye, Donna Campbell, Val Clemens, Joan Dougherty, Barbara Huber, Yukiko Imamura, Natalie Johnson, and Phyllis Portnoy have at various times and from various places formed a group on whom I rely for encouragement or commiseration as needed, and often over decadent desserts. I have also been sustained and inspired, beyond the bounds of this book and more than they know, by the teaching and friendship of Jack Woodbury and George Toles.

I am grateful, finally, to my family – to my parents, Harold Owens and the late Ruth Guinn Owens, for a lifetime of unstinting support; to my sister, Susanne Moroz, for timely help with family matters; to my brother, Kent, and sister-in-law, Myrna, for reminding me of life outside my borders.

I am beyond measure grateful to my husband, Gilbert Chartrand, for his support, expectations, and occasional prodding, and to our daughters, Madeleine and Adriana, for bringing me joy every single day and for helping me to keep all things in perspective.

Enabling Engagements

1 Contexts

To the most vertuous, and beautifull Lady,
the Lady Carew.

Ne may I, without blot of endlesse blame,
   You fairest Lady leave out of this place,
   But with remembraunce of your gracious name,
   Wherewith that courtly garlond most ye grace,
And deck the world, adorne these verses base:
   Not that these few lines can in them comprise
   Those glorious ornaments of hevenly grace,
   Wherewith ye triumph over feeble eyes,
And in subdued harts do tyranyse:
   For thereunto doth need a golden quill,
   And silver leaves, them rightly to devise,
   But to make humble present of good will:
Which whenas timely meanes it purchase may,
   In ampler wise it selfe will forth display. [1]

Edmund Spenser's address to Lady Carew, with whom he claimed kinship, brings together instructively several of the matters informing my study.[2] Lady Carew is one of only two women to be individually addressed in the sequence of dedicatory sonnets appended to the 1590 *Faerie Queene*. (The other is the Countess of

Pembroke, sister of Philip Sidney, and her presence seems primarily designed to permit Spenser's invoking the spirit of Sidney.) Since Lady Carew was not the most prominent of the women in Elizabeth's court, her inclusion in a socially astute sequence of dedications seems intended to promote Spenser's personal affiliation in a public, even "national," forum.[3] How are we to construe this forwardness? The short answer is that Spenser's loyalties generate their own decorum, a fact which militates against our accepting the view of Spenser, still prominently espoused, as the Elizabethan apologist par excellence.[4] Spenser never simply toes the party line. His responses to social and political exigencies are always imaginative – that is, uncategorical – and, at least from his perspective, morally responsible, as we shall see.

Another answer is suggested by Spenser's declaration that he includes Lady Carew to avoid "blot of endlesse blame." Because Spenser so consciously fashioned himself a writer, "blot" implies not simply "blemish" but also "ink blot" and "blotted out" – meanings which indicate how completely Spenser identifies himself with his writing. Spenser's metaphor thus also underlines the close connection between his personal loyalties – that is, loyalties without overtly political ends – and his sense of identity. We shall see that, especially in *The Shepheardes Calender*, Spenser constructs personal autonomy and inwardness largely in resistance to the public aspects of laureateship.

That Spenser feels extreme blameworthiness would be his were he to neglect Lady Carew directs us to consider his forwardness in yet another light – as evidence of his feudal sensibility.[5] We shall find that Spenser frequently configures both his clientage and his sense of corporate citizenship in relation to noble houses rather than to the Queen, resisting in this way courtly hegemony, drawing instead (and drawing on) alternative structures of power and authority.

Spenser's foregrounding of personal affiliation raises still more issues, especially in view of the fact that he takes his patron Sir Walter Ralegh thoroughly to task for construing *his* relationship with Queen Elizabeth as personal and private, as in effect outside professional courtiership. Spenser's censure extends particularly to Ralegh's adopting, after the fashion of Elizabeth's court, Petrarchan poetics and postures. What then do we make of Spenser's uncritical assumption of Petrarchism in his sonnet to

Lady Carew? The answer to this question is, in part, that Lady Carew is not the Queen: Ralegh's relationship with Elizabeth is political in ways that Spenser's with Lady Carew is not. Spenser can submit to Lady Carew's "tyranny" with relative impunity, because such submission is simply a compliment, because not much is really at stake, and because both parties surely recognize that Spenser's subjection is merely seeming. Spenser in fact manoeuvres freely within the apparent confinement of Petrarchism, playing wittily on Lady Carew's maiden name of Spencer to place himself at court and suggesting good-naturedly in the ambivalence of lines 12–13 that his good will towards Lady Carew is directly connected to her providing him with "timely means." It is not at all evident that Petrarchan courtiership offered similar latitude to the petitioner in Elizabeth's court.[6] In Spenser's estimation, it emphatically did not. Spenser, we shall see, objects to Petrarchan courtiership on grounds that are epistemological, philosophical, political, and, especially, Irish.

That such nuances inflect a sonnet forming just one cog in a larger dedicatory program helps point the complexity – indeed, even the suppleness – of Spenser's patronal relations. Recent critical attention to literary patronage has done much to fine-tune our understanding of a system that was at once pervasive and strained to the point of collapse, simultaneously cultivated and reviled. Armed with the conviction that literature does political work and taking its cue from new historicist interest in how literary patronage encodes the operations of power, this criticism has weighed, in particular, the socio-cultural effects of patronage – among which are to be counted, as Catherine Bates has recently remarked, "intense speculation about the worth of poetry" and "rigorous reassessment of the poet."[7] Critical revision has also encouraged the assumption that patronage fosters, not just the material production of literature, but also the production of literary meaning.[8]

We will see that Spenser's engagements with patrons mediate with particular subtlety, acumen, and audacity the anxieties and aspirations – both personal and cultural – investing the role of the poet. We will see also that Spenser's engagements with patrons and promoters elicit a wide range of his poetic powers, that literary meaning results from immediately felt pressures of patronage.

Spenser's address to Lady Carew alerts us not only to the dynamics of patronage but also to the potential for give-and-take within early modern structures of authority in general. Layered into Spenser's address to Lady Carew are indications that both the private Elizabethan subject and the corporate citizen could assume agency – and did so – within various structures of authority.[9] All avenues did not lead to or from the Queen and court. In stressing Spenser's resistance to the centripetal pull of the court, my study necessarily contributes to current debates regarding the degree of flexibility and freedom available to the corporate citizen in early modern England.[10] To locate Spenser's work more strategically in this broader context, I would like here to consider the challenges to institutional authority posed by the following wide-ranging and disparate group of practices, discourses, and texts: royal entertainments, pedagogy, forest law, and dramatic and lyric forests. Such a heterogenous grouping requires a word of explanation.

My reasons for bringing together royal entertainments and pedagogy are both general and specific. First, since they represent, respectively, aristocratic and middling social echelons, royal entertainments and pedagogical practices accommodate between them a wide range of subject positions; second, the important shaping forces of Spenser's career include his connections, however tangential, with aristocratic culture, and his schooling under the prominent Richard Mulcaster. I will not be arguing for direct lines of influence, but rather suggesting that, in articulating equivocal relationships with institutional authority, both pedagogy and aristocratic entertainments support our finding in Spenser as well the dynamics of challenge. My foray into forest law and literary forests proceeds from my conviction that at the intersection of law and landscape lies ground fruitful for analyses of both structures of authority – reproduced perforce in legal discourse – and constructions of that authority in imaginative literature. When this discourse treats a landscape feature – the forest – that figures prominently and materially in the lives of many early modern English subjects *and* resonates with extraordinary richness in much imaginative literature, the ground is especially productive. Again, the relevance to Spenser emerges both generally, in the way just sketched, and specifically, in that Spenser's literary forests often assume political valences and in that Spenser's land-holding in Ireland necessarily engaged him in legal constructions of landscapes. Moreover, the very frequency of "forest" as a literary trope makes it an exceptionally useful analytical tool, one which can cue us to often overlooked ways in which literature engages questions of authority. Accordingly, I will briefly examine Shakespeare's uses of the forest trope in *Henry IV, Part 1* and in *As You Like It*, as well as Wyatt's forest in "The long love."

By adducing this array of authors, texts, and practices – a sample sufficiently ranged across time, genres, and discourses to assume representative rather than eccentric force – I hope not only to demonstrate that early modern structures of authority admitted several kinds and degrees of freedom, but also to provide a context within which to gauge quite precisely Spenser's inventions of agency.

In examining the political dynamics of royal entertainments, I have chosen to concentrate on two of the entertainments offered Elizabeth on her progress in the summer of 1592, those presented at Bisham, the home of Lady Russell, and those at Rycote, the home of the Norrises. The 1592 date aligns these devices with the height of Spenser's career, their themes and issues parallel those with which Spenser grappled, and their sponsors had some connection to Spenser.[11] Additionally, the connections and influence of the Russell and Norris families help to illustrate that sovereign-subject relations must be plotted along complex, even convoluted, lines.

The Bisham entertainment at the home of Lady Russell celebrates Elizabeth's power and transformative presence while also demonstrating that Elizabeth's rule is and must be balanced with the strengths of the noble household.[12] Figures in all of the vignettes and speeches both cede authority to Elizabeth and retain, or reclaim, at least a portion of the ceded power, thus participating in a mutually constitutive sovereign-subject relationship. The wild man of the woods who greets Elizabeth upon her arrival declares himself reformed by her – "my untamed thoughts waxe gentle, and I feele in myselfe civility" – and prepared to follow her whose rule now supplants that of such woodland gods as Pan and Sylvanus: "Your Majesty on my knees will I followe, bearing this Club, not as a Salvage, but to beate downe those that are" (132). The wild man's assumption of a policing role (and his club identifies him as a whiffler, or crowd controller)[13] is double-edged: it attests to Elizabeth's executive control of force while also pointing the ever-present need to enforce subjection. Indeed, the environs of Bisham seem to be bristling with unruly subjects requiring not only the wild man's club but also Pan's intervention. Reformed, like the wild man, by Elizabeth's arrival, Pan promises that "[d]uring [Elizabeth's] abode, no theft shall be in the woods; in the fields no noise; in the vallies no spies: myselfe will keepe all safe" (135). While Elizabeth may be responsible for keeping the peace of foreign lands – one speaker reports that "one hande she stretcheth to Fraunce, to weaken Rebels; the other to Flaunders, to strengthen Religion" (134) – domestic peace is enforced by her subjects. In particular, the Bisham entertainment reminds Elizabeth that her safe progress through this landscape depends upon the vigorous and vigilant policing of the district. The promise of obeisance is thus also an assertion of autonomy. Implicit in this expressing of fealty is a demand for independence from sovereign, a point made humorously when the wild man offers his services by kneeling to the Queen and saying "on my knees will I followe, bearing this Club" (132). The posture of obeisance conflicts directly with the performance of duty, since on his knees the wild man could neither follow Elizabeth with much alacrity nor employ his club effectively! The wild man needs freedom to rise to a show of force.

Participants in a second strand of the Bisham entertainment similarly both defer to Elizabeth's control – here her power to reform wayward sexuality – and show that they already exercise some of that power themselves. Very likely designed to bring to Elizabeth's attention, and perhaps to promote to her court as Maids of Honour, Lady Russell's two daughters – the older of whom was a godchild of Queen Elizabeth – the Bisham entertainment emphasizes the virtues of chastity, a condition Elizabeth certainly encouraged in the women and men of her court.[14] The two daughters show themselves to be eminently qualified to serve Elizabeth with honour: dressed as shepherdesses, they ward off the importunate advances of a randy Pan, proving wittily and scornfully immune to his ignoble and self-serving posturing. Further, their rebuff of the lusty, dissembling Pan urges reform to all men minded like Pan to pursue lewd ambitions. The young women believe that to reveal Elizabeth to Pan will make him "surcease [his] suit ... and honour virginity" (134). Pan is, of course, duly reformed. "Give me leave to die with wondering," he says, and the ubiquitous pun on die as orgasm indicates just how thoroughly his libidinous energies have been chastened into obeisance (135). While it is the presence of Elizabeth which effects this reform, the two young women have nevertheless shown themselves more than able to resist Pan on their own. The stressing of chastity, while conventional in entertainments of the period, seems also to be politically canny, in view of Sir Walter Ralegh's being then in disgrace because of his clandestine marriage to Elizabeth Throckmorton. In late spring or early summer of 1592, Ralegh's marriage was discovered and by July of that year he was imprisoned in the Tower, unable to accompany the Queen, in his role as Captain of the Guard, on her current progress.[15] In assuming such topical point, the Bisham entertainment takes a calculated risk. Elizabeth, who could, and sometimes did, take umbrage if she believed she was being criticized or offered unsolicited advice, might well regard the entertainment's touting of chastity as an all too pointed reminder that her trust in Ralegh and Elizabeth Throckmorton had been misplaced, had proved an error in judgment. That Bisham runs this risk testifies to the strength of its initiative.[16]

The double-edged quality of Bisham's praise of Elizabeth continues unabated to the end of the entertainment when Ceres, like Pan before her, cedes her sovereignty and, further, ascribes to Elizabeth superior generative force. As Elizabeth nears the house, she meets "Ceres with her nymphes in a Harvest carte" wearing a "crown of wheat eares with a jewell" (135). Ceres' song, which flaunts her own reproductive power, marks female fertility and sexual appeal as intolerably presumptuous. When it confronts the virgin Queen, such pride must fall – as evidently Ceres literally does at the conclusion of her song:

> Cynthia shal be Ceres Mistres,
>   But first my carre shall rive asunder.
> Helpe, Phoebus, helpe; my fall is suddaine;
> Cynthia, Cynthia, must be sovereigne. (136)

Ceres acknowledges her erstwhile godhead to have been "feined" by poets, yields her crown to Elizabeth, and praises Elizabeth as supremely generative because the source of all: "To your Majesty ... we doe all Homage, accounting nothing ours but what comes from you." Elizabeth's very presence here has "added many daies to [Lady Russell's] life," a direct result of the "infinite joies [Lady Russell] conceyves in her heart" in response to Elizabeth's visit (136). But Lady Russell's becoming the mother of "infinite joies" does not, presumably, override her acutal motherhood; her daughters were, after all, front and centre in the entertainment, and her son is Elizabeth's host. Nor does Ceres' fall obliterate the presence of a fully laden cart. Thus, even while being, no doubt sincerely, celebrated as sovereign, Elizabeth everywhere at Bisham meets with signs of her subjects' autonomy.

A learned, eminent, and formidably determined woman, Lady Russell might well be expected to sponsor an entertainment which stresses familial independence, virtue, and initiative, while formulating these strengths in a tone of assumed intimacy with court and sovereign. Elizabeth Russell, Dowager – as she often signed herself following the death of her second husband – was connected by birth and by her marriages to the centres of courtliness and power. Her father, Anthony Cooke, had been tutor to Edward VI; one of her sisters, Mildred, married William Cecil, Lord Burghley; another sister, Anne, married Nicholas Bacon; Elizabeth Cooke married, first, Thomas Hoby, whose translation of Castiglione's *The Courtier* helped bring courtliness to England, and, second, John, Lord Russell, who was heir to the Earl of Bedford but who died before his father, preventing Lady Russell's rise to countess.

From the time of Thomas Hoby's death in 1566, much of Lady Russell's energy was directed toward the promotion of family interests, a campaign which ranged from erecting monuments in commemoration of her dead to the securing of marriage prospects for her surviving children – two sons from her marriage to Hoby and two daughters from her marriage to Russell, the daughters whose interests are especially advanced by the Bisham entertainment. Property and marriage matters occasionally required Lady Russell to deal directly with Queen Elizabeth. The lease of Donnington Castle from the Crown, which Lady Russell felt she had to retain to provide for her daughter Bess and which embroiled her in legal, as well as physical, wrangling with the nobleman granted the right of actual residence in the castle, apparently cost Lady Russell dearly in gifts to the Queen of gowns, fine cloth, and hats.[17] When in 1600 Queen Elizabeth delayed in naming a day for the wedding of Lady Russell's daughter Anne, Lady Russell approached Elizabeth in person, with apparent success – a day was named, and the Queen attended the wedding, which proved to be *the* London social event of that summer. More often, though, Lady Russell sought the intervention of her powerful brother-in-law, Lord Burghley, or his son, the likewise prominent Robert Cecil. In trying to negotiate a marriage for her son Thomas, Lady Russell persuaded Lord Burghley to write to the guardians of a wealthy and recently widowed heiress. She also suggested to her son that the young woman in question – whose guardians had other plans for her marriage – be more or less abducted and brought to where the Russells could press their suit. In all her endeavours, Lady Russell remained acutely conscious of what was due to her and her family, a preoccupation which fully informs the entertainments offered to Elizabeth.

The challenges to court- and sovereign-centredness posed by the September 1592 entertainment at Rycote emerge from the masculine, militaristic ethos characterizing its devices. From the start at Rycote, soldiering is opposed to eloquence and extolled as the most loyal profession. Having just come from Oxford, where she was entertained for six days, Elizabeth is met by Lord Norris with these words: "Vouchsafe, dread Soveraigne, after so much smooth speeches of Muses, to heare a rough hewen tale of a souldier: wee use not with wordes to amplifie our conceites, and to pleade faith by figures, but by deedes to shew the loyalty of our harts, and to make it good with our lives" (168). Not simply an apology for taciturnity, Norris's greeting suggests that eloquence might in fact constitute a dangerous excess in the citizen; to "amplify" conceits could well be to enlarge the subject unduly. In contrast to self-amplifying words, soldiers' deeds constitute them as loyal and faithful subjects. Further, speechlessness is offered as the response due to sovereignty. Entering the garden the second day, Elizabeth is met by music and this request from Lord Norris: "Pardon, dread Sovereraigne, the greatness of my presumption, who, having nothing to say, must follow still to wonder" (169). Ambiguous syntax permits our understanding stillness of the tongue as the very precondition for wonder. Far from a sign of presumption, therefore, silence is an emptying out of the subject, who can then be filled with sovereign wonder.

That nearly every recommendation of silence at Rycote comes armed with an apology, however, shows an edgy awareness of just how easily silence might be misconstrued as malfeasance, an awareness, in turn, of how much the militaristic ethos diverges from the norm of Elizabethan courtiership. The Rycote entertainment presents yet another gloss on contemporary courtiership in its light-hearted scorning of love. One of the letters heard by Elizabeth during her stay (a missive ostensibly opened and read aloud by mistake) represents soldiers as inconstant in love but thereby constant in service to the sovereign. Thus, at Rycote, the two mainstays of the Petrarchan courtiership favoured in Elizabeth's court – eloquence and the discourse of love – appear as disruptions of fealty.

Participants at Rycote not only scant these court-centred tropes of loyalty but also couch assertiveness in their professions of fealty. Son Thomas Norris, for example, sends a letter from Ireland which barely disguises discontent with his ten-years' absence from England. Moreover, his sending as a token a bejewelled Irish weapon, his affixing a motto in Irish, and his employing as a messenger an "Irish lacqué" become pointed reminders of his power to reduce – to ornamentation and to his purposes – potentially unruly Irish subjects. The point is made especially trenchant by Norris's strategic use of the Irish language. First, the Irish motto attached to the Irish weapon would have to have been translated for Elizabeth as "I fly only for my Soveraigne," a fact which seriously attenuates the connection between sovereign and this military officer (169). Second, in employing an Irish messenger to deliver the "wish of an English heart," Norris predicts that the messenger will not speak, explaining the silence thus: "I can scarce can write for joy; and it is likely this lacqué cannot speak for wondering. If he doe not, this is all that I should say, that my life is my dueties bondman; dutie my faiths soveraigne" (169). Built into this apology for the lacqué's silence is the distinct threat of insubordination. It may be wonder that stops the messenger's tongue; it may also be that his English is inadequate to express the "loyalty of an English heart." But given the frequency with which writers assumed a direct link between tongue and heart, Captain Norris's implication may be that the messenger does not express loyalty because he does not feel it.[18] Furthermore, while the Queen's command of this Irishman's loyalty and service may be thus tenuous, Captain Norris has clearly established his own command over him. Service in Ireland, it would seem, has provided Norris with an arena in which to act independently of Elizabeth – a circumstance also hinted at in Norris's declaring that it was only by chance that he heard his sovereign would be visiting his parents' home: "It is saide, the winde is inconstant: I am gladde it is; otherwise had not I heard that I most wished, and least looked for … [that] her Majesty would bee at Rycort" (169). If news of, and from, Elizabeth reaches Ireland with such inconstancy, Elizabeth's servants in Ireland must, it follows, proceed with at least some independence and initiative.

Three other letters – from sons Edward, John, and Henry, and delivered with, respectively, a key, a sword, and a truncheon – similarly balance professions of duty with insinuations of strength. These letters arrive from men who are either already, or about to embark, on military service abroad, in Flanders or Brittany. All three letters implicitly oppose personal attendance on the Queen to the performance of duty, and in doing so highlight the sender's exercising of agency in choosing *not* to be at Rycote during the Queen's visit.[19]

A final feature of the Rycote entertainment which counters court-centredness is its assumption of patrilineal imperatives. Rycote represents the Norris sons as having, quite rightfully, usurped their father's place and role. Old Norris's greeting of Elizabeth includes the disclaimer that he would yield to Elizabeth "my horse, mine armour, my shielde, my sworde," but his sons have taken them (168). Omitting any reference to court, sovereign, or state, this account of the Norris sons' careers establishes heroic enterprise (of the kind valued and deemed still necessary in post-Armada England) as the product of the noble household and a feudal dynamic.[20] Moreover, taken together, the four sons' letters, coming as they do from three military hotpoints of the day, serve as eloquent reminders of just how much Elizabeth needs the particular talents of the Norris men.

Lord Norris might well have had more personal reasons for offering entertainment to Elizabeth that eschewed courtly and court-centred tropes of power. His father, an intimate of Henry VIII's court, accused of being a lover of Anne Boleyn, had been executed in 1536. Queen Elizabeth is reputed to have believed him and her mother innocent, and to have considered Norris's execution – and his steadfast refusal to confess – a sacrifice on behalf of her mother, and accordingly to have subsequently extended favour to the Norris family. In view of this history, the stressing, in the Rycote entertainment, of silence as fealty takes on still more pointed meaning, as does the scorning of Petrarchan love as a figure for courtiership. The Norrises had also experienced at closer hand some of the lesser vagaries of court politics: ten years before the Rycote entertainment, Queen Elizabeth's expected visit to Rycote on that year's progress had not occurred, because – at least so Lady Norris maintained – the Queen had been persuaded by Leicester and Hatton to take another route. Given the considerable costs and inconveniences to the host of preparing for a royal visit and given the political importance attached to royal visits, the pre-emption of a visit was no slight matter on the political landscape. Careful to prevent the suggestion that the cancelled visit implied the suspicion of disloyalty on the part of the Norrises, Leicester reported that Lord and Lady Norris were "a hearty noble couple as ever I saw towards her highness."[21]

To argue that aristocratic entertainments challenged court- and sovereign-centredness is not to translate noble households into sites of subversion. Indeed, the subversion-containment model of early modern political culture has been thoroughly revamped of late to allow for more flexible readings of authority structures.[22] What Bisham and Rycote do demonstrate is that aristocratic subjects could imagine for themselves positions of relative strength and independence.[23] The very ease of these assumptions of strength presupposes a political milieu accustomed to considerable give and take, a climate in which both hosts and Queen could, as Mary Hill Cole observes, further their respective "agendas."[24] In her study of the progresses of Elizabeth I, Cole has recently demonstrated that the Queen – always parsimonious – remained committed to progresses in spite of the expense and inconvenience because she believed they helped her to govern by reminding participants and observers of her authority, by fostering an image of her as accessible and loved, by increasing her knowledge of local matters, and by keeping courtiers, councillors, and petitioners offbalance and so subject more completely to her dictates. Elizabeth, that is, relied on progresses to articulate royal prerogative. My reading of Bisham and Rycote emphasizes that royal entertainments articulated the hosts' prerogatives, expectations, and strengths just as fully.

To turn to discourses and practices more removed from the immediate political arena is to discover similar elasticity, a finding which suggests that, at several levels, early modern England accommodated a range of responses to institutional authorities. Richard Mulcaster's career and treatises offer a case in point. Eminent pedagogue, headmaster at Merchant Taylors' School and then St Paul's, Mulcaster regularly challenged authority, both ideologically and materially. In his 1581 treatise *Positions*, for example, Mulcaster justifies his handling of scholarly precedents, explaining at length that he will not simply adduce the authority of other writers on his topic. His diction and rhythms sustain even broader socio-political application: "Mastering the circumstance," he claims, "is the only rule that wise men live by." "It is not enough," he concludes, "to rule the world, to allege authorities; but to range authorities, which be not above the world, by the rule of the world, is the wise man's line."[25] The submerged claims here are large: for lineage (dynastic? social? political?) Mulcaster substitutes the line of the scholar's pen; for sovereignty, the ruled page.

Mulcaster's relationship with the structures of state authority thus adumbrated emerges as decidedly equivocal, even presumptuous. On the one hand, he firmly subordinates his pedagogical enterprise to the exigencies of corporate life. In considering what kind of pupil will prove "the fittest subject for learning in a monarchy" (105), for example, Mulcaster draws the analogy between school and state to argue that the child who remains obedient to "school orders," or who at least bears without repining the penalties for insubordination, will prove the ideal citizen. On the other hand, in representing pupils' obedience to the schoolmaster as a rehearsal for subjection to the monarch, Mulcaster necessarily represents the schoolmaster as a surrogate sovereign.[26] And at a particularly emphatic point in his argument about the judicious use of authorities, Mulcaster implicitly compares the relation between "truth" and writers to that between Elizabeth and her courtiers, saying that truth is the "lady and mistress whose authority and credit" entitles writers; he even ascribes Elizabeth's motto, "semper eadem" (always the same), to "truth," whom he extols as "still one" (43). More pragmatically, Mulcaster grants almost exclusively to the schoolmaster the task of choosing which "wits" should remain in school and which should be encouraged to take up a trade, thus giving to the schoolmaster a large role in the fashioning of corporate citizens.

The rhetorical supplanting of Elizabeth's rule and the assumption of pre-eminence in creating citizens do not just show Mulcaster's ability to think himself and his profession into a position of relative autonomy, but also, arguably, reflect some chafing against the restraints of subjection. Mulcaster's depiction of the ideal citizen in a monarchy, for example, suggests the extent to which this citizen must dissemble: his "natural towardness" must show itself to orderly, and with such modesty, as it shall soon appear to have no loftiness of mind, no aspiring ambition, no odious comparisons joined withal" (105). Behind this caution may well lie Mulcaster's own contentions with authorities over matters of school jurisdiction. Ambitious, irascible, and strong-willed, Mulcaster frequently ran athwart the governing boards, first of Merchant Taylors' School, and then of St Paul's. Notwithstanding his insistence in *Positions*, for example, that the number of scholars must be "restrained," Mulcaster regularly and in contravention of school statutes took into his home extra students, no doubt to augment his livelihood.[27]

Mulcaster's promoting of relative autonomy remains fundamentally self-interested; it does not extend to a wish for more generalized independence and social mobility. Indeed, what surfaces as an arrogation of authority in Mulcaster becomes at the same time a shoring up against inundation from the "multitudes" who seek advanced schooling. It is precisely the schoolmaster's authority which helps to "restrain" the number of scholars permitted to advance. Since the good of the country takes precedence over any one individual's desires to advance sons, not all who "throng thitherward" may continue in schooling "because of the inconvenience defeating other trades" (94). While Mulcaster's call for limits rests explicitly on premises about the "good of the country," his argument evinces some anxiety about maintaining distinctions between those who are learned and those who have acquired merely a show of learning. Although he would give to the "restrained" child the "skill to write and to read" (96), he "dare not venture to allowe so many the Latin tongue or any other language," not only because such an acquirement would breed discontent with low status, but also because those whose tongues are so trained may attract privileges which Mulcaster feels should go only to the learned. Mulcaster frames this objection obliquely, arguing that "it is not the tongue, but the treasure of learning and knowledge, which is laid up in the tongue, whereunto [the unlearned] never came, which giveth the tongue *credit* and the speaker *authority*" (97; my emphasis).

Mulcaster's discrediting of the tongue in favour of hidden treasure, his devaluing the merely outward in favour of the inward and immaterial, distinguishes his pedagogical project from that of a near-contemporary, Francis Clement. In *The Petie Schole* (1587), a work necessarily addressed to a wider readership than is Mulcaster's *Positions* in that Clement treats "petty" rather than grammar schools, Clement emphasizes pronunciation, thus crediting the tongue and speech over Mulcaster's "line."[28] In his prescriptions on spelling and punctuation, for example, Clement frequently refers these matters to questions of the breath.[29]

Clement and Mulcaster can be further opposed in ways which illuminate their very different assumptions about subject formation. Clement, for instance, stresses the speed and ease with which spelling can be mastered by "diligent reading over [his] few rules" (53-4), and promises nothing less than "marvaile at [the] sodaine change" (54). The title page claims that Clement's method will "enable ... a child to read perfectly within one moneth" (49). Mulcaster, by contrast, time and again insists upon the importance of "ripeness," of "readiness," stressing that learning cannot be rushed, that indeed time may give a sharp edge to a wit which had appeared dull. His asseveration that learning is like a "treasure" laid up, something with the strength to "shore up the person, because it is incorporate in the person, till the soul dislodge" (94), indicates that, for him, the scholar is informed by learning; for Mulcaster, subjects are formed through continuous and extended submission to the rule and lines of the master and book. Marvellous conversion of the kind promised by Clement would undermine Mulcaster's entire program of subject formation, not least, one suspects, because the speedy processing of students would cut into the schoolmaster's revenues as well attenuate the master's authority. The conversion promised by Clement also carries with it what would appear from Mulcaster's position to be a potentially explosive social charge. Through Clement's prescriptions for writing and spelling, scholars – even heretofore ill-taught pupils – might learn "to write true English," an accomplishment that, in "bettering" them, might elide distinctions between these pupils and "wise men" and even afford some advantage to the former:

As I covet an ende to all ignorant teaching, so I wish that such as have erste bene so taught, and never bettered by longer continuance, might now at the length (counting no time too late) helpe that by rule of due spelling, which tofore they could never cope and compasse in writing, I meane to write true English. The want whereof in wise men hath bene willingly confessed (53).

"Wisdom" – the incorporated treasure which in Mulcaster is a guarantor of class distinctions and privileges – becomes in Clement's formulation a far more transferable and elastic ascription. Such differences between treatises written within a decade of one another should serve as another caution against assuming hegemony in the Elizabethan state and in the means by which it produced and sustained its corporate subjects.

To turn to discourse of quite another kind – that concerning forest law – is likewise to find flexibility, and so to strengthen the supposition that early modern institutions accommodated contest and resistance. By Spenser's day, "forest" and "foresters" were long-established legal terms denoting territories and offices constituted under "forest law," legislation formally abrogated only in 1971. Introduced into England by the Norman kings and variously sharpened or moderated by their successors, forest law was designed to preserve forests – that is, areas of "woody grounds and fruitfull pastures" – in order to sustain "wild beasts and fowles in the safe protection of the king for his princely delight and pleasure."[30] Forest law, that is, primarily protected royal (and subsequently also aristocratic) prerogative. Legally construed, forests thus invite examination in small compass of early modern structures of authority.

Reviewing the history of the laws, John Manwood notes that the king "then might and may also make a Forest in every place where hee pleaseth" (Preface). In practice, however, monarchs from the time of Henry III frequently made or were forced to make concessions to their subjects and even sometimes to disafforest territory. And indeed Manwood suggests that from its inception (which Manwood erroneously ascribes to Canute) forest law instantiated certain rights of subjects. According to Manwood, prior to Canute all the beasts and fowl of England belonged to the king. In establishing laws of the forest, Canute decreed that "every free man [could] take his owne vert and venison ... upon his owne land" (Preface).

Forest law provided often stringent penalties for such offences as hunting the king's game, permitting one's swine to eat the acorns of forest trees, cutting up sod, felling trees for firewood or lumber, uprooting trees to make pasture, lopping and topping forest trees, and encroaching on forests with buildings. Offenders were tried in courts convened especially to hear pleas of the forest; and penalties ranged from death, castration, and maiming (in the early years of the law) to imprisonment, forfeiture, and fines. The Anglo-Saxon Chronicle for 1087 records the resentment stirred up by William the Conqueror's implementation of particularly harsh measures, including blinding for the killing of a hart or hind.[31] Again, in practice, forest law, from as early as the thirteenth century, was not often prosecuted to its full extent – at least partly because of frequently long intervals between court sessions – so long that often "attached" persons had died of natural causes by the time the court convened. Fines were usually assessed at rates commensurate with the offender's ability to pay; if the offender was sufficiently destitute, payment of the fine was often waived.

By the late sixteenth century, then, forests had long provided grounds of contention between subjects and kings, while the execution of forest law had admitted ambiguous effects, sometimes entrenching royal authority, sometimes diminishing it. Manwood's 1598 *Treatise of the Lawes of the Forest* provides a useful text for examining the contestative force, not only in the implementation of forest law, but also in assumptions about – representations of – forest law. I will argue that Manwood's Preface to the Matter, dedicatory epistle to Lord Howard, Earl of Nottingham, and Address to the Reader demonstrate Manwood's belief that forest law, in spite of its entrenchment of royal prerogative, can be wielded on behalf of subjects' rights. At the same time, however, the revisionary force of the treatise is limited in that the very rhetorical devices by which Manwood mounts an ideological challenge to aristocratic and royal interests also circumscribe that challenge.

The difference between Manwood's prefatory matter and the preface supplied by his early editors helps to gauge the particular socio-political charge of his enterprise. In their 1615 preface to the posthumous publication of Manwood's work, these editors (likely fellow Inns of Court men) represent the treatise as a sally in the ongoing debates about the relative merits of English common law versus Roman civil law – that is, law that relies on jurisprudence and precedence versus law codified under the Roman emperor Justinian. At a time when, as Richard Helgerson notes, the "uniqueness and antiquity of English law were being pressed with particular intensity,"[32] Manwood's editors stress precisely those features of his project which align it with the characteristics of English common law. In an "advertisement to the Reader," the editors state that Manwood "did first collect as wel out of the Statutes and Common Law of this Realme, as out of the sundrie ancient precidents and Records, much excellent learning concerning the Forest." They add that Manwood, moreover, "purposed" another labour, the publishing of the court proceedings for the forests of Pickering, Lancaster, and Woodstock. Clearly, Manwood's early editors conceive of his treatise as participating in the "gathering ... and writing down of English law," and so, therefore, as contributing to the still-emerging sense of English nationhood.[33]

Manwood himself inflects his enterprise even more particularly with concerns about nationhood, in so far as he converts forest law's monarchic entitlements into advocacy of subjects' rights. To be sure, Manwood begins his Preface to the Matter by acknowledging that the ancient laws of England, "having always had a speciall regard unto the continnuall studie and care that Kings and Princes have in great and weightie affaires of matters of Commonweale, for the good of their subjects," have quite rightly accorded to kings and princes "diverse royall prerogatives of most noble and princely pleasures to recreate themselves withall, to put away from them the remembrance of their laboursome toyle." Not least among these perks are the liberties of the forest. Manwood strengthens the royal claims by developing an implied analogy between kings and God: because biblical authority assigns to God all the beasts and fowl of the earth, and because English kings are God's divinely sanctioned representatives on earth, the beasts and fowl belong to the king. Manwood's position thus far is a seamlessly conservative defence of royal prerogative.

By the third paragraph of his Preface to the Matter, however, Manwood is distinguishing between "uncertain laws" which are commensurate with "the kings will and pleasure" and the "Certain laws and Canons which maintain the privileged places of pleasure." This distinction is a fine one, but far-reaching nonetheless, for it tells us that Manwood conceives of the monarch and the law as ideally separate and distinct. The separation between monarch and law which, as has long been noted, distinguishes English from continental (especially French) conceptions, is necessary to ensure the liberties of subjects. Manwood does not himself draw out this implication; perhaps he remains imperfectly aware of it. But his rhetorical strategies reveal a deep-rooted conviction about this necessary separation. When he rehearses the early history of forest laws, for example, Manwood offers what amounts to a dynastic record of the Norman kings, seeming in this way to resituate the law in the person of the king. He relates this history, however, as a prelude to a bitter complaint about the extent of the prerogative afforded the monarch, noting that the twelfth chapter of the Charter of the Forest

plainly shewed that the king then might and yet may also make a Forest in every place where he pleaseth, as well in the lands and inheritance of any of his subjects as in his desmeasne lands and inheritance, which was a great losse and hinderance to those that were owneres of those lands ... For after the same was so afforested, their pastures and profits of their lands was devoured by the wild beasts of the king without any recompense for the same to be made unto them.

Beasts may devour pastures, but only kings devour profits.

Like his Preface, Manwood's Dedication to Charles, Lord Howard, the Lord Chief Justice as well as Justice in Eyre of "all her Majesties forests, chases, parks, and warrens, by South Trent," moves from championship of royal and aristocratic authority to advocacy of commoners' interests. Noting that "many doe dayly so contemptuously commit such haynous spoiles and trespasses" against the forests over which Lord Howard extends his "provident care," Manwood seems poised to offer his treatise – with its enumeration of offences and penalties – as a useful punitive tool. And in some measure he does. But he also declares his intention to publish the treatise so that "men may the better know those Lawes, wherein they so often offend, and the danger thereof, which being knowne, they may the better avoide."

Manwood's alliance with subjects extends into his address To the Reader, where he imagines his own enterprise in setting forth forest laws as itself a kind of trespass against authority. "I am not ignorant, (gentle Reader)," he begins, "how dangerous a thing it is to range into so large a field, as I have undertaken ... considering how many sundry men may be able to control me." More than just a conventional modesty topos, Manwood's disclaimer tropes his work as a potentially punishable foray into territory – here a body of knowledge – possessed by others. His choice of the verb "range," with its senses of area, wandering, hunting ground, especially alerts us to his figurative meaning. This meaning emerges all the more prominently when we remark that Manwood was himself a gamekeeper, a duty often combined with that of ranger, whose particular job it was to drive deer in disafforested areas back into the royal forest. By the end of his address to the reader – having painstakingly established his right to enter this topic – Manwood more boldly draws the parallel between himself and subjects. Laying out his table of contents, he says he "began at [his] first entrance to step into a forest by the meeres and boundaries of the same." Manwood will begin his treatise, that is, by defining a forest. His figuring of his treatise as itself a forest suggests that at some level he conceives of his articulation of forest laws as an act of taking possession of the forest, perhaps even an act of creating the forest.

Manwood thus invests his treatise with a considerable sociopolitical charge, one moreover which mounts an ideological if not material challenge to aristocratic and royal interests. But the very device which underlines his arrogation of sovereign authority also highlights the limits of his challenge. When he metaphorically equates his treatise and the forest, the effect is not only to gauge his presumption, but also to define forest boundaries. By articulating the legal boundaries Manwood places the forest very securely within the law. Early in his treatise he speaks at some length about the demarcation of forests, noting that the "meeres and boundaries" which separate forests from non-forests are either set down in ancient records or are delineated by certain natural features of the landscape. In either case, forest boundaries seem only uncertainly knowable and so open to unwitting trespass. Manwood's treatise, on the other hand, offers certain knowledge of the law and so makes any trespass a witting one.

Once alerted to forest law and to its rhetorical constructions, we can turn to early modern literary forests to recover the revisionary vistas afforded by this trope, vistas available to early modern readers and play-goers, for whom "forest" would almost certainly, and readily, invoke assumptions and practices now lost to us. In Shakespeare's *Henry IV, Part 1*, for example, when Jack Falstaff urges Prince Hal to call Falstaff and his Boarshead cohorts not "thieves," but "Diana's foresters" (1.2.29), the audience, especially with its disproportionately high number of Inns of Court men, would likely have twigged onto Falstaff's "foresters" and so been alerted early in the play to the considerable subversive charge of the Boarshead world. Falstaff's metaphors for thieves – "Diana's foresters," "minions of the moon," "gentlemen of the shade," "squires of the night's body"(1.2.30) – do more than glorify thievery. "Diana" was a common appellation for Queen Elizabeth, while "minions," "gentlemen," and "squires" point to the offices and blandishments of courtiership – an effect underlined when Falstaff subsequently asks that he and his cohorts be considered "men of good government" (1.2.31). Falstaff's metaphors thus represent a translation upward of illicit into courtly activities. But Falstaff is not simply asking Hal to regard the world of Boarshead as an alternative court. Like a perspective picture, Falstaff's metaphors can yield a different configuration of meanings: to suggest that there is in fact little to distinguish courtiers from thieves. According to this metaphoric logic, in countenancing her courtiers and nobles, Queen Elizabeth is countenancing theft of the common wealth. Falstaff's implied criticism becomes more pointed when we remark that Queen Elizabeth rather liberally granted Crown woodlands to councillors and courtiers in return for "good, faithful, and acceptable service."[34] In the 1590s especially, such grants tended to result in serious deforestation as the grantees converted woodland to agricultural use and so personal profit. Such conversion would also, of course, preclude commoners' use of the woods for their cattle, encroaching in this way too on the common wealth.

Falstaff's critique of courtly authority emerges as less truncated than Manwood's – which is to say that the playwright can entertain a more sweeping range of possibilities than can the lawyer. Falstaff's subversion of authority extends well beyond this instance to call into scrutiny several matters of statecraft – from King

Henry IV's tainted ascension to the throne to abuses of the king's military press. Falstaff's initial metaphor of the forest thus sets the stage for a dynamic that thoroughly destabilizes assumptions about royal authority and statehood, contributing in this way to a new definition of kingship.

One of the reasons that Falstaff's renaming thieves as "Diana's foresters" can key so readily into the subversive potential of the Boarshead world surely lies in the long-established association, in England, of forests with outlawry. The same Norman invasion that established forest law made outlaws of certain dispossessed English nobles, who fled to William the Conqueror's New Forest to find both sanctuary and a "guerrilla" base from which to harass the much-despised Normans. From these historical outlaws, as Robert Harrison observes, grew the legends and ballads of "heroic outlaws" – the Gamelyns, the Robin Hoods, the Adam Bells. The fourteenth- and fifteenth-century folkloric memory of the forest as a place where, paradoxically, outlawry generates more justice than does the law endures in the literature and entertainment of the sixteenth century.[35] Shakespeare's *As You Like It* provides a case in point, and furnishes my next example of the revisionary force in literature.

Harrison refers, without elaboration, to this play's connection, via the Forest of Arden, to the forest outlawry that relied heavily on disguise to effect justice. My purpose in taking up the play will be to indicate more particularly the ways in which *As You Like It* accommodates revisionary possibilities. Louis Montrose and Richard Wilson have both offered cogent political readings of this comedy – on the centrality of family politics and on the subsistence crisis of the 1590s respectively – that suggest the extent to which socio-political concerns inflect the play's conflicts.[36] My emphasis on forest outlawry brings into purview larger questions of polity.

The association between the Forest of Arden and heroic outlawry is established early in the play when Charles, the court wrestler, tells us (and the villainous Oliver) that the rightful duke, banished by his younger brother, is "in the Forest of Arden and a many merry men with him," where they live "like the old Robin Hood of England … fleet[ing] the time carelessly as they did in the golden world" (1.1.120–5). Certain details suggest that Shakespeare conceives of Arden as, at least in part, a royal forest: the sheepfarm which figures in Rosalind's adventures is located in the purlieus, that is, a disafforested area within a royal forest; hunting – virtually the raison d'être of forests – is a popular pastime in Arden; the antique oak under which Orlando finds Oliver indicates the presence of a stand of preserved trees, another feature of royal forests. Together these motifs of the forest and of outlawry point Shakespeare's concern in this play with broad questions of political organization, particularly to do with royal and aristocratic authority.

Critics and audiences have long recognized that the Forest of Arden offers almost magical possibilities of transformation to the assorted characters who convene there. Among other things, Arden teaches the lovers and courtiers alike that process is preferable to hypostasis; that spirit and appetite must be balanced; that satire must give way to wonder; that real wealth is contentment; and that the conventions organizing lives and loves must be emptied out and then reconstituted. What is especially pertinent to my purposes is that Arden also effects a wholesale exchange of property which significantly reconfigures power relations. At the end of the play, the villainous older brother, Oliver, who had deprived his worthy younger brother, Orlando, of his deserved inheritance, transfers the entire family estate to Orlando; while the usurping duke, who had banished his worthy older brother, converts to religious life, letting the kingdom revert to Duke Senior. The peacefulness of these exchanges should not obscure the extent of the political transformation that Shakespeare imagines here. The bad duke's ruthless exercise of power, through intimidation, surveillance, and corruption, yields to the old duke's loving relations with his subjects. The bad brother's heartless economy in managing his estate, his family, and his servants yields to Orlando's heroic regard for servant and brother. The political order restored at the end of the play will thus reflect aspects of an idealized feudal order. As recent students of early modern England have observed in other contexts, the resurgence and celebration of feudal values in the 1590s in England frequently masked trenchant criticism of sovereign authority.[37]

At least part of the reason that the forest in *As You Like It* can work its magic lies in the fact that Arden teaches its visitors – with one notable exception – how to move out of hardened categories, how to entertain a range of possible responses to personal and political exigencies. The exception is Jaques, whose role as satirist effectively precludes, or at least postpones, his joining in the renewed community at the end of the play. Shakespeare suggests further that Jaques remains isolated partly because he constructs metaphors that collapse distinctions. When he "moralizes" upon the forest and its denizens, Jaques draws comparisons to city and court, but *only* in order to anatomize city and court. Somewhat like Manwood's legal metaphor, Jaques's metaphors delimit the play of meanings. Because his is a mind which does not allow full play to the vehicle in metaphors, Jaques remains an individual unable to benefit from the revisionary possibilities afforded by Arden. One suspects that Jaques could write good legal discourse.

Jaques's limitations highlight, by contrast, the fact that literary metaphor characteristically keeps in play a range of meanings. In literary works that treat questions of sovereign authority, such proliferation of meanings amply accommodates revisionary configurations of power. When the metaphor's vehicle is itself richly ambivalent, as is "forest," the possibilities multiply. Thomas Wyatt's "The long love that in my thought doth harbor" furnishes a particularly dazzling instance.

Michael Holahan's brilliant analysis of Petrarch's *Rime* 140 and Wyatt's translation of the sonnet, "The long love," aims to recuperate what have been regarded as Wyatt's "failures of art" in that poem, which I quote here in its entirety for ease of reference.

> The long love that in my thought doth harbor,
> And in mine heart doth keep his residence,
> Into my face presseth with bold pretense
> And therein campeth, spreading his banner.
> She that me learneth to love and suffer
> And will that my trust and lust's negligence
> Be reined by reason, shame, and reverence
> With his hardiness taketh displeasure.
> Wherewithal unto the heart's forest he fleeth,
> Leaving his enterprise with pain and cry,
> And there him hideth, and not appeareth.
> What may I do, when my master feareth,
> But in the field with him to live and die?
> For good is the life ending faithfully.

Holahan argues compellingly that Wyatt's departures from Petrarch reflect his "extension of Petrarchan language ... metaphor ... and idea ... into different regions of meaning," that "Wyatt ventures through and beyond the letter of the Italian text because he wishes to use it to affirm another kind of master, authority, and faith at court." In particular, he suggests, Wyatt's introduction of new metaphors of place, "the heart's forest" and "field," mark his departure from Petrarch in pointing an "activity beyond the world of romantic love" – specifically, the imperatives of Henry VIII's English court.[38] Noting the legal meaning of "forest," Holahan concludes that Wyatt's translation marks his commitment to King Henry. In retreating to the "heart's forest," contends Holahan, Wyatt represents himself as a willing vassal pledging faith to his King, as a subject willing to let service to his lord supplant romantic love. Elizabeth Heale follows Holahan in pursuing the specific – and specifically – Tudor English implications of "heart's forest," but reaches the quite different conclusion that Wyatt is "occupied by a love which is both rebel and monarch, a thing of nature and a natural lord." Wyatt's lover-speaker, in turn, "occupies a place of perplexing loyalties," at once "banish[ed] from the confines of courtly civility" *and* "seated in 'nature' and the manly-aristocratic domain of hunting, through which male desire is rendered natural and ... legitimate."[39]

Both Holahan and Heale usefully draw attention to Wyatt's invoking, through "forest" and "field," Tudor exigencies of courtiership, service, and courtship, but Holahan moves too quickly to read "forest" as exclusively Henry VIII's demesne, while Heale moves too quickly to understand the poem's implied monarch and desmesne as metaphoric. Neither presses "heart's forest" far enough. Doing so yields neither the willing and self-willed subjection to the King posited by Holahan's reading, nor the delimiting of the poem's tensions to conflicts among Love, lover, and Lady which results from Heale's reading. While "forest" does certainly connote the King's demesne, the legal boundaries of the forest were shifting and permeable, as we have seen, which means that forests could never *simply* be identified with monarchal privilege, as Holahan assumes. Moreover, the long-standing identification of the forest as a haven for outlaws whose rebellious actions in fact promote social justice surely comes into play in Wyatt's poem, as Heale nearly implies, but without applying this association to the historical particulars. According to this metaphoric logic, in retreating to the forest, the master (Love) and his faithful servant (Wyatt) withdraw to a space which technically belongs to the King, but which is effectively controlled by those in residence. Just as William the Conqueror's exercising of prerogative in creating the New Forest alienated English subjects, driving some of them at least to withdraw to the forest and convert it to their political uses, so Henry VIII's exercising of prerogative – notably in the matter of discarding and assuming wives – makes an outlaw of Wyatt, reportedly a lover of Anne Boleyn before Henry's eye fell on her.[40] The poem asserts in other ways that love – that is, Wyatt's love for Anne – has a prior claim to the political landscape figured here. This love keeps "residence" in Wyatt's "heart"; when he then retreats to the "heart's forest," it must be to the forest adjoining that residence. To recognize these claims to the forest is to see Wyatt as a creature – in the strictest sense – not of Henry's will but of his own will-to-love, exercised in contravention of Henry's.

To ground "The long love," by way of the forest, in professions of agency is not necessarily to promote what Jonathan Crewe calls "indulgence in the dream of the poet as an autonomous, masterful presence."[41] It is, however, to prompt another look at this poem's configuration of authority – reign – and rebellion, and to recognize the extent to which this sonnet represents the subject of love and of monarch as self-constitutive and unified. We can begin with a point of structure and observe that the *volta* does not, as might seem to be the case, mark a turning away from the Lady's lessons. Love, in response to the Lady's "displeasure" with his bold show, flees with "pain and cry" unto the forest where "him hideth, and not appeareth." Loyal to his master, Love, the lover-speaker determines "with him [i.e. Love] to live and die," to give his life the shape of faithfulness. What the sestet narrates, in effect, is the enactment – fulfilment even – of the Lady's lessons, strictures itemized in the octave's second quatrain. The Lady teaches the lover to suffer: Love flees with pain and cry. She teaches him to will himself reined by reason, shame, and reverence: Love hides, ashamed, in the forest; the lover's tone throughout registers the reasonableness of the participants in the drama; Love now fears – reverences – the Lady, and the lover reveres his master. What seems, in the sestet, like disorder, like a rout of Love and speaker by the Lady, then, amounts in fact to an ordering of speaker and Love. The speaker and Love are thus doubly disciplined, by the

Lady's displeasure and by her teachings. More interestingly, the effects of the Lady's teaching emerge in response to her displeasure – disapproval provoked by Love's "bold hardiness," that is, by rebellion against the rein (reign) of reason, shame, and reverence.

Thomas Greene has remarked of Wyatt's translation of *Rime* 140 that the dropping of Petrarch's "sometimes" ("Love ... sometimes comes all forth in armor into my forehead") transforms what in Petrarch is a ritualized encounter "played out an indefinite number of times" into a more dramatically intense event, into a "unique and unrepeatable plot" and therefore a situation which requires moral responses not demanded in Petrarch's poem, which fixes Love, lover, and Lady into conventional responses.[42] In so arguing, Greene neglects to register the full force of the word "harbor" in Wyatt's first line. Because harbour strongly connotes refuge or haven, Wyatt's point – made with brilliant economy – is surely that Love *has* rebelled at least once before, has already at least once before been forced to seek refuge from the Lady's displeasure. Wyatt's "harbor," that is, assumes a repeated display of "bold hardiness" on the part of Love, a display that proves self-constitutive (of Love and lover) in so far as it prompts the instruction of Love by the Lady.

We can gauge how thoroughly Love and the lover have absorbed the Lady's lessons – to the point of assuming agency – by noticing also the syntactical ambiguity, in lines 5–7, that makes the rein (reign) of reason, shame, and reverence an effect of *both* the lover's will and the Lady's will (or rather, perhaps, first of the Lady's, then of the lover's will). We can take the lines to mean that the Lady teaches the lover three things: to love and to suffer and to will the reining of his trust and lust's negligence. This reading is strengthened by the implied parallelism of the infinitives. We can also, however, take the lines to mean that the Lady both teaches the lover to love and suffer *and* wills that – "she will have it that" – his trust and lust's negligence be reined, a reading encouraged by the placing of "will" in a separate line and by an imagistic logic which predicts that the individual who is sufficiently powerful to exercise "displeasure" would also be the individual able to "will." The latter reading implies the complete subjection of the lover to the Lady. Arguably, however, the reading of lines 5–7 that highlights the Lady's will exerts only residual control, this reading having almost yielded to the reading that highlights the lover's act of will; the grammatical expectation that "will" is the third in a series of implied infinitives is strong, especially given the preponderance of parallelism in the poem, while the syntactical elision in the second reading ("she will have it that" contracted to "will") makes that sense less immediate. Such a structuring of meaning surely indicates a similar structuring of experience: the lover has learned so well from the Lady how to rein himself that such reining, and reigning, has become an act of his will.

Beyond this, we might also note, as does Crewe in connection with Wyatt's "Whoso List to Hunt," that it is the poet's exercising of his craft, his mastery of language, which makes possible the speaker's profession of agency;[43] we might also remark the less obvious implication: that Wyatt crafts this profession at the same time as he ostensibly demonstrates his loyalty, and subjection, to Henry VIII. Commentators concur that Wyatt's translations of Petrarch are the fruit of courtiership, the "by-product," in Holahan's terms, of Wyatt's work as Henry's envoy abroad.[44] Wyatt returned to Henry's court to write poetry which "Englished" Italian Renaissance values, in artful tribute to Henry, but also in performance of his own art.

The texts just discussed point us to large cultural dynamics that not only encourage citizen strengths but also decentralize power. Other socio-cultural forces bearing upon Spenser's work, however, presume the importance of centredness. Elizabethan processes of cultural commodification, particularly as manifested in the publishing and promoting of literary works, rely on centring the author in relation to social, moral, and economic forces.[45] We will see in subsequent chapters that Harvey, E.K., and Ralegh imagine Spenser as centred. Here, I would like to consider the assumptions about an author's relationship to authority which inform the presentation of Spenser by the publisher William Ponsonby, whose pre-eminence in the book trade ensures that his assumptions sustain considerable cultural currency.[46]

In Spenser's *Complaints* (1591), when Ponsonby addresses a preface to the "Gentle reader," he trades on a sense of Spenser – then newly minted and subsequently to remain current – as a writer of considerable cultural capital.[47] Spenser's work is sufficiently worthy of note to be the subject of rumour and report; Ponsonby has "heard" that some "small Poems" by the author of the *Faerie Queene* "were disperst abroad in sundrie hands." Moreover, these poems had been "diverslie imbeziled and purloyned" from Spenser (223). "Imbeziled," especially, registers the high value assigned to Spenser's work, since embezzlement was punishable as a felony. Ponsonby clearly imagines his own task to have been the rescuing of these sundry works from theft, fraudulent use, and possible destruction.

Ponsonby also, and more complexly, imagines his task to be a centring of Spenser and his work, as he implies when he writes of having "gathered togeather these fewe parcels" (223). The title-page ornament, four hands pointing inward, emblematizes succinctly this centring impulse while also indicating that centredness is established by the intersection of certain moral and social forces and institutions (216). Each of the four hands points beyond the circle, to figures of David with a harp and Moses with stone tablets, on the horizontal axis, and to "By Ed. Sp." and "London.," on the vertical axis. Because David and Moses appear, monumentally, in the woodcut border while the names of author and city appear within the border, this configuration suggests not only and generally the mutual reinforcement of 1) divine, poetic furor, 2) moral law, 3) temporal civic and market authority, and 4) individual author, but also and more particularly the close interdependence of author with civic and mercantile interests. Because the border figures of David and Moses are more visually imposing than "By Ed. Sp." and "London.," however, temporal interests remain firmly secured by atemporal imperatives – a structuring of authority echoed in the disposition of other information on the title-page. Within the border, and at the top of the title-page, we learn that the volume is entitled *Complaints* and that it contains "small Poemes of the Worlds Vanitie," while at the bottom of the page we learn that Ponsonby's bookshop is located in "Pauls Churchyard at the signe of the Bishops head."

I call attention to these features of the title-page, not to contend that Ponsonby (or the printer, or Spenser) consciously designed the page to produce these precise effects, but rather to delineate certain assumptions about an author's relationship to the structures of authority in early modern England. In Ponsonby's practice, cultural capital of the kind invested in Spenser accrues with centredness of the kind figured on the title-page and, as we shall see, adumbrated in the preface.[48]

In the preface, Ponsonby implicitly ascribes value to centredness, not only by speaking of his "gathering," by good as opposed to fraudulent means (note the claiming of moral high ground), but also by representing eccentricity as a condition which renders an author both vulnerable and, ultimately, profligate. Ponsonby's rhetoric implies that Spenser's removal from the centre, his "departure over Sea [to Ireland]," permitted the theft of his works while also leaving him unable to effect their recovery (223).[49] Ponsonby's omitting to name Ireland suggests how completely beyond the pale he imagines Spenser to be. Ponsonby himself, "dwelling in Pauls Churchyard," in the heart of London, remains positioned to collect the works; he has

> Endeuoured by all good meanes (for the better increase and accomplishment of your delights) to get into my handes such smale Poemes of the same authors; as I heard were disperst abroad in sundrie hands, and not easie to bee come by, by himselfe; some of them having bene diuerslie imbeziled and purloyned from him, since his departure ouer Seas. Of the which I have by good meanes gathered togeather these fewe parcels present, which I have caused to be printed altogeather. (223)

Ponsonby's are the hands which rescue Spenser's work from the mismanagement of "sundrie hands," thus adding Spenser's works to the store of cultural capital available for the "gentle reader's" "delights." The implicit claim here is that in centredness resides the competence to manage cultural commodities. The implication later in the preface, where Ponsonby emphasizes the moral profit to the reader of Spenser's work, is that movement away from the centre is somehow immoral. Having justified his publishing of the gathered works in one volume on the basis that they are all "meditations of the worlds vanitie," Ponsonby says he understands that Spenser wrote "sundrie others" to similar effect, adding that there are "[b]esides some other Pamphlets *looselie scattered abroad*" (224; my emphasis). Ponsonby's rhetoric even assumes an adversarial edge as he imagines that his endeavours to collect Spenser's scattered works may be resisted by Spenser: Ponsonby remains determined to collect the works "either by himselfe [i.e. with Spenser's help], or otherwise" (224).

Threading through what is already a complexly structured set of assumptions about the writer's relationship to institutional authority is the profit motive. By Spenser's day, the book trade was beginning to supplant patronage as a source to be tapped for livelihood. For Ponsonby the concentration of customers is clearly one of the virtues of the centre, London. Eager to cultivate a market, Ponsonby seems especially keen to appeal to women as potential customers: he stresses that the works he is offering bear an unworldly tenor (and would thus be suitable for women readers), and he points out that Spenser dedicated these poems to Ladies. When Ponsonby remarks that these poems are "verie grave and profitable" and when he hopes "for [the readers'] favour sake to set foorth" Spenser's still scattered pamphlets, he surely has in mind remuneration as well as approbation (224). We might also surmise that Ponsonby's insistence on the unavailability of Spenser's work amounts to a price-inflation ploy.

To focus on the book trade is to bring also into purview the continuing friction between print and manuscript circulation. Ponsonby's references to "hands" and "gathering" tap into precisely this opposition to suggest that print is the preferred medium for preserving and transmitting cultural commodities, at least partly because print centres the author and his work in fixed texts. As Arthur Marotti has recently demonstrated, manuscript miscellanies offered a means of literary transmission still viable in Spenser's day.[50] Such miscellanies could, however, corrupt the texts and authors so reproduced – through incomplete or inaccurate copying, or through dividing into smaller parts a work conceived by its author as a whole, for example. From the point of view of Ponsonby, a publisher who had recently begun to establish the Sidney "line," such reproducing no doubt appeared tantamount to embezzlement.[51]

Marotti has also observed pertinently that it was very often the "hands" – usually italic – of women that transcribed poetry into personal anthologies.[52] In remarking that the poems which *Complaints* comprises had been "dispersed abroad in sundrie hands ... [some] having been diversely imbeziled and purloyned," Ponsonby perhaps directs us to miscellanies assembled by the individual dedicatees of the poems in the volume. It is likely that Spenser would have given to each of the dedicatees a copy of the poem in her name, particularly when three of the dedicatees were members of the family with whom he claimed kinship. That in married life the homes of two were well removed from London perhaps helps to account for Ponsonby's "disperst abroad."[53] Ponsonby's hands, in contrast to those of various transcribers, have "caused to be printed altogeather" Spenser's poems; print thus restores to wholeness and correctness an author's opus. Ponsonby's reference to "gathering" suggests this also, in so far as a "gathering" is a collection of printed sheets in correct order. Ponsonby's prescriptions for the preservation of literary works remind us – and perhaps all the more forcibly for being implicit prescriptions – that cultural capital such as that invested in literary works remained very much up for grabs in Spenser's day.

I have dwelt at some length on what we can glean about the writer's position from the title-page and preface to *Complaints* for two reasons: first, to sketch in small compass the kind and complexity of pressures which could bear upon a writer, especially one with laureate ambitions; and, second, to prepare the ground for countering claims about the writer's (and, more generally, the corporate subject's) relationship with authority. It will be the burden of my argument to present these countering claims, in particular to show that Spenser's self-fashioning as well as his envisioning of nationhood involves resistance to the centre.

Ponsonby's appeal to the custom of women helps point the issue in so far as his appeal capitalizes on the virtues of centredness, including market concentration. Spenser's cultivation of female patrons in *Complaints* participates in a different dynamic, which, while not necessarily eschewing the marketplace, contributes to the larger, centrifugal, anti-court movement which defines the volume as a whole. In three of the four dedications to women, Spenser relies on his female patrons to deliver him to the world. In addressing Lady Strange, for example, he says he wants to make his affection for her "universallie knowen to the world; that by honouring you, they might know me, and by knowing me they might honour you" (268). In his dedication to Lady Carey (Carew), he vows to esteem her "for that honorable name, which you have by your brave deserts purchast to your selfe, and spred in the mouths of al men: with which I have also presumed to grace my verses, and under your name to commend to the world this smal Poeme" (412). Spenser's dedicatory sonnet to Lady Carey in the the 1590 *Faerie Queene* plays wittily, as does this dedication, on their sharing of a name. In the sonnet, the name helps Spenser to place himself at court. Here, he turns the coincidence in their names to the purpose of securing esteem from a wider audience.

Spenser speaks of Lady Carey's, and by implication his, name as being "*spred* in the mouths of *al men*" (my emphasis), a dispersal which contrasts succinctly with Ponsonby's inclination to gather. Notably, too, the spreading abroad which Spenser hopes will develop carries none of the opprobrium assigned to such broadcasting by Ponsonby. Nor does making readily available one's self, one's work, one's name, diminish value. Unlike Ponsonby, Spenser does not fabricate an economy of scarcity. Indeed, Spenser seems deliberately and provocatively to deploy a vocabulary of promiscuity in recurring to the pleasures and virtues of being so "thoroughlie known to al men." He seems, as well, little concerned with drumming up sales. His remarking that by "honouring" Lady Strange the world might "know" him remains something of a throw-away sentiment unless one surmises that he hopes that Lady Strange, honoured by requests to read a poem conceived under her auspices, will lend to friends the poem given her by Spenser, or perhaps include Spenser's poem in a reading circle of the kind recently described by Louise Schleiner.[54] Such free exchange might be just the sort of purloining that Ponsonby inveighs against.

One could argue simply that Ponsonby's business was selling books while Spenser's business was to extend his reputation. Nevertheless, Spenser's inversion of Ponsonby's marketplace assumptions about supply, demand, and value helps pinpoint the folly of relying on any one model to explicate relations between writer and institutions. Even within the same volume and between men who had (presumably) already collaborated, and would again, to publish Spenser's work, one cannot expect coincidence of views and design. What this means for critical practice is a curtailing of the search for large, totalizing paradigms, the impetus which characterized the inception of new historicism and cultural studies, in favour of detailing local effects and causes and retailing contexts. What this means for critical pleasure is the proliferation of unexpected moments and sites of discovery.

In the case of Spenser, too long regarded as the Elizabethan propagandist par excellence – as Marx's "arse-kissing" poet – the licence to localize and to multiply contexts has been especially salutary.[55] When placed in such varied contexts as those provided by the material conditions of early modern publishing or by Irish matters, Spenser's politics and poetics prove more nuanced and more independent of the court than has, at least until very recently, been too often supposed. Spenser's assured independence of mind and position will remain a keynote in the following chapters. Here, I would like to sketch the ways in which the *Complaints* volume traces a firm trajectory away from the court.

Richard Helgerson has argued cogently that the Gothic character of *The Faerie Queene* makes that poem an "implicit advocate of a partially refeudalized English polity."[56] He does not, however, read other works by Spenser in light of this advocacy. But Spenser's *Complaints* does represent alignment with noble houses as an important counteraction to the gravitational pull of the court; does extol as patrons figures who preserve detachment from the court; and does censure Leicester for excessive attachment to court and Queen.

The dedicatory program of *Complaints* features the celebration not only of female patrons but also of noble houses and families, to whom Spenser generally and repeatedly declares himself "bound." Indeed, the three dedications to the Spencer sisters trace a gradual strengthening of the bonds which tie Spenser to that family, moving from, simply, "some private bands of affinitie" (268) to bands which exact his "faithfull duetie" (334) to bands which require him to "give [him]selfe wholy" (412). Spenser likewise attaches himself closely to the Sidney-Russell-Bedford families. In these dedications, intimacy between poet and noble houses operates as a vocational as well as a political ideal, Spenser's "vassalage" promising poetic fecundity.

In certain of the volume's poems, most notably "The Ruines of Time," Spenser advances similarly feudalized poetics and politics. In that poem, he develops extensive and pointed contrasts – between the speakers Verlame and Colin Clout, between Leicester and Sidney, and between Leicester and other members of his family – in order to censure court- and sovereign-centredness and to suggest that an English empire depends upon noble houses.

Although Verlame's lessons – remonstrations drawn from her own and Leicester's demises – are ostensibly those of the *de casibus* and *contemptus mundi* traditions, she in fact demonstrates excessive attachment to worldly and ungodly empire, a predilection which in turn colours our perception of Leicester, whose portrait is delineated by Verlame, not by Spenser or Colin Clout.[57] Verlame stresses in particular Leicester's status and his position in "the bosome of his Soveraine" (line 188). Colin Clout, for his part, remains conspicuously silent when urged by Verlame to mourn Leicester's "decease" (line 237). What Colin proffers in place of the requested lament for Leicester are "remembrances" of the other Dudleys and the Bedfords, portraits which contrast with Verlame's lament for Leicester in emphasizing family life and communities of affection – the noble household, in other words – as well as happy after-lives.[58] Moreover, while the worthies, Leicester included, in Verlame's *ubi sunt* catalogue have vanished without trace, the men and women of Spenser-Colin's eulogistic catalogue, as well as the virtues which they espoused and embodied, remain eternally present, held in living memory and preserved in the poet's immortal verse. Thus the noble household rather than the court proves the repository of the strengths and arts of (godly) empire.

This point emerges with particular clarity in the contrast between Leicester and Sidney, a "gentle spirite breathed from above, / Out of the bosome of the makers bliss" (lines 281–2). Sidney's Christlike proximity to God contrasts with Leicester's favoured position in the "bosome of his Soveraine," the two men thus representing two kinds of fealty, to otherworldly and to temporal authorities respectively. But though Sidney's service is to an otherworldly control, he seems neither reclusive nor ineffectual in advancing secular Tudor causes: it is Sidney and not Leicester who is represented as having died for his country's good and from active service to his country – this despite the fact that exhaustion and sickness contracted in the Netherlands no doubt hastened Leicester's death.[59]

In evaluating the careers of Leicester and Sidney, Spenser suggests that Leicester's was flawed to the extent that he depended upon sovereign, rather than divine and familial authority. Leicester's very closeness to the Queen undoubtedly precluded his forwarding the militant Protestant cause as unreservedly as its adherents might have wished, since Leicester had to contend with Elizabeth's reluctance to support military expeditions. Her dislike of militancy is reflected in the hollowness with which she countenanced the military exploits of some of her courtiers. The lavish public spectacle which marked Sidney's funeral and sanctioned his conduct on the field at Zutphen did not match her private reaction to his death, her complaint that he "had thrown away a noble life with an ordinary soldier's death, as if he had never fully understood rank."⁶⁰ Several years later, with much the same sentiment, Elizabeth recalled Essex – another favourite, Leicester's stepson, and bearer of the militant Protestant cause – from Rouen, where he was commanding an English force sent as part of Elizabeth's half-hearted commitment to lend military aid to the cause of Henri IV in France, saying the expedition was beneath his dignity.⁶¹ Elizabeth's hobbling of militant enterprise no doubt helped to strengthen Spenser's belief that the noble household was more apt than was the court to produce the heroes deemed necessary to the militant Protestant cause.

Spenser's championing of militancy and its masculine ethos, support expressed not only in *Complaints* but also and more significantly in *The Faerie Queene*, marks him as one of those men, chiefly of the Sidney circle, recently described by Jean Brink as favouring the "heroic enterprise" of military service and colonial exploration over the "frivolous activities of the court."⁶² Spenser's censure of the court extends well beyond charging it with frivolity, however; we shall see that for Spenser court-centredness imperils both corporate subject and the project of nationhood, particularly as that project entailed Ireland.

Everywhere in Spenser one finds evidence of his grappling with the moral imperatives of fashioning self and nation. That Spenser stakes his ground very surely even within the potential confinements of patronage speaks at once to his boldness of enterprise, tenacity of purpose, and amplitude of imagination, features of his mind and art which remain foremost in the following pages.

In chapter 2, I argue that Spenser in *The Shepheardes Calender* resists the "laureate" poetics promoted by patrons E.K. and Hobbinol, tendering instead a poetics at once more "homely" and more eccentric. Spenser's inaugural work also addresses extensively the issue of subjectivity, sounding depths of inwardness in Colin (and by extension himself) – again, against the limited possibilities afforded by patronal relations.

If the patronal apparatus of the *Calender* provides Spenser with a mechanism for self-definition, the patronage which accompanies the 1590 *Faerie Queene* mediates individual and cultural assumptions about the corporate, rather than the private, subject; at stake in Spenser's poem of nationhood is the relationship between sovereign and citizen. In the 1590 commerce between

Spenser and patrons, we witness competing versions of that relationship and so measure the boldness of Spenser's enterprise. In chapter 3, on the commendatory verses appended to the first instalment of *The Faerie Queene*, I demonstrate the heterogeneity in the praise of Spenser, stressing that to broaden his constituency is to bring into view a range of subject positions and to release him from the limited (and limiting) economies imagined by courtly observers such as Ralegh and Harvey. To extend the horizons of the 1590 *Faerie Queene* is to bring into purview not only London, with its particular commercial and market forces, but also Ireland, whose influence on the 1590 (as opposed to the 1596) volume remains little recognized and under-documented. The Irish connection recruits for Spenser a constituency more potentially unruly than the ones usually imagined in criticism, while inflecting his project – to fashion a sovereign, a nation, corporate subjects, and heroes – with specifically Irish reformist designs. Spenser's 1590 sequence of dedicatory sonnets, the subject of chapter 4, also reflects his Irish tenure, not simply by including dedicatees with Irish connections, but by articulating a far-reaching militaristic ethos with specific application to Ireland. Viewed in this context, Spenser's dedicatory sonnet to Ralegh, long considered the pre-eminent patron of the 1590 *Faerie Queene*, assumes a burden of censure, as Spenser scrutinizes this powerful man's Petrarchan (and so, courtly) politics and poetics, and finds them inadequate to the reformation of Ireland. In Spenser's dedicatory sequence we can not only gauge Irish pressures but also weigh some effects of the material conditions of early modern publishing, conditions which, like the Irish context, invite us to regard the 1590 volume as less court-bound than has been customary and to suppose its audience and constituency to be wider than has often been assumed.

Not mere puffs, Spenser's dedicatory sonnets thus engage issues of moment, matters at once poetic and political. When we cross the threshold into the poem proper, we find Spenser grappling with some of these same concerns, again through patronal relations, as I demonstrate in chapter 5. In the fiction of Timias and Belphoebe in Book 3, as well as in the proem to that book, Spenser marks, on largely Irish grounds, the limits of Ralegh's court-centred, Petrarchan tropes. In place of those tropes, Spenser offers a reformative mirror of Ralegh's poetics and Irish career. Behind his censure lies the conviction that Petrarchism vitiates the heroic form and energy required to recreate Ireland.

2 *The Shepheardes Calender*

The patronly relations of the *Calender* are subtle, complex, and multi-layered: in the introductory and editorial apparatus of the volume, Spenser-Immerito solicits patronage from Sidney and, perhaps, from the Earl of Leicester; E.K. (who may well be Spenser himself)[1] patronizes and presents the "new Poete," asking Gabriel Harvey to act as patron as well; within the fiction of the *Calender*, Spenser's relationship with Harvey is figured in that of Colin and Hobbinol, whose relationship is itself subject, I will argue, to differing constructions by E.K. and Spenser. In this chapter I will contend that to follow closely the very intricate lines of patronage in the *Calender* is to highlight Spenser's concern to preserve poetic and moral autonomy, and to find such autonomy associated with selfhood, private experience, romantic love (what E.K. terms "gynerastice"), and an anti-courtly poetics. It is to discover that Spenser challenges the very pressures in patronage designed to mould the court-centred, laureate poet.[2] I wish to emphasize in particular that, while the patrons represented in the *Calender* (E.K. and Harvey) assume Spenser's willingness to be made public, Spenser systematically resists these designs and Colin becomes the figure for this resistance.

Richard Helgerson, David Miller, and Louis Montrose, among others, have demonstrated amply that Spenser's self-fashioning involves his projecting a Virgilian, that is to say, laureate's, role for himself. Features which distinguish the *Calender*'s publication – its annotated format, as well as the remarks and tone of E.K., its formal, metrical, and thematic virtuosity, its deliberately ambiguous use of the humility topos, its promise that more works will follow – signal an active and determined aim on Spenser's part to make himself the "new Poete," a national, public poet after the manner of Virgil. At the same time, the commentators note, the *Calender* projects failure, whether through default, as Helgerson suggests, or through design, as Montrose and Miller argue. Spenser's persona, Colin Clout, a poet of promise celebrated by his peers and capable of overgoing Pan and rivalling Apollo, fails to secure the laureate's mantle: overwhelmed by personal misfortune in love, Colin withdraws from public function. The relationship between Spenser-Immerito and Colin Clout has been examined extensively in recent years, with the consensus being that Spenser represents in Colin a negative example, that Colin's career follows a pattern against which Spenser defines his own, that Colin's self-absorption demonstrates the dangers of the selfhood to poetic vocation, that Colin, in short, is a figure from whom Spenser dissociates himself.[3]

Without unequivocally identifying Spenser with Colin and without ascribing to Spenser the intemperateness which threatens at times to overwhelm Colin, my own argument nevertheless construes Colin more positively as a figure through whom emerges Spenser's resistance to publication and the laureate's role. This reading emphasizes, not the intransigence of available poetic roles or the strategically sharp self-consciousness of Spenser's poetic debut, but the radical, if not always consciously articulated, ambivalence in Spenser's pursuit of a public poetic career. This reading also produces a Spenser who is not so single-mindedly the careerist that Richard Rambuss, in *Spenser's Secret Career*, has made him out to be.

Spenser's resistance to laureateship emerges most fully in connection with E.K. and Hobbinol; accordingly, those patronly relations will occupy most of this chapter. In the envoy and epilogue which frame the *Calender*, however, Spenser adumbrates the kind of patronage within which his poetic aspirations could be realized. I will thus turn first to consider this set of relations.

The dedicating and publishing of the *Calender* were matters of concern to Spenser, these issues being among his "principal doubts" regarding Harvey's plans for Spenser's career.[4] In a letter to Harvey dated October 1579, Spenser voices reservations about dedicating the *Calender* to Leicester, as originally planned by him or urged by Harvey, his qualm hinging at least partly upon his perception that it would be indecorous to dedicate a work celebrating a "private personage" (Rosalind? Colin? Spenser?) to so eminently a public figure as Leicester. His choice of Sidney as dedicatee presumably involves for him no such breach of decorum. Spenser may have felt that in Sidney he addressed a patron less exclusively oriented than was Leicester toward public, national life. Katherine Duncan-Jones observes in her biography of Sidney that from about 1577 he cultivated a role and persona "that released him from political pressures while liberating him to speak freely about private emotions."[5] Spenser may have been counting on Sidney to act as an intermediary through whose hands and favour the *Calender* could make its way to Leicester. But even if Leicester's is the patronage Spenser hoped to ultimately secure, the indirection and hesitancy of his approach reflect much ambivalence.

Listing for Harvey his doubts regarding the promotion of his career, Spenser in the letter writes that he "was minded for a while to have intermitted the utterings [i.e. publication] of [his] writings" (635). By this time engaged by Leicester and having tasted "some sweetnesse" (i.e. "gain or commodity") from the employment, Spenser feared that publishing might result in "overmuch cloying their noble eares" (635). "Cloy" works instructively here: to suggest that Spenser fears that in this economy of patronage his words may be considered by his audience (immediate and extended) to be a kind of currency, a purchasing of "commodity," and so fulsome; or that he fears that in such an economy of exchange – his words in return for favour and promotion – his poetry would be heard in *only* flattering ways, regardless of his own intended meaning; or that surfeit would stop up altogether the ears of the noble audience. In any of these cases, Spenser would "gather a contempt of my self," while his words would remain essentially unheard. Spenser's reservation makes it clear that he is a poet who is from the start of his career keenly aware that poetic meaning, as well as the estimation of the poet, is produced in an exchange fraught with social, political, and economic pressures. The submerged harvest metaphor in "gather" intimates that Spenser's concern lies more in reaping identity and reputation than reward, that he recognizes that moral agency depends upon his preserving a sense of self, and that he fears that the economy of exchange in patronage might produce in him self-alienation (he would harvest only his own contempt for himself). At the heart of Spenser's doubts about public service and patronage lies the fear that he will lose himself – a qualm registered obliquely in his disingenuous declaration that he is prepared to "adnihilate mine owne determinations" in response to Harvey's advice.

That the pressures to devalue both poet and poetic meaning would in Spenser's view only be intensified by his proximity to the centres of power seems apparent from the letter: its keynote of complacency – "here I am at Leicester House" – is muted by indications that he cannot subscribe wholeheartedly to the poetic and political program at Leicester House. Spenser's several references to the debate regarding rhymed versus quantitative poetry provide a case in point. Although Sidney and Dyer have "proclaimed ... a general surceasing and silence of balde Rymers," and although Harvey has promoted "English Versifying" rather than "Ryming," Spenser himself seems reluctant to follow suit. He notes that Sidney's and Dyer's proclamations have silenced not just "balde Rymers," but "also of the verie best to[o]" (635); and in an enclosure appended to the October 15th letter, but written ten days earlier, he says that he "was minded also to have sent [Harvey] English verses: or Rymes, for a farewell" (638). Whether Spenser here is implicitly defining "English verse" as rhyming verse or posing the two as alternatives, the point remains that he will not dismiss rhyme.

In order, then, for his words not to be considered mere currency (and that of a kind quickly devalued through surfeit), for his words to be heard and his meaning taken, and for his sense of self to remain secure, Spenser in his dedicatory poem to Sidney fashions an exchange between poet and patron in which his poetic talents and fecundity are not figured (in two senses) in strictly economic terms. More notably, Spenser presents himself as removed from the centre of power. His assumption of social distance from his dedicatee – he is simply a "shepheards swaine" while Sidney is "the president / Of noblesse and of chevalree" – is matched by a geographical distance which Spenser-Immerito seems determined to maintain: he will not follow his *Calender* to court; he will only "send more [works] after" this "little booke."[6] Moreover,

Spenser-Immerito seems particularly to draw attention to his *not* being situated at Leicester House. In advising his book to present itself as a "child whose parent is *unkent*," Spenser puns on his no longer being in Kent, in the Bishop of Rochester's employ, and so alludes to his public, civic identity as an up-and-coming secretary – a gesture which makes that much more pointed the lack of reference to his current position with Leicester.

Removal from the centre not only licenses Spenser's fecundity – "I will send more after thee" – but also permits him to establish moral autonomy. Although he presents himself as a "parent ... unkent" ("unknown" and no longer in Kent – but not at Leicester House), Spenser gives himself an occupation:

> asked, who thee forth did bring,
> A shepheards swaine saye did thee sing,
> All as *his* straying flocke he fedde. (lines 8–10; my emphasis)

Because Spenser presents himself as being a "shepheards swaine," and so not the owner of the flock, the possessive pronoun in line 10 acquires ambiguous reference. If it does not refer to the "shepheardes swaine," it must refer to "him that is the president / Of noblesse and chevalree" (lines 3–4), that is, Sidney. Notably, his flock is "straying." Spenser's dedication thus offers veiled censure of Sidney and his circle, targeting their remissness as Protestant leaders, perhaps, or (what may be more likely in view of the eminence of his patrons) warning them that their flocks need more vigilant shepherding. Spenser's implied censure makes more significant his requesting "pardon for [his] hardyhedde," a request which demonstrates how far he now feels himself to be from "cloying noble ears." Because the possessive pronoun in line 10 retains as well its reference to Spenser, the "shepheardes swaine," Spenser not only censures his potential patron(s), but also promotes his own important role in this shepherding; the flock is "his" in that he ministers to it.

Such details of the poem might readily be absorbed into the conventions of pastoral or dedicatory verse were it not that, first, the poem formally draws attention to the details and, second, the epilogue to the *Calender* picks up these details to transmute them in significant ways. Formally, the poem to Sidney stresses line 10, with its reference to the feeding of the straying flock; it is with this line that Spenser's handling of his rhyming triplets changes. Until this point, he enjambs his triplets, moving us on too briskly for reflection. But lines 9 and 10, which mark the end of the third triplet and start of the fourth, are not enjambed, even though line 10 remains part of the syntactical unit begun in the second line of the third triplet. Thus, although line 10, an adverbial clause, is grammatically subordinate, in effect it emerges from that subordination. Moreover, for the remainder of the poem, the triplets also form self-contained syntactical units, giving us in this last half of the poem, the half concerned with the poet rather than his "little book," more frequent pause for registering the features of this fictional self-presentation, for remarking in particular the poet's assumption of moral agency.

In the epilogue, details about shepherding reappear, but in a revealingly altered context. Here Spenser unveiledly adopts the role of teacher:

Loe I have made a Calender for every yeare,
That steele in strength, and time in durance shall outweare:
And if I have marked well the starres revolution,
It shall continewe till the worlds dissolution.
To teach the ruder shepheard how to feed his sheepe,
And from the falsers fraud his folded flocke to keepe.
   Goe lyttle Calender, thou hast a free passeporte. (lines 1–7)

From its position of moral, religious, and ecclesiastical certainty, Spenser's work will instruct "ruder" shepherds, teaching them how to keep their sheep, now, significantly, "folded" rather than straying as in the dedicatory poem to Sidney. The implication to be drawn is that it is the *Calender* itself which enfolds the sheep; through Immerito's agency, the sheep have been made safe from "falsers fraud." In view of the *Calender*'s ecclesiastical eclogues, the falseness here is probably not a generalized evil, but rather a specific allusion to Catholics or Catholic sympathizers.[7] In 1579, the year of the most intense marriage negotiations yet between Elizabeth and the Catholic Alençon, such claims about the moral efficacy of the *Calender* denote Spenser's sense of his volume as a significant sally in the efforts of the Leicester circle to persuade Elizabeth not to marry. That Spenser deliberately positions himself outside that circle indicates his sense that a poet's moral agency depends upon establishing distance within patronly relations.[8]

Spenser's removal of himself from the centre creates tension with the volume's more explicit and ostentatious display of the "new Poete" as soon to be very much the centre of attention – "beloved of all, embraced of the most, and wondred at of the best" (13), as E.K. says. The new Poet's prominence is implied even in the formatting of E.K.'s dedication to Harvey:

> To the most excellent and learned both
> Orator and Poete, Mayster Gabriell Harvey, his
> verie special and singular good frend E.K. commen-
> deth the good lyking of this his labour,
> and the patronage of the
> new Poete. (13)

Placed in this way – at the apex of an inverted pyramid, or the narrow end of a funnel – the "new Poete" is the point toward which "excellence" and "learning" and "oratory" and "poetry" have been tending or the fulcrum upon which rests the weight of accumulated learning and arts; in the latter rendering, the new Poet sustains his culture's learning and lore. Centred in these ways, the "new Poete" occupies a position analogous to that of Sidney, addressed on the title-page as follows:

> Entitled
> TO THE NOBLE AND VERTU-
> ous Gentleman most worthy of all titles
> both of learning and chevalrie M.
> Philip Sidney. (2)

With respect to their cultural positions, then, "Philip Sidney" and the "new Poete" are made to mirror each other in a way which collapses distances between the "uncouth" new Poet and the prominent Sidney.

In the prefatory material, E.K. remains determined to elide distances between the new Poet and cultural/political centres. He secures the proper orientation toward Immerito by suggesting that the new Poet will be, like Chaucer and like Virgil, a "loadstarre" (13). Even while acknowledging that certain features of the *Calender* appear "strange," almost alien, E.K.'s rhetorical strategies figure and refigure the work, as well as the new Poet, as centralized. Although the new Poet's words "be something hard, and of most men unused," for instance, this diction in fact testifies to the poet's learning, fits the "rusticall rudenesse of shepheards," and brings "great grace and ... auctoritie to the verse" by providing "an eternall image of antiquitie" and making the "style seeme grave ... and reverend" (14–15). The only effect of diction which seems out of place in this list is rusticity. This is also the one effect regarding which E.K. expresses some uncertainty about Immerito's intentions and regarding which we may detect implicit conflict between Immerito and E.K. Whereas E.K. assures the reader that Immerito's unusual words reflect his being "much traveiled and throughly redd" in the "most excellent Authors and most famous Poetes," he cannot be certain that Immerito shares this understanding:

But whether he useth them by such casualtye and custome, or of set purpose and choyse, as thinking them fittest for such rusticall rudenesse of shepheards, eyther for that theyr rough sounde would make his rymes more ragged and rusticall, or els because such olde and obsolete wordes are most used of country folke, sure I think, and think I think not amisse, that they bring great grace and, as one would say, auctoritie to the verse. (14)

E.K. acknowledges the possibility that rusticity remains Immerito's intended or prime effect, but he deliberately attenuates this possibility – grammatically, through expressing it in a subordinate clause, and rhetorically, through the marked alliteration (a device elsewhere mocked by E.K. and Harvey), through the doubled either-or construction, and through the verbal schemes (such as epizeuxis and polyptoton) which return us insistently to what E.K., rather than Immerito, thinks. And what E.K. thinks is that the new Poet and his work should, and will, become the cynosure of a courtly culture and aesthetic.

Certain of E.K.'s other tropes confirm the impression that, in presenting the new Poet, E.K. wishes to fashion him as a courtly figure and his work as primarily a source of aesthetic pleasure rather than moral or reformist instruction. Speaking still of Immerito's archaic diction, E.K. develops analogies which marginalize the rustic elements of the *Calender*:

But all as in most exquisite pictures they use to blaze and portraict not onely the daintie lineaments of beautye, but also rounde about it to shadow the rude thickets and craggy clifts, that by the basenesse of such parts, more excellency may accrew to the principall; for oftimes we fynde ourselves, I knowe not how, singularly delighted with the shew of such naturall rudenesse, and take great pleasure in that disorderly order. Even so doe those rough and harsh termes enlumine and make more clearly to appeare the brightnesse of brave and glorious words. So ofentimes a dischorde in Musick maketh a comely concordaunce: so great delight tooke the worthy Poete Alceus to behold a blemish in the joint of a wel shaped body. (15)

Construed in this way, the rusticity of the volume becomes little more than a foil to promote the excellency of "brave and glorious words."

Aware, perhaps, that his vision of the *Calender*'s rusticity does not accord entirely with Immerito's, E.K. seemingly reverses himself in a subsequent analogy, when he praises the new Poet for having "laboured to restore, as to theyr rightfull heritage such good and naturall English words, as have ben long time out of use and almost cleare disherited" (16). His analogy plays out, however, as a story which reconfigures the rustic (and therefore marginalized) as "stately," and implicitly urbane and well-tailored, while diction which borrows from French, Italian, and Latin (the diction, presumably, of the fashionable young man on the rise) is figured as a disinherited bastard, a cast-out wearing "peces and rags." Thus, even when seeming to subscribe to the rustic element of the *Calender*, E.K. in fact espouses the values of the centre.

E.K.'s patronage of the new Poet relies, then, on an orientation toward the centre, an orientation to which Spenser himself seems implicitly but insistently opposed, as the dedication to Sidney and the envoy attest. In related ways, E.K.'s introduction of the "new Poete" involves his articulation of a homosociality (to be reiterated within the *Calender* through Hobbinol) against which Colin Clout's career and poetics – informed with "gynerastice" – take shape: as truancy, according to the patronal relations conceived by E.K. and Hobbinol, but as resistance to the elision of selfhood, according to Spenser's construction of Colin.

E.K.'s advocacy of homosociality appears throughout his dedicatory epistle to Harvey as he establishes a male community of fellowship to surround the new Poet, a community of orators and poets, ancient and contemporary, a community of those dedicated to language and poetry. In smaller compass, he draws particular attention to the bonds of fellowship uniting Immerito, Harvey, and himself. E.K. closes his epistle to Harvey on this note:

And thus recommending the Author unto you, as unto his most special good frend, and my selfe unto you both, as one making singuler account of two so very good and so choise frends, I bid you both most hartely farwel, and commit you and your most commendable studies to the tuicion of the greatest. (20)

When E.K. says he makes "singuler account" of his two "so very good and so choise frends," he conflates Immerito and Harvey through amibiguous pronoun reference at the end of the sentence. The conflation is strengthened by the postscript, which urges Harvey to do what E.K. has said he hopes Immerito will do: publish previously composed works. Not only does E.K. establish in this way a mirror relation between Immerito and Harvey, he presents that mirroring expressly in terms of public identity, as a matter of their respective publications. As these last points suggest, the homosociality of E.K.'s epistle remains public, tied to civic identity and to matters of literature, rhetoric, and language. Almost as a corollary, E.K.'s articulation of homosociality takes on a misogynous cast. As well, his rhetorical turns shunt matters to do with women and with love ("gynerastice") to the private as opposed to the public sphere. Accordingly, tension between public and private underwrites E.K.'s presentation of the new Poet in such a way that homosociality and matters literary and rhetorical come to be signs for public identity, while "gynerastice" comes to be a sign for the private sphere, for private identity.

These tensions and alignments extend beyond E.K.'s epistle to inform his glosses to the *Calender*. One of E.K.'s first glosses provides us with a way to focus these matters. In introducing Colin to us, the narrator in "January" offers the following description:

All as the Sheepe, such was the shepeheards looke,
For pale and wanne he was, (alas the while,)

May seeme he lovd, or els some care he tooke:
Well couth he tune his pipe, and frame his stile (lines 7–10)

E.K. singles out "couth" for discussion, glossing it in ways pertinent to issues which are raised in the epistle and which will figure largely in the eclogues. E.K.'s choice of spelling, "couthe" as opposed to Spenser's "couth," signals a connection to the first words of the epistle, the proverb "Uncouthe, unkist," and so to E.K.'s presentation there of the new poet. E.K. employs that proverb centrally, substituting "uncouthe" for Chaucer's "unknowe"[9] in setting out the new Poet's campaign for public esteem, a campaign to make famous (couth), and central, the learned (couth) poet. Beyond that, E.K.'s gloss reflects his continuing emphasis on male fellowship; eagerly, he informs us of his happening to have a borrowed copy of Thomas Smith's book, lent to him by his good friend, Harvey. Significantly, too, the book which offers the interpretation of "couth" is a "booke of government," devoted to civic matters, language, and etymology. What E.K.'s gloss presents in little is a community of like-minded men engaged in humanistic pursuits, centred on Gabriel Harvey and fostered by his gift of a book to E.K.[10] The insistent intertextuality of this gloss is characteristic of E.K.'s annotations: his economy of hermeneutics is a hermetic one in so far as it precludes exclusively private mattters.

What Harvey effects in the margins of the *Calender* he also effects, E.K. implies, in his relationship with Spenser outside the volume. In a gloss which follows closely the one just discussed, E.K. considers the character of Hobbinol:

Hobbinol) is a fained country name, whereby, it being so commune and usuall, seemeth to be hidden the person of some his very speciall and most familiar freend, whom he entirely and extraordinarily beloved, as peradventure shall be more largely declared hereafter. (33)

The coyness here does not make for much of a puzzle; Hobbinol can be readily identified as Harvey. Indeed, E.K. wants Harvey disclosed. E.K. presents Hobbinol-Harvey's relationship with Spenser as close and sustaining and calculated to promote Spenser's civic role. One of E.K.'s glosses to "June" strengthens this impression, casting Hobbinol-Harvey in the role of mentor. E.K. says that it is "no poetical fiction" that Hobbinol advises Colin to move to the south; rather this is

> unfeynedly spoken of the Poete selfe, who for speciall occasion of private affayres (as I have bene partly of himselfe informed) and for his more preferment removing out of the Northparts came into the South, as Hobbinoll indeede advised him privately. (114)

E.K.'s co-ordinating conjunction "and" makes Spenser's "private affayres" seem, at the least, well sorted with his civic aspirations. E.K.'s assurance that Hobbinol "advised [Spenser] privately" to move south "for his more preferment" goes even further, to virtually subsume private concerns under public ambitions by implying that the "speciall occasion of private affayres" *was* Harvey's private advice to move. In this way, E.K. turns even private commerce to public ends.

E.K.'s presentation of the "new Poete," then, involves his elevating public roles, promoting homosociality at the expense of private experience and "gynerastice," and figuring Harvey-Hobbinol as particularly pivotal in sustaining the new Poet's proper community. Within the fiction of the eclogues, Spenser represents his relationship with Harvey very differently from E.K.'s conception.[11] Unlike Harvey's gift to E.K., Hobbinol's gifts fail to win Colin. Preferring to turn toward Rosalind, Colin scorns Hobbinol's gifts and by this gesture refuses to complete the circle of fellowship which began with Harvey's lending a book to E.K.:

> It is not *Hobbinol*, wherefore I plaine,
> Albee my love he seeke with dayly suit:
> His clownish gifts and curtsies I disdaine,
> His kiddes, his cracknelles, and his early fruit.
> Ah foolish *Hobbinol*, thy gyfts bene vayne:
> *Colin* them gives to *Rosalind* againe. (lines 55–60)

In this opening gesture begins the series of oppositions that reverberate throughout the *Calender*, oppositions between the eclogues and the gloss, Colin and E.K., Colin and Hobbinol-Harvey, gynerastice and homosociality, private and public concerns. Hobbinol, along with E.K., looks toward a public world and seeks to turn, or rather return, Colin to that world.[12]

In its distribution of the proper names "Hobbinol," "Colin," and "Rosalind," the stanza rehearses on a visual level the results of Colin's gesture. Hobbinol's name, appearing in the first and fifth lines of the stanza at about the same mid-line point, mirrors itself, while the names of Colin and Rosalind, yoked together in the final line of the stanza, remain outside the circuit formed by the repetition of "Hobbinol." To recall the terms in which Immerito's dedicatory verse and E.K.'s epistle play against each other, Hobbinol is in the centre while Colin and Rosalind inhabit the margins – situations which anticipate the dispositions of Hobbinol and Colin in "June," the eclogue in which Hobbinol urges Colin (who apparently resides in the north country when not being pursued from coast to coast) to relocate to the courtly dales.

We can suppose that, in speaking of Hobbinol's "gifts" to Colin, Spenser has in mind the passing on of rhetorical and literary skills. That "January" is the most rhetorically adorned of the eclogues offers support for this supposition.[13] Lines 61–6 dramatize Colin's turning of Harvey-Hobbinol's gifts to the private matter of love, when Colin laments:

> I love thilke lasse, (alas why doe I love?)
> And am forlorne, (alas why am I lorne?)
> Shee deignes not my good will, but doth reprove,
> And of my rurall musick holdeth scorne.
> Shepheards devise she hateth as the snake,
> And laughes the songes, that *Colin Clout* doth make.

Admiringly, E.K. draws attention to the rhetorical play in the first two lines: "I love) a prety Epanorthosis in these two verses, and withall a Paronomasia or playing with the word, where he sayth (I love thilke lasse (alas etc" (34). As E.K. judges so approvingly, Colin demonstrates here his facility in poetic-rhetorical skills.[14] E.K. identifies first "epanorthosis," a figure in which a word is recalled in order to substitute a more correct or stronger term. His emphasis indicates that he reads Colin's "alas why doe I love?" as Colin's self-correction, as Colin's asking, in effect, "why do I love a lass and not Hobbinol?"[15] Such emphasis remains in keeping with E.K.'s promotion of fellowship with Harvey and of (proper) "pederastice" over "gynerastice." Closer attention to the pun suggests that Colin is here turning his rhetorical skill to private matters, to "gynerastice," and not, as E.K. implies, expressing the desire for correction. Colin's pun, "a lass/alas," establishes an equivalence between the object of unfulfilled desire and the expression of unfulfilled desire, suggesting precisely that for Colin gynerastice offers the proper subject for – proves commensurate with – his rhetorical gifts.

If Hobbinol's gifts, his "kiddes, cracknels, and early fruit," are literary and rhetorical skills, then Colin's recycling of them also involves a "ripening" and translation upward; what Colin gives to Rosalind are "songs" and "rurall musick." The sly suggestion may be, not only that Hobbinol-Harvey's literary skills and devices are relatively immature, but that it is the redirecting of such talents toward gynerastice which (Rosalind's scorn notwithstanding) makes poetry. And Colin's renaming of Hobbinol's "clownish" gifts as "songs" and "musick" shows Colin's wish to make himself unlike Hobbinol: whereas E.K. emphasizes likenesses between patron and poet, Colin insists on distinctions. Further, the turn of phrase in Colin's report of Rosalind's scorn – she "laughes the songes, that *Colin Clout* doth make" (line 66) – permits a double reading: reversing the subject and object, one can read "songs" as the grammatical subject and "Colin Clout" as the object.[16] Such a reading points to Colin's understanding of the intimate relationship between poetic-rhetorical practice and identity, or selfhood. Colin implies that he is making himself through his songs, that in directing his skill away from public or civic purposes he fashions himself.

"January," then, opposes the conceptions of the poet fostered by E.K. and Hobbinol. Our gauging of this implicit opposition must measure more directly the degree to which Spenser holds a non-ironic view of Colin, since my argument requires our accepting Spenser's treatment of Colin as essentially sympathetic. Brief consideration of the differences in this eclogue between E.K. and the narrator helps to define the narrator's, and arguably Spenser's, sympathetic treatment of Colin. The narrator certainly mocks Colin's excesses, putting them in perspective; he does so gently, though, and without calling into question the seeming genuineness of the emotions, leading us, indeed, to register the "sincerity" of Colin's emotion through those very distancing techniques. Conversely, E.K. consistently collapses distinctions between

Immerito and Colin and directs us to consider Colin's articulation of love woes as artifice.

The opening stanzas emphasize the narrator's distance from Colin, through the narrator's insisting on Colin's station – "A Shepeheards boye (no better doe him call)" (line 1) – and, especially, through his observing that on this "sunneshine day" (line 3), "Winters wastful spight was almost spent" (line 2). While the narrator finds the promise of winter's relenting, Colin hypostatizes "winters wrath" (line 19), drawing (and drawing out) in this "myrrour" (line 20) the lineaments of his woe. Colin's anatomizing of his woe thus strikes us as self-indulgent.[17] Similarly, the narrator draws an analogy between Colin and his sheep, "All as the Sheep, such was the shepeheards looke" (line 7), after having first pointedly attributed the condition of the sheep to the privations of winter (lines 4–6). It is, however, just this emphasis on their privations – an emphasis which precludes pathetic fallacy and so again underscores Colin's self-indulgence – which prepares the ground for a reversal and shift in perspective in the closing stanza of the eclogue. There we read that Colin "Arose, and homeward drove his sonned sheepe, / Whose hanging heads did seeme his carefull cases to weepe" (lines 77–8). Here the narrator makes a point of construing the continued downcastness of the sheep as commiseration for Colin: "sunned," they are no longer suffering terribly the privations of winter.

The narrator's closing perspective, then, focuses sympathy on Colin, a sympathy which gains definition through being counterpointed to the narrator's opening, distanced, perspective. It is as if Colin's complaint itself has moved the narrator. In a volume replete with in-house audiences, the narrator's implicit response to Colin's complaint should claim our attention: his sympathetic response permits our accepting, if only provisionally, the sincerity of Colin's sorrow in love.

E.K.'s presentation, on the other hand, continually alerts us to the artifice in the figure of Colin. In the Argument prefacing the eclogue, E.K. assumes that Colin's complaint involves posturing with respect to love:

In this fyrst Eglogue Colin cloute a shepheardes boy complaineth him of his unfortunate love, being but newly (as semeth) enamoured of a countrie lasse called Rosalinde. (29)

Alerted by E.K.'s parenthetical demurral, which ambiguously qualifies "newly" or "enamoured" – and either qualification looks askance at Colin's love – we might turn to E.K.'s gloss on Rosalind's name to find that the whole tenor of the note suggests a firmly established relationship: "Rosalinde," E.K. informs us, "is also [like Hobbinol's] a feigned name, which being well ordered, wil bewray the very name of hys love and mistresse" (34). Rather than being an instance of pleonasm, the phrase "love and mistresse" reflects E.K.'s belief that Spenser-Colin is not in fact *newly* enamoured. As well, the reader who has been attending punctiliously to E.K.'s presentation of the "new Poete" might well recall that in his epistle to Harvey E.K. writes that Immerito-Spenser's love woes stem from an

unstayed youth [which] had long wandred in the common labyrinth of Love, in which time to mitigate and allay the heate of his passion, or els to warne (as he sayth) the young shepheards .s. equalls and companions of his unfortunate folly, he compileth these xij Eglogues. (19)

Having offered in explanation of the volume's composition a version of circumstances in which at least some time intervenes between the new Poet's entering the labyrinth and his determining to "mitigate ... or warne," E.K. reminds us, in the Argument and gloss looked at already, that Colin's love is only seemingly, fictively, new.

Set against E.K.'s cool presumption that Colin remains a figure of artifice, the narrator's, and so Spenser's, attitude toward Colin in "January" emerges as essentially sympathetic and non-ironic, giving us surer ground for assuming that Spenser countenances Colin's turning poetry toward private purposes rather than the civic ones championed by E.K. and Hobbinol.

In "Aprill," Spenser formulates more extensively this opposition, strengthening Hobbinol's association with the public sphere and confirming Colin's truancy from that world. The centre-piece of the eclogue, Colin's "laye of Eliza," is framed by expressions of regret that the Colin who can produce such commendatory verse has grown "alienate" (Argument, "Aprill," 70) from the community of shepherds and their pursuits. Spenser, however, does not share the judgement of E.K., Hobbinol, and the pastoral auditor, Thenot, regarding Colin's truancy from the laureate's sphere. Instead, Spenser indicates the limitation inherent in the public-mindedness of Hobbinol, Thenot, and E.K., namely, their inability to register depths of private experience or even recognize the boundaries which define Colin.

In his Argument prefacing the eclogue, E.K. stresses that Colin's truancy is a matter for correction. "Hobbinol," says E.K.,

is here set forth more largely, complayning him of [Colin's] great misadventure in Love, whereby his mynd was alienate and with drawen not onely from him, who most loved him, but also from all former delightes and studies, aswell in pleasaunt pyping, as conning ryming and singing, and other his laudable exercises. (70)

E.K.'s designation of Colin's exercises as "laudable" underscores his sense that Colin's skill should be directed toward public ends: Colin's exercises are "laudable," that is, praiseworthy, in so far as they are intended to praise, presumably, Elizabeth. In this regard, E.K. conflates Colin and Immerito-Spenser, for he reads the entire eclogue, not just the "laye of Eliza," as "purposely intended to the honor and prayse of our most gracious sovereigne, Queene Elizabeth" (Argument, "Aprill," 70). Clearly, E.K. conceives of "Aprill," with its framing story of Colin's truancy, as designed by Spenser to point the need to recover Colin's poetic voice for laureate purposes. E.K. thus fails to register Colin's private experience.

In this connection, E.K. focuses informatively on the periphrasis for Rosalind, "the Widdowes daughter of the glenne":

The Widowes) He calleth Rosalind the Widowes daughter of the glenne, that is, of a country Hamlet or borough, which I thinke is rather sayde to coloure and concele the person, then simply spoken. (77–8)

Apparently unwilling to let Rosalind remain concealed and countrified, E.K. goes on:

For it is well knowen, even in spighte of Colin and Hobbinoll, that shee is a Gentle woman of no meane house, nor endewed with anye vulgare and common gifts, both of nature and manners: but suche indeede, as neede nether Colin be ashamed to have her made knowne by his verses, nor Hobbinol be greved, that so she should be commended to immortalitie. (78)

The translation of Rosalind to social eminence, from the marginalized private space where Spenser-Immerito has concealed her, indicates just how firmly E.K. remains committed to the conception of Immerito's career and poetry as culturally centred and very public in nature. In what seems a glib disregard of boundaries, E.K. wishes to make known what Spenser-Immerito desires to keep private.

E.K.'s Argument produces a corollary effect in a momentary conflation of Hobbinol and Colin. According to E.K., Hobbinol as the guardian of Colin's civic career, takes

> occasion, for proofe of *his* more excellencie and skill in poetrie, to recorde a songe, which the sayd Colin, sometime made in honour of her Majestie, whom abruptly he termeth Elysa. (70; my emphasis)

The ambiguous antecedent of "his" permits our attributing Colin's "excellencie and skill in poetrie" to Hobbinol, an effect which recalls E.K.'s mirror tricks in the Epistle. Once again E.K. collapses distinctions – here between patron/mentor and poet – in a way which elides literary subjectivity.

In the framing fiction of "Aprill," Spenser extends through Hobbinol and Thenot the matters raised by E.K., developing the issues to emphasize that laureateship not only elides private concerns but also precludes uniqueness of poetic voice. With the exchange of Hobbinol and Thenot, Spenser highlights Hobbinol's promotion of public concerns and homosociality. Hobbinol's complaint of Colin's "misadventure in Love" moves quickly from considering Colin's "payne" to assessing the loss to the pastoral community; the aural pun in line 11 – we can hear Hobbinol's "a lasse" as "alas" – stresses that Hobbinol's regret is specifically occasioned by Colin's loving a lass, rather than his fellow shepherd:

> the ladde, whome long I lovd so deare,
> Nowe loves a lasse, that all his love doth scorne:
> He plongd in payne, his tressed locks dooth teare.
>
> Shepheards delights he dooth them all forsweare,
> Hys pleasaunt Pipe, whych made us meriment,
> He wylfully hath broke, and doth forbeare
> His wonted songs, wherein he all outwent. (lines 10–16)

Like Hobbinol, Thenot does not remain focused on Colin's painful experience. His question, "Ys love such pinching payne to them, that prove," prompts him to another, seemingly more pertinent question, "And hath he skill to make so excellent, / Yet hath so little skill to brydle love?" (lines 18–20). After hearing Hobbinol's rehearsal of Colin's "laye of Eliza," Thenot rues the "foolish boy, that is with love yblent," concluding that "Great pittie is, he be in such taking, / For naught caren, that bene so lewdly bent" (lines 155–7). Thenot's diction places him in E.K.'s camp with respect to "gynerastice." In calling Colin "lewdly" inclined, Thenot maintains E.K.'s distinction between (proper) "pederastice," to which the learned incline, and "gynerastice," which draws men – and has drawn Colin – away from humanistic, that is, learned and civic, pursuits. Moreover, in accusing Colin of "naught caren," Thenot echoes the phrase so often assigned to Colin's condition, "careful case," in which "careful" implies that love has filled Colin with "care" (in the sense both of worry and of solicitous regard). Thenot's use of the phrase, however, effectively obliterates the implications which cluster around "careful case," for Thenot's phrase implies that the only thing worthy of "care" is learning. Because Colin no longer has care of, or from, learning, he is empty, he is "naught." In making the lovelorn, "lewd," Colin a cipher, Thenot denies the fullness of Colin's experience of love. The pun on "naught" as cipher and as slang for vulva confirms how thoroughgoing and how thoroughly contemptuous is Thenot's denial of such fullness.[18]

As does E.K., then, both Hobbinol and Thenot refuse to register the fullness and the depth of Colin's inner life. Thenot's greeting of Hobbinol at the start of the eclogue suggests that Spenser indeed intends to represent the pastoral world conceived, inhabited, and articulated by Hobbinol and Thenot as one which does not accommodate inwardness or literary subjectivity. Thenot wishes to know why Hobbinol is weeping:

Tell me good Hobbinoll, what garres thee greete?
What? hath some Wolfe thy tender Lambes ytorne?
Or is thy Bagpype broke, that soundes so sweete?
Or art thou of thy loved lasse forlorne?

Or bene thine eyes attempred to the yeare,
Quenching the gasping furrowes thirst with rayne?

Like April shoure, so stremes the trickling teares
Adowne thy cheeke, to quenche thy thristye payne. (lines 1–8)

Thenot's survey is not only perfunctory but parodic in the short shrift it makes (in lines 3–5) of the concerns which distinguished and preoccupied Colin in "January." It is a canvassing of the conventional pastoral roles of shepherd, poet, and lover, moreover, which emphasizes precisely the conventionality – and so repeatability – of such roles: if Hobbinol's sufferings can be likened to Colin's, then a "careful case" seems like mere mask or role. Thenot's most expansive surmise, that Hobbinol is "attempred to the yeare," works more subtly still to deny Hobbinol the proprietorship of his careful case by leaving "payne" without any fixed antecedent. Hobbinol's "payne" seems to have no cause beyond "attemperment to the yeare." In describing Hobbinol's weeping as intended to "quench [his] thristye payne," Thenot repeats images from his description of the rain's "Quenching the gasping furrowes thirst," forging in this way an echoic connection between Hobbinol's pain and the season. Such "attemperment" leaves no place for the inwardness or depth of experience which a less generalized source of "payne" might betoken.

Hobbinol's introduction to Colin's song of Eliza turns upon a similar congruence – in this instance, of poet's mind and external circumstance – to suggest that his vision of the world, and of Colin's place in that world, likewise does not accommodate inwardness or unique literary subjectivity. In consenting to Thenot's request that he rehearse Colin's song, Hobbinol locates the genesis of Colin's poetry in an outward-turning gesture, scanting in this way whatever might have been Colin's private impetus:

Contented I: then will I singe his laye
Of fayre *Elisa*, Queene of shepheardes all:
Which once he made, as by a spring he laye,
And tuned it unto the Waters fall. (lines 33–6)

Uncharacteristically, the first and third lines of this quatrain have identical rhyme words. The coincidence of "laye" as song and "laye" as a figure for pastoral *otium* suggests that, for Hobbinol, Colin's public poetry expresses fully his experience, that Colin's "life," as we would say today, does not extend beyond the poetry. This means that Hobbinol's "recording" of Colin's lay is more than a rendition of Colin's song: it is a rehearsal of Colin. A more radical loss of autonomy could scarcely be imagined than the state of being *repeatable*.

Spenser's fears about the dangers to self of laureateship and patronage thus strikingly underwrite his self-presentation in the eclogue which helped to inaugurate the cult of Elizabeth and which established Spenser in the minds of his contemporaries, and ours, as laureate *nonpareil*. Spenser criticism provides us with an indication of just how justifiable were Spenser's fears that laureateship would elide personal concerns. With few exceptions, and following E.K.'s silence in the gloss, critics have assumed that in stanza 9 of the "laye of Eliza" Colin nominates Queen Elizabeth as the fourth grace:

> Lo how finely the graces can it foote
>   to the Instrument.
> They dauncen deffly, and singen soote,
>   in their meriment.
> Wants not a fourth grace, to make the daunce even?
> Let that rowme to *my Lady* be yeven:
>   She shalbe a grace,
>   To fyll the fourth place,
> And reigne with the rest in heaven. (lines 109–18; my emphasis)

Arguably, though, by "my Lady" Colin means his love, Rosalind.[19] That E.K. neglects to note Rosalind's presence in Colin's song and poetics, that he directs us to hear only praise of the Queen, which by and large we do, gauges in small compass the pressures of patronage on poetic meaning.

With regard to Rosalind in "Aprill," E.K. faces a conflict between his unwillingness to let Rosalind remain countrified and unknown and his unwillingness, or inability, to allow room for Rosalind in Spenser's song of praise. In his gloss on line 26 of the eclogue, E.K. insists that since Rosalind is "a Gentle woman of no meane house, nor endewed with anye vulgare and common gifts both of nature and manners," Colin need not "be ashamed to have her made knowne by his verses" (78); yet in his gloss on the "graces" E.K. does not follow the logic of his own estimation of Rosalind to identify her as the "Lady" celebrated in Colin's verses. Tellingly, too, E.K. reconfigures as "shame" what is in Colin the impulse to turn inward and away from the centre, suggesting again just how thoroughly E.K. identifies as normative, and as a sign of healthy self-esteem, the impulse to publish (make public): literary subjectivity, according to E.K., is exclusively a public enterprise.

E.K. remains staunchly, sometimes otiosely, opposed to the desires animating Colin and informing his poetics. But Hobbinol in "June" participates in an exchange with Colin which, while developing very fully the oppositions between Hobbinol's laureate poetics and Colin's "homely" poetics,[20] opens up space for empathy in patronly relations even if it does not entirely reconfigure those relations.

Hobbinol, initially, tries repeatedly and in vain to recover Colin, to woo him back to the community of shepherds, to a pleasaunce public in orientation, to the "harbour" afforded by the patronage of "shepheards ritch." He extols the virtues of his pleasaunce, in a truncated rehearsal of the song of Elisa:

> Here no night Ravens lodge more black then pitche,
> Nor elvish ghosts, nor gastly owles doe flee.
>
> But frendly Faeries, met with many Graces,
> And lightfote Nymphes can chace the lingring night,
> With Heydeguyes, and trimly trodden traces,
> While systers nyne, which dwell on *Parnasse* hight,
> Doe make them musick, for their more delight;
> And *Pan* himselfe to kisse their christall faces,
> Will pype and daunce, when *Phoebe* shineth bright:
> Such pierlesse pleasures have we in these places. ("June," lines 23–32)

Art flourishes in Hobbinol's pleasaunce, art centred upon Elizabeth. Indeed, it is Elizabeth who makes possible this poetry: Pan will pipe and dance *"when* Phoebe shineth bright" ("June," line 31; my emphasis). Enabled by Elizabeth-Phoebe, such poetry is courtly poetry par excellence, preserving detachment from anything outside or, more precisely, underneath the song. The "systers nyne" of Hobbinol's state "Doe make them musick, for their more delight" ("June," lines 28–9). Whether the "their" of this line refers to the "systers nyne" or to the fairies, graces, and nymphs of the earlier lines, the poetic revels evoked in this stanza remain self-enclosed. And the faces, kissed by Pan, are "christall," transparent, able to reflect the beholder, with no depth of shadow beneath: this poetic pleasaunce does not accommodate inwardness.

A well-tempered site, Hobbinol's pleasaunce is untroubled by "wolves," or "ravens," or "elvish ghosts," or "gastly owles" because the poetry produced in this pleasaunce does not sound the depths of political or personal shadows. The "ayre[s]" here are "simple"; uncompounded by political allusion or personal reference, these "lovely layes" may be "freely boste[d]" because they *mean* so transparently and innocuously. E.K., whose pedantry often makes him an unwittingly reliable guide, reminds us of what this poetry excludes when he glosses "faeries" and "elves" with details which, while drawn from bygone eras, nevertheless target the deep religious and factional divides of the Elizabethan court. "June"'s pleasaunce also excludes shadings of moral or reformist purposes, as Hobbinol intimates when he names its pleasures "pierlesse" in pointed rebuttal of Piers, the moral, reformist voice of "May."

The poetry conceived by Hobbinol does not sound any of this, not only because of the crystal lyricism which precludes referential meaning, but also because this poetry remains univocal. Although this pleasaunce shelters "Byrds of every kynde," the songs do not reflect diversity of voice: all the birds "To the waters fall their tunes attemper right." And, since these birds refrain from all but "chereful cheriping," the poetry seems generically uniform.

Such collapsing of distinctions – in voices, kinds, poets, poetic effects, and purposes – contrasts significantly with the poetics espoused and figured by Colin in this eclogue. Colin's business here is precisely to distinguish himself and his poetics in ways which permit proliferation of, and increased resonance in, poetic voices, kinds, and purposes. Colin's distinctions rest particularly upon centrifugal movement away from the courtly centre touted by Hobbinol. Colin begins by reminding us and Hobbinol that he has no place, no patronly "harbour" of the kind promoted by Hobbinol as centred and available in the courtly dales. Nowhere does Colin appear so lamentably "alienated" as here: pursued by "angry Gods ... from coste to coste," he "Can nowhere fynd, to shroude [his] lucklesse pate" (lines 15–16). As the allusion to the *Aeneid* insinuates, however, heroic poetry, ambition, and accomplishment originate from the periphery. Moreover, in a reversal of what Helgerson has identified as the typical pattern of the

Elizabethan poet, and what Hobbinol represents as maturation – "Lo *Collin*, here the place, whose pleasaunt syte / From other shades hath weand my wandering mynde" (lines 1–2) – Colin represents as growth the movement away from the poetic delights of the courtly milieu.[21]

As a corollary to Colin's removal from the centre, his "sovereign" is not the Phoebe whose shining provides the occasion, cause, and object of courtly poetic revels, but *"Tityrus,"* that is, Chaucer, from whom Colin learned "homely, as I can, to make." This is not the Chaucer esteemed by E.K. in the epistle to Harvey as a "Loadestarre" for "his excellencie and wonderful skil in making" (13), and commended by E.K. in his "June" gloss, again for "hys excellencie" in poetry (117). Indeed, E.K.'s gloss distorts Colin's praise of Chaucer by failing to register at all just what it is that elicits Colin's regard for Chaucer: his position as "the soveraigne head / Of shepheards all, that bene with love ytake" and as a writer whose "mery tales" keep shepherds sufficiently awake to tend their sheep (lines 88–9). Not merely a source of aesthetic pleasure and Anglo-lingual pride to Colin (as it is to E.K.), Chaucer's poetry serves diverse purposes, of love, therapy, and morality. Metaphors alert us to the centifugal force of Colin's poetics. The difference between E.K.'s metaphor of the "loadstarre" and Colin's metaphor of Chaucer as a wellhead ("spring") provides an elegant measure of the differences in their Chaucerian poetics: E.K.'s Chaucer exerts regulatory force, drawing poets from errancy to a single point or centre; Colin's Chaucer sustains more fecund, diverse, even errant poetry.

While Colin espouses a poetics which resists the cynosural pull of the court – and so licenses fecundity and diversity in voice, genre, and purpose – and which finds epic potential in the restlessness of marginal wandering, his poetry remains in its own way centred: in and on himself. "I wote," says Colin,

> my rymes bene rough, and rudely drest:
> The fytter they, my carefull case to frame:
> Enough is me to paint out my unrest,
> And poore my piteous plaints out in the same. (lines 77–80)

Critics who simply regret Colin's focus on his "carefull case," regarding his expression of his sufferings as intemperate and self-indulgent, miss much of the vocational dynamic of this eclogue. In his fervent wish that poetry could be the vehicle by which he could make the world and Rosalind feel his pain, Colin dreams of a literary subjectivity inconceivable to E.K.:

> But if on me some little drops would flowe,
> Of that the spring was in [Chaucer's] learned hedde,
> I soone would learne these woods, to wayle my woe,
> And teache the trees, their trickling teares to shedde.
>
> Then should my plaints, causd of discurtesee,
> As messengers of all my painfull plight,
> Flye to my love, where ever that she bee,
> And pierce her heart with poynt of worthy wight:
> As she deserves, that wrought so deadly spight.
> And thou *Menalcas*, that by trecheree
> Didst underfong my lasse, to wexe so light,
> Shouldest well be knowne for such thy villanee. (lines 93–104)

E.K.'s glossing of "poynt of worthy wight," which picks up on only one of several possible puns, signals his failure once again to respond to Colin's poetics: "Poynte of worthy wite) the pricke of deserved blame" (117). E.K.'s substituting the spelling "wite," with its visual pun on "wit," for Colin's "wight" reflects his continued focus on Colin's "excellencie in making," his "wittiness in devising," as E.K. phrases it in the epistle to Harvey. As well, E.K.'s pun shows his continuing insistence that Colin's are, as he says in the Argument to "Aprill," "laudable" poetic exercises, directed in good epideictic fashion toward praise and blame. Finally, E.K.'s pun on "wit" obscures Colin's own pun on "wight" as both blame and man. Colin wishes Rosalind to feel the point of his blame and also his worthiness as a man, to feel that the point of the blame *is* his worthiness. Colin's pun thus establishes an equivalence between his sense of self and his poetic exercise: his blaming of Rosalind signals, not his skill, as E.K. would have it, but his conception of self.

As does his gloss, so does E.K.'s Argument to "June" consider Colin's "carefull case" to be an effect of poetic device and wit. "This Eglogue is wholly vowed to the complayning of Colins ill successe in his love," says E.K., "For being (as is aforesaid) enamoured of a Country lasse Rosalind, and *having (as seemth)* founde place in her heart, he lamenteth to his deare frend Hobbinoll, that he is nowe forsaken unfaithfully, and in his steed Menalcas, another shepheard received disloyally" (109; my emphasis). "And this," concludes E.K., "is the whole Argument of this Eglogue." E.K.'s "(as seemth)" registers something other than scepticism regarding Rosalind's intial acceptance of Colin; such suspicion would not call into question the "reality" of Colin's experience. E.K.'s doubt is more profound; his qualification in fact disqualifies Colin's experience *as* experience, making Colin's finding and losing of a place in Rosalind's heart to be merely poetic seeming and artifice. A far-reaching corollary effect of E.K.'s scepticism is to discount the very possibility of inwardness, or interiority: places in and of the heart are, for E.K., merely rhetorical and poetic topoi without ontological standing.

E.K.'s urbane scepticism reverberates hollowly against the eclogue and particularly against Hobbinol's empathetic response to Colin's plight. "O carefull *Colin*," says Hobbinol, "I lament thy case, / Thy teares would make the hardest flint to flowe" (lines 113–14). Moved by Colin's suffering, Hobbinol is moved also to a muted acknowledgment that the courtly poetic pleasaunce to which he tried to recruit Colin proffers delights that are delightful by virtue of detachment from experiences (whether personal, political, or spiritual) that include depths and shadows. Hobbinol closes the eclogue with a benediction, tacitly reforming the landscape he celebrates early in the eclogue as one where "frendly Faeries, met with many Graces, / and lightfote Nymphes can chace the lingring night, / With Heydeguyes, and trimly trodden traces" (lines 25–27). "Now is time," says Hobbinol in closing,

> homeward to goe:
> Then ryse ye blessed flocks, and home apace,
> Least night with stealing steppes doe you forsloe,
> And wett your tender Lambes, that by you trace. (117–20)

This landscape retains little of Hobbinol's courtly poetic pleasaunce, assuming instead some of the moral and social imperatives of Colin's "homely" poetics as Hobbinol admits night's "stealing steppes," regards the "traces" of vulnerable flocks, and locates "home" in movement away from the centre.

With its accommodations of Colin's desires and poetics, "June" presents a patronal structure which is potentially more enabling than that within which E.K., and sometimes Hobbinol, seek to situate the poet. "June" remains a special case in the *Calender*, however, its accommodations tested and only imperfectly realized in subsequent eclogues, a fact which supports our reading the *Calender* as largely concerned to adumbrate failures of patronage. In "August," for example, we learn that Colin's "June" wish to make the community of shepherds (poets) respond to his plight seems to have taken some effect. Offering to rehearse a "doolefull verse / Of Rosalend ... / That Colin made," Cuddie asks, "who knowes not Rosalend," bearing witness in this way to Colin's careful case (lines 140–1). In other ways, though, "August" demonstrates a poetics that does not accommodate literary subjectivity and interiority. Perigot's lovelorn condition parodies Colin's plight, while the singing match, in performing Perigot's pain, renders as poetic, aesthetic object what in Colin signals subjectivity. Perigot responds with admiration, as E.K. might, to Cuddie's performance of Colin's "doolefull verse":

O *Colin, Colin* the shepheards joye,
   How I admire ech turning of thy verse:
And *Cuddie*, fresh *Cuddie*, the liefest boye,
   How dolefully his doole thou didst reherse.

The emotional charge of Colin's case has become an aesthetic dimension of the performance and therefore something rehearsable by others rather than something informing Colin.

More than any other eclogue, "October" is systematic, though far from coherently resolved, in its consideration of the poet's position in Elizabethan social, political, and patronal structures. From its often shifting (and often cross-purposed) lines of argument emerge clearly opposed positions on poetic autonomy and agency, with Cuddie consistently imagining the poet as subject to, and subjected to, extrinsic forces, and Piers just as consistently imagining the poet as autonomous. It is Cuddie who represents poets as reliant on patronage and as ill-served by love, while Piers downplays the force of patronage and celebrates the influence of love. It is Cuddie who is esteemed by E.K. as representing "the perfecte paterne of a Poete." Arguably, it is Piers whose poetics more nearly approximates Colin's and Spenser-Immerito's. Piers's metaphors very confidently ascribe not just autonomy, but also sovereignty, to the poet. "Lyft up thy selfe out of the lowly dust," he admonishes Cuddie, "Turne thee to those, that weld the awful crowne, / To doubted Knights" (lines 38–41). Piers's is a vision of the poet as self-sustaining and as able to, in some sense, become the monarch or the knight. Such a poet can establish the "kingdom of his language," when his muse "stretch[es] her selfe at large from East to West" (line 44).[22] "There," says Piers, "may thy Muse display her fluttrying wing" (line 43). Piers's "there" very emphatically centres the poet at court, but this is a court of his own making. Moreover, Piers's defence of love's effects on Colin articulates even as it idealizes the desires which animate Colin and his poetics.

When in "December" Colin reviews his life and career, he does so in a way which points to his understanding of divergences between public and private poetics. He laments what E.K. in the Argument calls his "unseasonable harveste wherein the fruits fall ere they be rype":

Thus is my sommer worne away and wasted,
Thus is my harvest hastened all to rathe:
The eare that budded faire, is burnt and blasted,
And all my hoped gaine is turned to scathe.
   Of all the seede, that in my youth was sowne,
   Was nought but brakes and brambles to be mowne.

My boughes with bloosmes that crowned were at firste,
And promised of timely fruite such store,
Are left both bare and barrein now at erst:
The flattring fruite is fallen to grownd before,
   And rotted, ere they were halfe mellow ripe:
   My harvest wast, my hope away dyd wipe.

The fragrant flowres, that in my garden grewe,
Bene withered, as they had bene gathered long.
Theyr rootes bene dryed up for lacke of dewe,
Yet dewed with teares they han be ever among.
   Ah who has wrought my *Rosalind* this spight
   To spil the flowres, that should her girlond dight? (lines 97–114)

E.K. alerts us to the extended metaphors here when he glosses "fragrant flowres" as "sundry studies and laudable partes of learning, wherein how our Poete is seene, be they witnesse which are privie to his study" (211).[23] Coercing this stanza into supporting his presentation of the "new Poete" as learned, as qualified to be a public poet par excellence, E.K. thus shows himself to be, characteristically, blinkered with respect to Colin's meaning. In these stanzas, Colin distinguishes between two kinds of poetry, linking "fragrant flowres" explicitly to the "girlond" that should adorn Rosalind and so to private matters. He alludes to public poetry in the images of trees and fruit, as his reference to "flattring fruite" in particular indicates. More generally, his reliance on metaphors of husbandry suggests that he has in mind here poetry which is public in orientation.[24]

The discrepancy between E.K.'s gloss and Colin's meanings suggests, once again, Spenser's attunement to problems of patronage. That Spenser models "December" after Clement Marot's *Eglogue de Marot au Roy* confirms the suggestion, for Marot's eclogue is an appeal to Francis I for continued patronage.[25] Spenser's poem, though, does not so much extend a plea for patronage as it presents intimations of the ways patronage has failed him. The stanzas on Colin's wasted harvest again point the matter, for they image a failure of husbandry, a failure to foster and sustain the growth of the orchard and the garden. Given the logic of the metaphor, the role of husbandman must be assigned to the patron. The *Calender* inscribes this failure in its fiction, the story of Hobbinol and Colin, and in its very production, in the interaction between the editorial apparatus and the eclogues.

3 Commendatory Verses

At stake in Spenser's poem of nationhood, more so than in the *Calender*, is the relationship between sovereign and subject – the corporate, rather than private, subject. In the commendatory poems by patrons, in Spenser's dedicatory sonnets and Letter, and in the commerce between Spenser and patrons, we can both register the boldness of Spenser's enterprise and witness competing versions of the relationship between subject and sovereign. Such measures help us to gauge more precisely the subject position from which Spenser launches his national poem. Andrew Hadfield has recently argued that, while both "nation" and "literature" were shifting, permeable categories in sixteenth-century England, we too often read back into them what they came to represent.[1] I hope to avoid this teleological fallacy by stressing hetero- rather than homogenous elements in the patronly apparatus of *The Faerie Queene*.

The commendatory verses appended to the 1590 *Faerie Queene* have received only sporadic attention – this despite the fact that they provide fruitful grounds for considering the socio-political charge of the work.[2] My argument in this chapter begins to redress this neglect. I demonstrate the heterogeneity in the praise of Spenser, thereby broadening Spenser's constituency and bringing into view a range of subject positions for the poet. Extending in this way the horizons of *The Faerie Queene* brings into purview London's social, commercial, and market forces, as well as Ireland. The former context moves us beyond the confinements of court; the latter informs with specifically Irish reformist designs Spenser's project of fashioning sovereign, nation, corporate subjects, and heroes.

One feature of the commendatory poems which lends itself very profitably to an analysis of the social relations informing Spenser's inauguration as national poet is the range of social places represented by these poems – from court to university to city, from powerful courtier to university don to purveyor of wares. Each speaker inflects Spenser's epic project differently. What the social range of the commendatory sequence helps us most immediately to see is that expressions of cultural anxiety about Spenser's ambitions concentrate in the courtly milieu; those who commend Spenser from other social vantage points do not show similar anxiety. Indeed, the movement away from the court in these poems easily grants autonomy to Spenser.

Long regarded as the pre-eminent patron of the 1590 *Faerie Queene*, Sir Walter Ralegh commends Spenser's work in two poems fraught with unresolved ambivalence, not so much about the poem as about the poet. In this ambivalence we can trace aristocratic cultural reluctance to grant status to poets, as well as assumptions about nation-building which (we will see later) run counter to Spenser's.[3] On the one hand, Ralegh has high praise for Spenser's poem as a work which supplants those of Petrarch and Homer and so carries forth the project of nationhood. Ralegh also admits the exhortatory power of Spenser's fashioning of Elizabeth when he claims that if "ought [in Spenser's poem] be amis," Elizabeth as the privileged and ideal reader can "mend it by her eine" ("Another of the Same," line 6). Although Ralegh here may simply be asking Elizabeth to overlook deficiencies in the poetic portrait, or urging her to recreate her image in her own interpretation of the poem, he may well be admonishing her to correct anything amiss within herself. Her eyes will reflect that improved self and so "mend" Spenser's poem – Spenser's mirror of her – by presenting an improved object for reflection in his poem.

The latter reading of "mend with her eine" presupposes the idea that Elizabeth and the poem reflect each other, not in the static way fixed by a printed text, but in a process of revision (re-vision). This assumption about poetic production, along with Ralegh's references to "Angels quill" and Spenser's "lines" and "letters" ("Another of the Same," lines 12–13), locates Ralegh in the coterie manuscript culture within which his own works circulated, placing him implicitly at odds with Spenser's active cultivation of the print market. The stigmatizing effects which accompanied the transition from manuscript to print culture significantly underwrite Ralegh's representation of Spenser. [4] While Ralegh can imagine an intimate scene in which Elizabeth's "sole looks divine" peruse Spenser's lines and in which Spenser can "behold [Elizabeth's] Princely mind aright," he cannot, it seems, imagine Spenser himself in physical proximity to the Queen. His representing as co-ordinated actions Spenser's "beholding" of Elizabeth's mind and his "writing" her anew indicates that in Ralegh's version of Spenser's relationship with the Queen there is only a meeting of minds, with poet and sovereign each alone sequestered with Spenser's manuscript. Since Ralegh's position as Captain of the Guard from 1587 involved him officially in matters of access to the Queen, his figurative excluding of Spenser from her presence seems especially telling.

When Spenser recalls in *Colin Clouts Come Home Again* Ralegh's introducing him to the Queen, he emphasizes his being in Elizabeth's presence: "that same shepheard [Ralegh] still us guyded, / Untill that we to *Cynthiaes* presence came."[5] Just as significantly, Spenser claims that Ralegh "enclin'd [Elizabeth's] ear" to Spenser's "oaten pipe," with the result that Elizabeth "gan take delight, / And it desir'd at timely houres to heare" (lines 360–2). Not just once, then, but repeatedly Spenser comes into the Queen's presence. Moreover, Spenser's claim to have been listened to more than once by the Queen occurs in a poem which begins with an account of the powerful effects of Colin Clout's pipe: "The shepheards boy," we read,

> Sate (as his custome was) upon a day,
> Charming his oaten pipe unto his peres,
> The shepheard swaines that did about him play:
> Who all the while with greedie listfull eares,
> Did stand astonisht at his curious skill,
> Like hartlesse deare, dismayed with thunders sound.
> At last when as he piped had his fill,
> He rested him. (*Colin Clouts*, lines 1–11)

Spenser's "listfull," in suggesting the senses of both "leaning toward" and "desiring," prepares us to understand Elizabeth's "enclining" toward Colin's pipe as a sign of her strong desire to hear Spenser's voice, to have him in her presence. Spenser thus converts what in another context would be a sign of Elizabeth's condescension into an index of the potency of his own presence. I am not interested here in which of these accounts is "true." What is interesting is that these competing versions of Spenser's inauguration as national poet represent so differently the relationship between subject and sovereign, with Spenser's version granting stronger agency to the subject and reducing the distance between this subject and his sovereign. Elizabeth "inclines" toward Spenser, while Spenser's praise of Elizabeth – as one of the auditors in *Colin Clouts* notes astutely – "doest [Spenser] upraise" (355).

In keeping with his reluctance to figure Spenser in the presence of the Queen, Ralegh imagines Spenser as a properly humble and anxious suitor seeking countenance from the powerful courtier. Although Ralegh defers to Spenser's talent, casting himself as the cuckoo to Spenser's "Philumena," he nevertheless composes his commendatory poem as if in answer to such implicit questions from Spenser as "is there anything amiss in my portrayal of virtue, beauty, chastity, or temperance?" and "will the Queen think that I am too audacious?" Ralegh's marginalization of Spenser sorts oddly with Spenser's presentation of himself both in the dedicatory sonnets (which, I will argue, figure much audacity) and in the Letter, where Spenser undertakes, in a tone always assured, to furnish – apparently at Ralegh's own request – "better light" for Ralegh's reading of *The Faerie Queene*. More, the confidence of Spenser's stated primary aim, "to fashion a gentleman," his arrogation almost of the sovereign right to "create" noblemen, bears no traces of the anxiety which Ralegh projects.

The relationship between aristocratic patron and poet clearly provides ample grounds for contesting versions of the corporate subject; that Spenser and his publisher expected no repercussions from the rehearsal of this contest suggests that the book world provided a relatively open arena for such contests. We would do well today to allow similar room for flexibility and negotiation. Ralegh's construction of Spenser – as a suitor whose approach to the court is duly tempered by humility and anxious eagerness and as someone whose text, but not his person, is admitted to the Queen's presence – finds a parallel in one of the few recent critics to accord any extended treatment to Spenser's sequence of dedicatory poems. David Miller reads the sonnets as a barometer for gauging Spenser's anxiety in approaching the courtly hierarchy figured by the sequence. Building on Carol Stillman's demonstration that Spenser's ordering of the sonnets follows heraldic rules of precedence, Miller concludes that Spenser evinces anxiety in the first two sonnets (those addressed to Hatton and Burghley), that he confidently stresses the "didactic and memorial" services of poetry in the sonnets addressed to those who are neither powerless nor too powerful, and that he adopts a tone of playful, "patronizing intimacy" when addressing the relatively powerless ladies of the court.[6] But Miller's reading of the court produces a static and rather flattened view of what was dynamic and multidimensional. As Linda Levy Peck's careful analysis of the structures of court patronage suggests, we cannot assume that an individual whose place and office were formally quite limited did not wield considerable power more informally.[7] The avenues of access and influence were complex, and nuanced in ways unaccounted for in rules of precedence.

The view of the hierarchy implicit in Miller's reading neglects to weigh, moreover, the function of the Privy Chamber. While Elizabeth's Privy Chamber – staffed, naturally, by women – did not retain the political and administrative power it had acquired under Henry, it remained informally influential. Since access to the sovereign was, as Pam Wright notes, still "the key to political power," the Ladies of the court were singularly well placed in their proximity to the Queen "to operate a free market economy of favours."[8] Keeping in mind the constitution and functions of the Privy Chamber, we can read the concluding sonnets of Spenser's dedicatory sequence, not as evidence of his assuming the most confidence only in addressing the "relatively powerless" Ladies of the court, but as evidence of a rather bold imaginative foray into Elizabeth's very presence. In "To all the gracious and beautiful Ladies in the Court," Spenser imagines himself enjoying the right of entrée to the Privy Chamber, a right which was emininently desirable and, in practice, very scrupulously guarded.[9] It is only in the sonnets addressed to women that Spenser speaks as if he is in view of those he is addressing.

Ralegh would, of course, have been all too familiar with the dynamics of the court; his marginalization of Spenser thus proceeds on grounds quite different from those of Miller, whose rendering of Spenser as relatively powerless rests on a view of the court flattened by the centuries. Ralegh's marginalizing of Spenser is edgier, admitting as it does the possibility that Spenser could work court structures to his advantage. It is this uneasiness with up-and-comingness, visible on the larger socio-political canvas (in the pervasive fear of "masterless men," and, more generally, social mobility, for example), that accounts perhaps for the apocalyptic tone Ralegh assumes even when he seems most to praise Spenser.

The first of Ralegh's commendatory sonnets represents the arrival on the literary scene of Spenser's "conceit of the Faery Queen" as an enormously disruptive event which threatens to crack the very cosmos. Upon the Faery Queen's supplanting of Petrarch's Laura and her stealing of the graces which formerly attended Laura, the "hardest stones were seene to bleed, / And grones of buried ghostes the heavens did perse. / Where *Homers* spright did tremble all for griefe" ("A Vision," lines 11–13). Ralegh's proclaiming of Spenser, and so of England, as the successor to the Greeks and Italians is thus double-edged in its imaging of Spenser's triumph as disastrous. Moreover, Ralegh's casting of himself as a virtual tourist at Laura's tomb – "Me thought I saw the grave, where *Laura* lay," "and passing by that way, / To see that buried dust of living fame" (lines 1–4) – figures England as an absence, an impression reinforced by Ralegh's seeming desire to linger (regretfully?) at the site of Laura's obliteration. Rather than remove, with the graces, to the court of the Faery Queen, Ralegh remains focused on Laura's tomb:

> All suddenly I saw the Faery Queene:
> At whose approch the soule of *Petrarke* wept,
> And from thenceforth those graces were not seene.
> For they this Queene attended, in whose steed
> Oblivion laid him downe on *Lauras* herse. ("A Vision," lines 6–10)

The full stop at the end of line 8 sounds Ralegh's seeming regret at the passing of the graces from Laura.

Louis Montrose has encouraged us to see in Ralegh's commendation of Spenser this patron's understanding of *The Faerie Queene* as "parallel in strategy and purpose" with his own *Cynthia* poems. Whereas Spenser "had declared a public, Vergilian vocation in his *Letter* to Ralegh," Montrose continues, Ralegh "transform[s] Spenser's declaration into intimate Petrarchan terms" and in so doing "illuminates a characteristic stance of the Spenserian persona: a humble poet celebrates a sublime female figure."[10] My reading of Ralegh's commendation suggests, in contrast, that Ralegh recognizes and regrets (as the tone of his first sonnet indicates) that Spenser's enterprise both erases Petrarchan tropes and refigures as more public the relationship between subject and sovereign. I will take up this point in detail in the next chapter, but for now would like simply to remark a corollary effect of reading this regret in Ralegh's commendation: my emphasis permits us to read Ralegh's poem as illuminating, not Spenser's humble posture, but his boldness. Ralegh's poem seeks to contain that audacity.[11]

To move from Ralegh's poems to Gabriel Harvey's commendation, from court to university, from powerful courtier to inveterate place-seeker, is to encounter a new set of parameters within which to measure both the boldness of Spenser's approach to the court and cultural anxiety about Spenser's project. Precisely because Harvey invariably lacks literary as well as social tact (solecisms for which Thomas Nashe will take him to task), his poem exposes more obviously than do Ralegh's poems the fault lines in the social terrain which Spenser traverses in his move from pastoral to epic.[12] In Harvey's construction, Spenser and his enterprise are made to rely almost entirely on ingratiation; this commendation converts Spenser's ambition into abasement.

Harvey's is a representation which allows Spenser no autonomy, in spite of Harvey's seeming to hold forth as an ideal an unmediated relationship between Spenser and sovereign. Disregard courtiers, advises Harvey, and "Subject thy dome to her Empyring spright, / From whence thy Muse, and all the world takes light" ("To the learned Shepheard," lines 35–6). This Spenser remains entirely subjected to Elizabeth, however: the available senses of "dome," as judgment, church, house, or head, suggest spiritual as well as temporal and political subjection. In Harvey's conception, Elizabeth's "Empyring spright" colonizes Spenser as well as territory. Such a vision of Spenser's subject-hood suggests that Harvey understands Spenser's project of fashioning sovereign, nation, vocation, and self to be everywhere coextensive with Elizabeth's rule: in such a conception, the body politic and the individual corporate subject cannot be distinguished.

Harvey's limited, and limiting, understanding of Spenser's laureate aspirations shows itself as well in his cynical assumption that Spenser can only reach the Queen through ingratiation, through flattering the court. Spenser will, Harvey presumes, "with pleasing style / ... feast the humour of the Courtly traine" (lines 31–2). Harvey's diction and metaphor indicate that he imagines Spenser as hosting the Queen and her large entourage on one of her progresses. One can only speculate about how much Harvey's own experience at Audley End during Elizabeth's 1578 progress through East Anglia slants his take on courtly relations, but he certainly construes courtly commerce as asymmetrically structured: the host must please the "courtly train," humouring even the most vain and idle wishes.[13] Indeed, Harvey cannot imagine any genuine or mutually profitable commerce between host (poet) and court: he cautions Spenser not to be "beguiled" into self-satisfaction by, presumably, favourable responses, or to be "daunted" by the (apparently inevitable) envy and disdain which his work will excite. In construing flattery as the only channel for Spenser's laureate ambitions to follow, Harvey betrays his uneasiness about the scope of his friend's ambition, uneasiness reflected as well in Harvey's difficulty in establishing and maintaining a commendatory tone. Harvey sounds by turn condescending and reproachful (stanzas 1 and 2) toward Spenser, as well as unctuous in his reference to powerful courtiers, the "higher powers" whose "deepe skanning skill" may "Allow and grace our Collyns flowing quill" (stanza 3).

Harvey's "our" here is especially telling in identifying the extent of his sycophancy. Having reproached Colin for abandoning his pastoral purposes and auditors and for "loathing" his former pastoral pleasures, and having implied that Colin's epic purposes are a "maske" – in short, having noted, and marked as disloyalty, Colin's wilful alienation from the pastoral community for which Harvey/Hobbinol seems here to speak – Harvey now reclaims proprietorship in Colin. Indeed in the closing stanza, Harvey reiterates Colin's pastoral identity in naming him "jolly Shepheard." Harvey's initial castigating of Spenser thus does not so much express genuine regret at Spenser's leaving of lowly places as it apportions the kind of blame which Harvey imagines might fall on Spenser from "higher powers." Harvey, that is, constructs Spenser (on behalf of the "higher powers," as it were) as blameworthy in his ambitious attempt to abandon his low designs.

Harvey is far from alone in being able to imagine only flattery as Spenser's objective in treating courtly figures. The editors of the *Variorum* prominently cite Warton's contemptuous dismissal of Spenser's "compliance with [the] disgraceful custom" of writing "unpoetical and empty panegyrics."[14] A.C. Hamilton's estimable Longman edition of *The Faerie Queene* relegates the dedicatory sonnets, along with the Letter to Ralegh and the commendatory poems, to an unannotated appendix. When such assumptions about Spenser's purposes direct analysis of *The Faerie Queene*, Spenser emerges as Marx's "arse-kissing" poet or, more recently, Gary Waller's "first and most prominent poet of British imperialism."[15]

We might well be tempted to excuse Harvey's assumptions as clear-eyed pragmatism, and so, perhaps, to accept wholesale the "imperialist" Spenser: many of the vehicles for advancement, poetry included, were well oiled by flattery.[16] But the poverty of Harvey's imaginings about the sovereign's subjects, and so the limitations of readings which turn on Spenser's complicity with imperialist designs, appear not only in the contrast (which I will go on to develop) with Spenser's poetry, but in contrast with other contemporary views and social practices. As I demonstrated in chapter 1, for example, in her progresses Elizabeth frequently met, not just with flattering representations of her rule, but also with displays of political and ideological strength, even resistance. Even such a signal event as Elizabeth's coronation entry into London in mid-January 1559 involves, as Susan Frye has recently argued, a largely successful attempt by civic authorities to set the terms for their relationship with the Crown.[17]

As Frye's emphasis on relations between Crown and city reminds us, our understanding of early modern political structures – too often weighted toward Crown and court – needs to be balanced by a sense of civic politics and authority. By Spenser's day, life in England was increasingly urban, and London was a major European city. Spenser himself keeps in view city prospects even when articulating his faeryland and imperial geographies. In book 3 of *The Faerie Queene*, for instance, Britomart sets against Paridell's reductive (and self-serving) retailing of epic and imperial struggle a vision of the city as gloriously reconstitutive of epic Troy. Britomart prophesies that "a third kingdome" will "arise / Out of the *Troians* scattered of-spring / That in all glory and great enterprise, / Both first and second *Troy* shall dare to equalise"

(3.9.44.6–9). A salient feature of Britomart's Troynovant is the fact that it "with the waves / Of wealthy *Thamis* washed is along" (3.9.45.1–2). "Wealthy" here surely glances at the commercial and shipping interests which plied the Thames and on which much of London's prosperity rested.[18] In Britomart's vision, an urban commercial ethos, rather than martial struggle, underwrites empire. Her redefining of epic values also reconfigures epic conflict as struggle between humanity and nature, not between nations, and in consequence seems to purge the epic process of the sin and guilt attendant upon martial struggle: Troynovant has "fastened her foot" upon the "stubborne neck" of the Thames, whose raving waves in turn "wash" the city (3.9.45.1–6). That the idea of the city can exert such pressure upon Spenser's epic vision in a relatively subordinate moment testifies to the importance, often overlooked, of the city in early modern imaginative and material experience.[19]

We can gauge further the ways in which a London-based perspective might expand our sense of Spenser's independence from courtly figures, actual and imagined, by turning to consider a species of epideictic entertainment not usually aligned with Spenser's poem of praise and blame – the London mayoral pageant.[20] With its focus on interests, influences, and ideologies operating with relative independence from the monarch, the mayoral pageant provides a salutary reminder that early modern political life did not always start and end at Westminister. The mayor himself, elected annually from the ranks of the twelve great livery companies, represents the forces of trade and industry, interests concentrated in, and administered by, the guild structure of London. For many Londoners, guild courts, rather than the royal court, regulated the pressing issues of day-to-day life.

Thomas Dekker's *Troia-Nova Triumphans* (1612), the only mayor's show to have New Troy in its title, traces spectacularly and discursively what might be called the "westering" of Troy, and thus participates in a cultural project similar to that which underwrites Spenser's *Faerie Queene*.[21] What is especially pertinent here about Dekker's handling of this motif is the thoroughness with which he translates the martial values of epic nation-building into the values of city industry, trade, and commerce. In the sequence of devices and speeches, Dekker moves from Greece and Troy to London, from myth to epic to English dramatic and chronicle and lyric traditions, while representing the mayor's progress through the city as a heroic journey comparable to that of Aeneas. Dekker's pageant, in other words, recasts heroic endeavour, not only as English, but also as civic rather than martial or knightly. It is, perhaps, only to be expected that a form of entertainment designed to ritually install the mayor should celebrate civic virtue, and virtu. But the implication bears repeating: the tendency to emphasize courtly hegemony in all matters political and cultural has too often led us to overlook the alternative structures of power, authority, and autonomy that must have helped form the early modern subject.

The commendatory sequence itself offers us alternative ways to understand Spenser's relationship to the Crown, to find in that relationship not just (as do Ralegh and Harvey, as well as some contemporary critics) the dynamics of subjection, but also configurations which minimize sovereign authority. The fourth poem, by R.S., begins by arresting and reversing the centripetal force of the poems by Ralegh and Harvey, whose focus had been directed toward court and Queen.[22] "Fayre *Thamis* streame," R.S. begins,

>   that from *Ludds* towne,
> Runst paying tribute to the Ocean seas,
> Let all thy Nymphes and Syrens of renowne
> Be silent, whyle this Bryttane *Orpheus* playes. (lines 1–4)

The concern with nationalism which informed Ralegh's verses is still here; as Britain's Orpheus, Spenser helps to translate classical authority and status to his nation. But nationhood no longer centres exclusively on Elizabeth or her court – or even on England, as aguably it does in Ralegh's commendation with its reference to "Angels [angle's] quill" ("Another," lines 12–13). The person of Elizabeth remains absent from R.S.'s poem: unlike the poems by Ralegh and Harvey, which image the sovereign through references to her face, her beauty, her eyes, this poem relies on metonymy ("sacred crowne") and synecdoche ("hand") to represent the Queen. Notably, too, whereas Ralegh and Harvey both refer to "the faery queen," concentrating the exemplary power of the poem in the single figure of the Queen, R.S. refers to faeries in the plural, dispersing authority into multiple heroic figures.[23] Furthermore, the poem's opening figure is topographical, directing attention to the land itself.²⁴ More revealingly, in this setting, sovereign attributes and prerogatives do not pertain exclusively to the Queen: "stateliness" is ascribed to London and the Thames runs in "tribute" to the oceans. Pride of place in this scene goes to the London commercial and shipping interests which could and did rival monarchal authority.

It is surely no coincidence that this commendatory poem, the first in the sequence to sideline sovereign influence (literally, in the imagery of poem: the "sacred crown" lives "Nere [the] sweet bankes" [line 5] of the Thames), is also the first to construe not only Spenser but also his work as independent of the Queen. Both Ralegh and Harvey stress Elizabeth's role in producing *The Faerie Queene* and so, by extension, Spenser: Ralegh in imagining a process of revision, Harvey more conventionally in asserting that "high conceites" were "Enfus[ed]" into Spenser's "humble wits" by the "fiers devyne" of Elizabeth's eyes. R.S. grants to Spenser alone proprietorship of his conception: "For he hath taught hye drifts in shepherdes weedes, / And deepe conceites now singes in *Faeries* deedes" (lines 9–10). This Spenser possesses considerable collateral, as it were: two substantial works which originated with, and belong to, him.

R.S.'s version of Spenser's inauguration as national poet also differs signally from those of Ralegh and Harvey in being free of anxiety about Spenser's advancement. This Spenser is brought suddenly to the attention of the Queen, with the unanimous acclaim of the Thames's voices (the support of Londoners?); the senses of unexpectedness and consensus both seem implied by R.S.'s directive: "Let all at once, with thy soft murmuring sowne / Present [Elizabeth] with this worthy Poets prayes" (lines 7–8). Ralegh, we recall, finds disturbing Spenser's momentous and sudden entry onto the literary scene; R.S. evinces no such qualm. Harvey, we recall, is unsettled by the presumption in Spenser's ambitious leap from pastoral to heroic literature. R.S. accepts matter-of-factly this generic shift, equanimity signalled by the structural balance of lines 9–10, the balancing of the "hye drifts" of Spenser's pastoral poetry with the "deepe conceites" of his heroic poetry, and by the rhyming of "shepeherdes weedes" and "*Faeries* deedes" in the closing couplet.

In yet another way the poem by R.S., as well as the next poem in the sequence, challenges courtly absolutism: by brokering praise of the poet. R.S. urges the Thames to "present" Elizabeth, not with Spenser or even with his poem, but "with this worthy Poets prayses" (line 8). In the next poem, by H.B., "Grave Muses march ... with prayses" for Spenser, "this rare dispenser of [Muses'] graces" (lines 1, 3). Such a presentation of Spenser, especially that conceived by R.S., demands, defiantly almost, that Elizabeth honour Spenser. The praise of Spenser is presented to Elizabeth as a gift and thus exacts, as social anthropologists have shown us, acknowledgement and recompense.[25]

The exchanging of gifts in Elizabethan culture was a carefully observed and orchestrated business. Lists of the New Year's gifts given and received by Elizabeth meticulously recorded descriptions and monetary values; court officials routinely made recommendations about gifts to be presented to the Queen and her retinue on progresses; debt-burdened lords and ladies continued to present (often very costly) gifts to Elizabeth.[26] Gift-giving was strictly regulated by and in turn helped to articulate social hierarchy, the value of the gifts given by Elizabeth, for example, being determined by a precisely graduated scale. Gifts carried political and ideological values as well; Susan Frye's discussion of the gifts presented to Elizabeth on her coronation entry indicates just how potently charged gifts and the process of giving and receiving could be.[27]

Within such an economy, the presenting of praise of Spenser to Elizabeth becomes an assertive gesture putting the Queen in the position of being obligated to bestow honours on Spenser. Ralegh, in contrast, remains far more circumspect in praising Spenser, devaluing his own words of praise with "The prayse of meaner wits this worke like profit brings, / As doth the Cuckoes song delight when *Philumena* sings" ("Another," lines 1–2). In the context just sketched, Ralegh's reluctance to praise appears less a sign of modesty than a sign of his unwillingness to subject Elizabeth to obligations.

R.S.'s indication that praise of Spenser is sufficiently significant in degree and kind to offer as a gift to Elizabeth is worth considering for what it suggests about the constituency which Spenser in 1590 might represent. Who was praising Spenser in the years between the appearance of *The Shepheardes Calender* (1579) and his being brought formally to the attention of Queen and court? The appearance of the *Calender* won its author immediate acclaim and popularity – two subsequent editions of the *Calender* appeared in 1581 and 1586, before the first instalment of *The Faerie Queene*;

allusions to, and imitations of, the *Calender* began soon after its publication.[28] In 1585, John Dove translated the *Calender* into Latin, an exercise which David Radcliffe terms "a mark of high approbation." William Webbe in *A Discourse of English Poetrie* (1586) singles out Spenser for much praise and draws on the *Calender* to illustrate "the forme and manner of our English verse." In his ambitious *The Arte of English Poesie* (1589), George Puttenham awards "the hyest price" to the "Gentleman who wrate the late *shepheardes Callender*." *The Faerie Queene* was known, and at least portions of it circulated, prior to its publication. Abraham Fraunce draws on both the *Calender* and *The Faerie Queene* to illustrate precepts of logic and rhetoric.[29]

In his study of Spenser's reception history, Radcliffe notes that, from the 1580s until the twentieth century, "Spenser's readers and critics tended to be ... young scholars at the public schools, universities, and Inns of Court," with "the typical age of those who comment on Spenser ... prior to the twentieth century ... likely to be under twenty-five."[30] Arguably, then, youth and learning make up Spenser's largest constituency – a supposition supporting the contention that the giving of praise of Spenser as a gift to Elizabeth is an assertive gesture. Elizabethan youth were regularly construed as unruly and were subjected to cultural and political measures designed to rein them in; learning was habitually conceptualized and represented as something which granted a degree of independence from socio-political structures of authority.

To these suppositions about *The Faerie Queene*'s constituency, we should adduce Spenser's attachments in Ireland, connections well established and increasing by 1590. Although accustomed to regard the second instalment of *The Faerie Queene* (1596) as reflecting, in the darkened visions of Books 4–6, Spenser's Irish experiences, we need to remember that by 1590 Spenser had been in Ireland for a decade, acquiring properties and positions.[31] About the time Spenser was preparing his poem for publication, he was in the last stages of acquiring the patent for Kilcolman. It is even likely that his trip to England in the fall of 1589 provided not only the occasion to present *The Faerie Queene* to Elizabeth (and deliver it to the printer) but also to secure more householders for his Kilcolman estate. Moreover, since the term "Britain" was by 1590 charged with the politics of union, R.S.'s referring to Spenser as "Britain's" rather than "England's" "Orpheus" directs us again to Spenser's Irish tenure and audience.[32] Certainly, given Orpheus's customary association with the power to civilize, the Orphic analogy applies more aptly and immediately to Ireland, habitually construed by the English as a savage place in need of "civilization."

In extending to Ireland the horizons of this commendatory poem, we recruit for Spenser a constituency which is potentially even more unruly than that comprising youth and learning. Relations between Elizabeth and the new English in Ireland – the officials, administrators, and planters charged with the governing of the colony – were frequently strained, if not openly hostile. It was not only Elizabeth's Irish "subjects" who "muttered," to use Christopher Highley's adopted term, against her authority. [33] Clare Carroll has demonstrated recently that at least some of the English tracts on Ireland contained muted criticism of Elizabeth.[34]

R.S.'s commendatory poem thus keys into cultural, social, and economic practices and assumptions which configure Spenser's relationship with court and Crown along lines very different from those which confine Ralegh and Harvey to imagine only subjection. Like R.S.'s, the fifth commendatory poem conceives for Spenser a position of strength in relationship to the Queen. To begin with, H.B. imagines as imminent Elizabeth's awarding of honours to Spenser. "Our Goddesse," declares H.B, "biddes" Spenser "Bow downe his brow unto her sacred hand" (lines 2–4). Like R.S., H.B. challenges Elizabeth to reward Spenser. In the poem's closing lines ("Faire be the guerdon of your *Faery Queen* / Even of the fairest that the world hath seene" [lines 9–10]), the phrase "of the fairest" sustains multiple senses: it could mean that Spenser's "guerdon" will come from the "fairest," that is, most beautiful and most just woman; or, more assertively, that the reward itself will be the fairest that has ever been granted a poet; or, still amplifying Spenser's role, that the poem *The Faerie Queene* is the fairest such work that the world has seen.

More interestingly, while H.B. speaks of Elizabeth as one "In whose sweete brest are all the Muses bredde," he identifies Spenser as the "rare dispenser of [the Muses'] graces" (lines 6, 3), with the pun on Spenser's name – dispenser, steward – seeming to secure for Spenser alone the honourable function of distributing these graces. Within this economy of "graces," Spenser acts as an executive power, or perhaps comptroller, without whom significant cultural capital would remain undistributed. This cultural capital, moreover, performs substantial political work, as the (fairly standard) comparison of Elizabeth and Spenser to Augustus and Virgil (lines 7–8) insinuates: Spenser's dispensing of graces helps to articulate the English nation. Ralegh's commendation, we recall, similarly connects Spenser to a nationalist project; however, the calculated and unresolvable ambiguities of H.B.'s closing two lines, quoted above, show that H.B. is much more prepared than is Ralegh to amplify Spenser's role in nation-building. Ralegh's first sonnet, which rehearses the English supplanting of Italians and Greeks, grants virtually all agency to the Queen; his second sonnet underlines Elizabeth's role in producing the *Faery Queene*. H.B.'s poem, in contrast, equivocates in ways which leave open not only the matter of subjection but also the question of who effectively produces a nation to rival those of Italy and Greece: the pronomial "your *The Faerie Queen*" could either grant to the poet possession of the Queen represented in his poem or emphasize the Queen's sovereignty over the poet; Elizabethan pronunciation could readily conflate "guerdon" and "garden," a common image for England, to permit our reading line 9 to mean that the state as represented in Spenser's poem is the "faire," that is, beautiful and just, one. Moreover, H.B. alludes suggestively to Spenser's Irish tenure in his representation of the Muses, and so their "dispenser," as arriving in London from off-shore and proceeding in triumphant march – quite unlike recent lord deputies of Ireland – to Elizabeth's court.[35] The vision of nation-building which underlies H.B.'s poem thus includes Ireland.

As do R.S. and H.B., W.L. awards "immortall" praise to Spenser, appealing to posterity rather than to sovereign (line 21). Even more thoroughly than do R.S. and H.B., W.L. imagines Spenser's enterprise to be independent of the sovereign; W.L. places Spenser in a community of competitive-minded poets where Spenser wins the "Laurell quite from all his feres" (line 22). Notably, as the coincidence of "feres" (companions) and "fears" implies, Spenser's growth in self-assurance takes place independently of sovereign countenance.

W.L.'s scenario reminds us, moreover, of what Ralegh and Harvey in their promotion of sovereign power would obscure: the extent to which Elizabeth was the subject in, and so her image subject to, a burgeoning literary industry, one that could and did (as W.L.'s "so large" [line 7] insinuates) take liberties with her reputation, in spite of censorship and callings-in.[36] It is this feature of the literary world which accounts for W.L.'s otherwise curious comparison of Elizabeth to the abducted – "rape[d]" – Helen.

W.L.'s allusion to the Trojan War reminds us that Elizabeth's fame, her image, was manipulated by conflicting factions, as well as by disgruntled subjects and foreign observers. By representing a retiring Spenser as enlisted by Sidney ("So Spencer was by Sidneys speaches wonne, / To blaze her fame not fearing future harmes" [lines 15–16]), W.L. advertises *The Faerie Queene*'s partisanship with the Sidney-Leicester-Essex faction, implying at the same time, in the assurance that Spenser need not fear repercussions, that Spenser's sally is countenanced by powerful people. W.L. implies more. In decidedly ambiguous lines, he writes of Sidney's persuasion of Spenser: "For well he knew, his Muse would soone be tyred / In her high praise, that all the world admired" (lines 17–18). The pronominal ambiguity makes several readings possible, all plausible. Perhaps W.L. means that Sidney, anticipating that his muse would be "retired" in his forced absence from court over his criticism of the Alençon marriage negotiations, convinced Spenser to take up the torch. Perhaps the lines mean that Sidney knew that Spenser's muse would soon be covered (attired) in praise from Elizabeth in addition to already being "admired" by all the world. The latter reading grants much agency to Spenser and, like the poem by R.S., accords Spenser a large and relatively powerful constituency.

W.L.'s Trojan analogy points as well and even more aptly to Ireland, whose relations with England more nearly approximated a war, of course. W.L.'s concern with Elizabeth's "fame" (image, reputation) is especially pertinent in connection to Ireland, where the managing of Elizabeth's image was a perennially troublesome matter. Further, the Irish context explicates certain oddities in W.L.'s use of the Trojan-Greek story. Because the story was customarily interpreted by the English with a Trojan bias, it seems curious that W.L. should identify Spenser with the Greek hero Achilles – until we recall that by this time Spenser calls Ireland home. Like the Greeks, the Irish were regularly denigrated, in Spenser's own works and the works of others, as barbarous.[37] While W.L. is not, of course, insinuating that Spenser is barbarous, his comparison effectively implies that Spenser's literary treatment of Elizabeth can become *the* Irish image of her, an image to countervail the less-than-celebratory images of her which circulated in Ireland.[38]

That W.L. frames concern for Elizabeth's "fame" with references to, in particular, Achilles and the rape of Helen establishes an especially instructive point of contrast between Spenser's handling of

Elizabeth's image and the notorious (mis)handling of Elizabeth's image by the rebel Brian O'Rourke. In a widely known incident, O'Rourke and a band of gallowglass were reputed to have subjected an image representing Elizabeth to particularly scurrilous treatment.[39] Writing to Burghley from Dublin on 9 April 1589, Lord Deputy Fytzwilliam reported that "having found in a church or in some other place an image of a tall woman [O'Rourke] wrote upon the breast thereof Queen Elizabeth, which done he presently fell with such spiteful and traitorous speaches to rail at it, and otherwise so filthily to use it." Meanwhile, his "barbarous gallowglass ... with their gallowglass axes [struck] the image ... until with hacking and mangling they had utterly defaced it," at which point they "fastened a halter about the neck of the image and tying it to a horse tail dragged it along the ground ... beating it ... and railing ... [and] finished their traitorous pageant."[40] As rehearsed here, the incident clearly recalls key details of the killing of Hector – his being hacked to death by Achilles' myrmidons and then dragged by horse around the walls of Troy – with O'Rourke as Achilles, his gallowglass as the myrmidons, and Elizabeth as Hector *and*, given that the violation is so emphatically directed against the image of a female, Helen. The conflation of Helen and Hector in the image of Elizabeth thus makes the Greek Achilles the ravisher of his own countrywoman and so emphasizes that, in rebelling against Elizabeth, the Irish are turning against their own sovereign. W.L.'s poem conceives of Ireland's Spenser as someone whose vision of Elizabeth can correct Irish misprision.

The Irish context illuminates yet another curious feature of W.L.'s poem: the designating of Spenser's pastoral persona as effeminate, in the comparison of Spenser's decision to "seeme a shephearde" to Achilles' disguising of himself in "woman's weeds" to avoid the wars. Implicitly, then, W.L. promotes as more manly the writing of heroic verse, a belief that makes particular sense in connection to Ireland. As Christopher Highley has recently demonstrated, a masculine, military ethos thoroughly permeated the English administration in Ireland.[41] Resonating in these several ways with Irish implications, W.L.'s poem helps us further to imagine for Spenser a subject position of considerable latitude.

As a final measure of the range of subject positions imagined for Spenser in the commendatory sequence, we might remark that, while the sequence begins with a patron firmly located in the manuscript culture, it ends with an entrepreneur who thinks of Spenser's *Faerie Queene* as a physical, marketable object – a "worke" for sale. With Ignoto's poem we enter the marketplace for the first time in the sequence, as Ignoto advertises Spenser's "worke of rare devise" (line 1) in the hope of earning the publisher a fair return. Having earlier likened himself to the host of an inn and compared Spenser's poem to the wine served therein, Ignoto urges potential buyers of Spenser's book to "give [their] hoast his utmost dew" (line 24). It is tempting to speculate that Ignoto is in fact Spenser's publisher, Ponsonby, particularly when Ignoto, taking charge of the whole commendatory sequence, says "And thus I hang a garland at the dore" (line 19), extending his proprietorship beyond Spenser's poem to the entire 1590 *Faerie Queene* volume. Notably, Ignoto plays down patronly commendation – claiming that he hangs the "garland" of commendation only because it's customary – and relies instead on the buyers' discrimation in recognizing the "goodnes of the ware" (line 20), insisting that the buyers' "tast," not commendations, will tell them the product is truly good (line 23). Astute businessman that he is, Ignoto nevertheless recognizes the "customary" value of commendations as hooks to draw in customers and so "custom," that is, money. Ignoto's appeal to the book trade and a (potentially) wide readership removes Spenser from the very limited economies imagined by Ralegh and Harvey – circuits of exchange which subject the poet to sovereign influence; in widening the audience to literate "men" with some purchasing power (line 11), Ignoto resists the centripetal force of Queen and court even more thoroughly than do R.S., H.B., and W.L.

In sum, the sequence of commendatory verses appended to the 1590 *Faerie Queene* mounts a considerable challenge to courtly absolutism and demonstrates, once again, that we need to remain flexible in our understanding of the subject positions available to Spenser as he embarked on his epic project. I have stressed the heterogeneity in the praise of Spenser in order to recover some of the liveliness and range of expectations that must have attended the appearance of the poem. We will see, in the next chapter, that in his own promotion of his poem, Spenser consistently imagines for himself positions of strength and independence.

4 The Dedicatory Sonnets

The Faerie Queene has for long been regarded as the most sustained and articulate paean to Elizabeth produced in Elizabethan or any other times. And Spenser's epideictic purposes do shape his vision in fundamental ways.[1] Such a reading can, however, unduly narrow Spenser's audience, and find in his relationship with court and Crown only the dynamics of subjection. We have seen that the commendatory verses attached to the 1590 *Faerie Queene* render competing versions of that relationship. Close attention to the printing of the volume, and to Spenser's promotion of it, confirms that the politics of his poem of nationhood are more nuanced than have often been supposed and that his sense of agency is assured and finely tuned. In this chapter, I will consider in particular the significance of *The Faerie Queene*'s being printed by John Wolfe; the effects of the print-house miscalculation which displaced prefatory matter to the back of the volume; and the kinds of liberties imagined (and taken) in Spenser's sequence of dedicatory sonnets. To adduce these more materialist contexts is, as I hope to demonstrate, to appreciate more fully just how clearly and creatively Spenser's poem engages its historical moment.

Ignoto's grounding in the book trade directs us, not only generally to the marketplace, but specifically to the print shop, to consider the implications of the 1590 *Faerie Queene*'s being printed by John

Wolfe.² Since, in many cases, we do not know how authors, publishers, and printers got together, arguments about the material conditions of early modern publishing necessarily rest often on conjectures which then shape our take on a given text. The 1590 *Faerie Queene* was printed by John Wolfe and published by William Ponsonby. Joseph Loewenstein, one of the few critics to take up these matters, assumes that Ponsonby, being asked or having asked to publish *The Faerie Queene*, hired on Wolfe as printer. Part of Loewenstein's sophisticated and wide-ranging argument is that Ponsonby, having begun to publish the "Sidney" line, wished to add Spenser to the fold – as indeed he did, eventually publishing all Spenser's verse with the exception of the *Shepheardes Calender*.³ From this premise, Loewenstein surmises that Ponsonby hired Wolfe for mere expedience: that is, Ponsonby wanted Spenser to be able to read proof before returning to Ireland and so wanted the poem printed quickly. Wolfe had the second largest print shop in London and thus might be expected to print the poem in about twelve weeks.⁴ On this premise, Loewenstein builds the argument that Spenser – ever the poet of deliberate sequence – felt rushed by the industrial pace of Wolfe's print shop and, being called upon for unknown reasons to write seven additional dedicatory sonnets, used the occasion to meditate upon his own cultural belatedness and to ponder the grim implications of presswork. Loewenstein's argument thus produces a very conservative Spenser, one whose gestures are recuperative and whose vision is retrospective. In presuming that Ponsonby hired Wolfe and that he did so for mere expedience, Loewenstein occludes a line of argument that generates quite a different Spenser and text. To focus instead on Wolfe – either as the one who initiated the publishing venture, or perhaps as someone hired by Ponsonby for political and ideological reasons – is to align Spenser's 1590 *Faerie Queene* with progressive thinking, with a nationalism that was not parochial, and with challenges to authority and absolutisms, courtly and otherwise.

Wolfe's relationship to institutional authority was decidedly equivocal. On the one hand, he was a rabble-rouser: he was a sometime book-pirate, a printer of surreptitious texts, and he was the leader of the printers' revolt in the early 1580s against the granting of royal patents – in effect monopolies – to certain privileged printers.⁵ While his interests in the latter cause may have been primarily financial, his rhetoric at the time at least gestures toward a strongly principled position. Defending his actions, Wolfe compared his attempts to reform the printing trade with Luther's reformation of the church. Wolfe also seems to have assumed that being a "subject" of the Queen should not involve being subject to invasive force. In a deposition to the Star Chamber regarding a May 1582 raid on his printing house, Wolfe complains vigorously that armed men broke in "most forcibly and riotously" in his absence. Wolfe figures the raid as a series of break-ins – the men first forcing the hall door, then "breaking up" the "Lockes and doors of the chambers, Counting houses, chestes and other places." Wolfe thus multiplies the boundaries, or thresholds, that the raiders violate in their "spoyl[ing] and undoing" of him, the "said Subject," suggesting that he imagines the subject as deeply ensconced within what should be inviolable boundaries. Wolfe's description of his "dwelling" as "scytuate and beinge in the parishe of Saincte Nicholas Gold abbey in London" implies similarly that multiple jurisdictions mediate between subjects and sovereign power, here manifest in the actions of the armed men.[6] Wolfe's deposition also reveals how very closely he identifies his subjecthood with the printed books he produces. He complains that the men "spoyled and took away with them printed books and diverse other goods." Such "extreme spoil and havock," says Wolfe, have resulted in his "utter spoyle and undoing."[7]

I have dwelt on Wolfe's version of this incident for two reasons. First, the recounting reveals resistance to royal authority at deeply imagined levels, and so can encourage us to expect such resistance in others and in other contexts, in Spenser, for example. Second, Wolfe's recounting forges a close connection between autonomy and the printing industry, to suggest that, in spite of fairly rigorous policing – through such means as licensing, callings-in, and raids – those in the industry could still conceive of print as promoting agency and autonomy.

Wolfe's contesting of the authorities governing his trade represents just one facet of his career. In 1587, Wolfe became the beadle of the Stationers' Company, that is the member of the company charged with policing fellow printers, with finding out illegal presses, for example. In this capacity, Wolfe participated in the crackdown on the Marprelate pamphlets.[8] That Wolfe was still someone who did not rest content with regulations, though, may be surmised from the fact that when he took on the job of beadle, the salary was increased by 66 per cent.⁹ He apparently struck a hard bargain. In the pattern of Wolfe's career, it is possible to find a paradigm for manoeuvrings within the structures of authority in Elizabethan England, a flexible paradigm which accommodates both acquiescence and challenge.¹⁰ Equipped with this paradigm, we can then turn to a writer such as Spenser to find in his gestures of seeming subjection the performance of challenge.

I also want to suggest that despite Wolfe's coming into the fold and assuming the role of beadle, his name quite possibly still carried a certain cachet, a hint of insubordination. The printers' revolt of the early to mid-1580s had been much talked about in the bookstalls and inns of London.¹¹ In the minds of the book-buying public, Wolfe in 1590 might still have been linked with insubordination. Wolfe's printing of *The Faerie Queene*, then, may very well have prompted potential buyers to regard it as a poem whose celebration of Elizabeth – its title and dedication notwithstanding – would be equivocal.

Wolfe's connection with Spenser's book could also be expected to attract buyers accustomed to works showing cosmopolitanism, reasoned positions, and, above all, independence of mind. In his extensive study of Wolfe's career, Clifford Huffman demonstrates that Wolfe was a man who "prosecuted a vision of printing and what it could be in the London of his time," and a man whose printing served – indeed helped to create – various communities of writers and readers, communities diverse in their interests and aims, but alike in being prepared to hold their ground even in the face of entrenched, institutionalized positions.¹² Issuing from Wolfe's print shop and from such a context, Spenser's *Faerie Queene* would likely have appealed to potential buyers, not as (or not simply as) a royal paean, but as a work likely to have a judicious mix of celebration, vision, and censure. Focusing on the printer Wolfe rather than the bookseller Ponsonby thus invites us – as do the commendatory verses – to reorientate the 1590 *Faerie Queene*: to regard it as less court-bound than is customary and to suppose its audience and constituency to be wider than is often assumed.

Such reorientation invites us to reconsider the socio-political charge of the sequence of dedicatory sonnets appended to the volume – verses long dismissed as mere puffs, tritely conventional at best, the effluvia of abasement at worst. Close attention to carefully orchestrated sutleties in diction, syntax, imagery, and tone, however, dispels any lingering sense of Spenser's servility. Once again, attention to the printing of the volume especially helps to recover evidence of Spenser's agency and audacity, because anomalies in the printing of the volume permitted him, I will argue, to intensify his claims for autonomy and prerogative.

The significant anomalies are, first, the fact that all the prefatory matter actually appeared at the end of the volume and, second, the fact that at some point in the print run seven additional dedicatory sonnets were added to the initial ten.[13] The displacement of the prefatory matter seems to have been by default rather than by design. Ignoto's remarks about the garland at the door suggest as much. Also, prefatory matter was usually printed last. Presumably Wolfe– expecting only the typical amount of prefatory matter – left what he thought would be sufficient room and began printing the poem on A2r. In the event, however, the preliminaries included the dedication to Elizabeth, the Letter to Ralegh, six commendatory poems, and – atypically – many subsidiary dedications. The dedication to Elizabeth appeared on A1v and all the rest of the supporting matter was displaced.

The result was sufficiently noteworthy to attract comment and imitation from Thomas Nashe. Toward the end of his 1592 *Pierce Penilesse*, Nashe belatedly makes his own dedicatory gestures, arguably in imitation of *The Faerie Queene*'s leaving these till last. In formulating his dedication, Nashe alludes to the unusual feature of Spenser's volume, referring to "that honourable catalogue of our English *Heroes*, which insueth the conclusion of [the] famous Faerie Queene." Nashe claims to have been alerted to the displacement of the patronal apparatus by the title-page of Spenser's book. In his own dedicatory sonnet to the Earl of Southampton, Nashe writes:

Perusing yesternight with idle eyes,
   The Fairy Singers stately tuned verse:
And viewing after Chap-mens wonted guise,
   What strange contents the title did rehearse.
I streight leapt over to the latter end,
   Where like the queint Comedians of our time,
That when their Play is doone do fal to ryme,
   I found short lines, to sundry Nobles pend.
Whom he as speciall Mirrours singled fourth,
   To be the Patrons of his Poetry.[14]

Nothing in the title-page as we know it would invite a reader to leap immediately to the back of the book. Presumably Nashe is referring to a title-page posted by the bookseller, one which directs the reader explicitly to the dedications at the back.[15] Perhaps Ponsonby was anxious to reassure potential buyers that the volume did make the customary dedicatory gestures, that Spenser had not audaciously omitted all such matter. But Nashe's describing the volume's contents as "strange" invites an alternative supposition. The 1590 *Faerie Queene* was remarkable for the number of subsidiary dedications; perhaps my hypothesized title-page alerted readers to this unusual feature as something worth remarking. It is, then, worth our asking what might have been the effects produced by and the intentions behind the extended catalogue of heroes.

We can begin with Nashe's response, which moves from "idle" perusal of Spenser's "stately" poem to a vigorously kinetic, even interactive, response as he leaps to the end of the volume, finds the sonnets, reads them, reverences the addressees, and proceeds to write his own contribution to the catalogue. Spenser's multiplying of dedicatees – itself an act which decentres the Queen and represents the body politic, the state, as separate and distinct from her – thus generates more multiplying, which disperses authority still more widely.[16] The effect of Nashe's response is also to destabilize authority, to render authority – here represented in a catalogue of heroes – as not yet permanently, perhaps never to be permanently, fixed or constructed: poets can always reconfigure authority by adding new figures. Spenser's own apparent change of mind regarding dedicatees, his adding seven more, similarly shows the figuring of authority to be an ongoing process, one finely tuned to shifting political pressures. The added sonnets respond at least in part to the post-Armada anxieties of 1589–90 as well as to Irish exigencies.

Nashe's own displacement of dedicatee, from the front to the back, is far more irreverent than Spenser's, of course. Nashe converts the patronal occasion to mockery of the gestures of clientage. But, while his irony distinguishes him from Spenser, it may well be that it was in Spenser's book, with its accidental displacement of authorizing figures, that Nashe found authority for his own more irreverent displacement.

The possibility that the displacement in Spenser's book somehow licensed Nashe's audacity invites us to look intently at how

Spenser responded to the print-house miscalculation that required moving preliminaries to the back. The seven sonnets added at some point in the print run provide rich grounds for just such an analysis. I have referred already to Loewenstein's conclusion that Spenser's being subjected to the demands of the print-shop produced in him recuperative gestures and retrospection. I wish to argue, in contrast, that the added sonnets reflect, not a rearguard action, but intensified claims for autonomy and agency, as well as a sharpened sense of the sometimes paradoxical and almost always ambivalent power of print. Spenser's alertness to the power of print includes particularly the understanding that state power, or royal authority, cannot entirely appropriate print for its own purposes or completely efface traces of challenges to its rule.

The added sonnets reflect in several ways Spenser's intensified claims for autonomy and agency. The sonnet to Lord Burghley, for example, inserted after the opening one to Hatton, turns, as does the sonnet to Hatton, on the relationship between poetry and affairs of state; but the sonnet to Burghley makes much larger and more specific claims for poetry's efficacy. Playing with the idea of gravitas, the Burghley sonnet implies that Spenser's poem is as weighty in its way as the "burdein" – borne by Burghley – of this "kingdoms government" (line 4).[17] In a mini-sequence beginning with the sonnet to Grey and extending through two added sonnets, "To Buckhurst" and "To Walsingham," Spenser moves from modest claims about what he expects his epic poem to do, to very grand claims about its cultural and political significance. Similarly, compared to the sonnet which precedes it, "To Cumberland" makes more elaborate and particularized claims about the relationship between poetry and martial glory. As a corollary to Spenser's extended claims about the moral and political efficacy of his poetry, two of the added sonnets represent the reading of his poem as an act of apprehending inwardly, of being "in-formed" by the poem. Generally, too, the added sonnets show Spenser's increased willingness to compose *and* to censure the body politic comprised by the dedicatees.

Spenser's intensified claims for agency and for poetry's efficacy emerge provocatively in a four-sonnet grouping which places, on one page, "To Ormond," "To the Lord Admiral," and on the facing page, "To Lord Hunsdon" and "To Lord Grey." Only the Hunsdon sonnet is new, but its insertion turns the grouping into a meditation on both the containment of threats to England's security and the role of writers in helping to secure the English nation. The grouping begins and ends with sonnets about Spenser's tenure in Ireland, not as administrator or landholder, but as poet. Between these sonnets, the poems to Howard (the Lord Admiral) and to Hunsdon celebrate victories over enemies of Elizabethan security: the Spanish in the Lord Admiral poem, the rebellious northern earls in the Hunsdon poem.[18] The reference to the Armada is only to be expected: that victory and its anxious aftermath still pressed on the minds of the English. The citing of the northern rebellion of 1569 seems less immediately interpretable. To emphasize simple retrospection, as might Loewenstein, would be to neglect the pressure exerted by the Hunsdon sonnet on the Howard poem and on current anxieties about renewed Spanish threats. With the Hunsdon sonnet, Spenser reaches back two decades to find an instance of a threat having been – reassuringly – contained. Spenser's wish that his readers draw the comforting parallel is suggested by, among other things, his implying that the "case" in which Hunsdon found himself resembles Howard's. Notably, the two martial poems are themselves framed – contained – by sonnets to do with Spenser as poet in Ireland. These pages thus emblematize something about the relationship between martial acts and poetry that goes well beyond the conventional theme, developed conventionally enough in some of the first-state sonnets, that poets make heroes famous and so should be countenanced by heroes. Spenser's claim stakes much more substantial ground, implying that writing and publishing help to secure the English nation.

The added sonnets reflect an imagination very actively engaged with the publishing industry. And *pace* Loewenstein, I would argue that for Spenser the implications of presswork are not grim, but ultimately salutary. In even small details, the dedicatory sequence shows Spenser's thinking to be increasingly informed by the business of printing. For example, three of the added seven sonnets address men who acted as licensers for the press, whereas only two of the original ten did.[19] Moreover, two of the added sonnets reflect the decorums of the print house by adopting the language of "correctors" in speaking of "faults" and "mending." One could, I think, make the case that the added sonnets mark a significant shift in Spenser's thinking, away from imagining his poem as enmeshed in the traditional patronage system and toward imagining it as a work which, because licensed and published, depends for its continued circulation on the discrimination of individual readers. Engaged with the business of the printing industry, Spenser is much less inclined in the added sonnets to make the conventional request for patronal countenance.

I would like to return to the Hunsdon sonnet to suggest that it reflects in particularly far-reaching ways Spenser's increasing alertness to the power of print, a power which Spenser recognizes to be ambivalent but also able, in that very ambivalence, to resist wholesale appropriation by state authorities. As with several of the added sonnets, Spenser seems certainly to have composed the Hunsdon sonnet with the immediately preceding one in mind, the Lord Admiral sonnet in this instance. But while the two sonnets share vocabulary and theme, the Hunsdon sonnet extends these shared elements into a meditation on the publishing industry. Both sonnets concern a victory, and both sonnets employ vocabulary of the print house, a feature noted by Loewenstein. But only the Hunsdon sonnet deploys this vocabulary. For instance, while Spenser figures the Lord Admiral's Armada victory as an allegorical pageant not at all, or not yet, dependent on the press to give it currency, he represents knowledge of Hunsdon's victory over the northern earls as almost exclusively a function of the press and reading. The term "Chace" – c-h-a-c-e in the Howard poem remains a "chase," c-h-a-s-e (the Lord Admiral's chasing of the Spanish ships); while in the Hunsdon poem, the phrase "your owne high merit in like case" (7) sustains multiple meanings, two of which pertain to the print-house: Hunsdon's merit appears in the chace and in the type case, as well as in the armour and circumstances of his victory. The term "deface," appearing in both poems, invites similar scrutiny, especially in view of the Star Chamber decree of 1586 which made the defacing of presses one of the penalties for illegal printing.[20] In each poem, the term appears in a syntactically ambiguous unit referring initially to the wiping out of enemy power and secondarily to the wiping clean of a record. In the Howard poem this ambiguity is resolved to leave only the first meaning of "deface" possible (lines 7–14). In the Hunsdon sonnet, on the other hand, the ambiguity remains in play to suggest that Hunsdon's victory both defaced the power of the rebellious earls and defaced the evidence of their power from the "record of enduring memory" (lines 11–12). Spenser seems here to allude to the many printed works which appeared in the months after the quashing of the rebellion, to imply that repeated recording of the victory in print leaves the impression in the collective memory of only the victory.[21] Since the many printed works about the rebellion were state-sanctioned, Spenser's allusion reveals his sense of the extent to which print extends royal, or state, power.

There remains, however, a final irony in Spenser's meditation on the power of print, one which implies Spenser's recognition that royal, or state, power can never entirely appropriate the power of print: the very works which celebrate state victories – works such as Spenser's own "lasting verse" ("To Hunsdon," line 13) – necessarily identify enemies, leaving impressions of those threatening forces. The proliferation of print means that the traces of challenges to state power can never be entirely effaced.

Clearly, Spenser experienced the print shop as enabling. But even apart from the intensified claims for agency produced by the miscalculation, Spenser's dedications figure much audacity in establishing distance from the court and maintaining pronounced social, political, and ideological positions, as I will argue in the remainder of this chapter. We will see that Spenser aligns himself firmly with the militant Protestantism of the Leicester-Essex faction and elaborates a militaristic ethos, particularly with respect to Ireland. His implicit claims for autonomy run still deeper. We will see also that the sonnet to Ralegh offers an especially sensitive and informative index to Spenser's maintaining of poetic and imaginative freedom. In this sonnet Spenser grapples intensively with the figure of Elizabeth as Petrarchan mistress, one of the definitive court-centred and court-sanctioned tropes of Elizabeth's reign, and of Ralegh's own poetry, developing a thoroughgoing, if oblique, critique which goes beyond the dedicatory sonnet into the very matter of *The Faerie Queene*.

Spenser's opening dedication, "To Hatton," establishes assurance and audacity, not anxiety and subservience, as the keynotes of the dedicatory sequence. Spenser's likening of Hatton to the "prudent heads" who "taught ambitious Rome to tyrannise" (lines 1–3) is equivocal praise indeed, evoking as it does a whole complex of associations to do with St. Augustine's and Protestants' view of the godlessness of Rome and the pride and ambition of the Roman church.[22] That Spenser's enditing here inclines to censure rather than to composition appears more likely given Hatton's reported Catholic leanings.[23] Less obviously, but no less instrumentally, subtle imagistic and rhythmic constrasts between octave and sestet undermine Hatton's position of authority. In the octave's description of ancient Rome, firmly end-stopped lines and a preponderance of masculine rhymes reinforce the point that "Those prudent heads" "with theire counsels wise / Whylome the Pillours of th'earth did *sustain*" (lines 1–2; my emphasis). In contrast, the sestet, which turns to Hatton, begins with enjambed lines which, while seeming flatteringly expansive, also figure dangerous precariousness: "So you great Lord, that with your counsell sway / The burdein of this kingdom mightily" (lines 9–10). Although "sway" means primarily influence or control, the enjambment makes us feel "sway" as oscillation. And to sway rather than to sustain the burden of government seems to court collapse. Spenser's ostensible praise of Hatton's "might" thus registers discordantly ambivalent notes.

At the same time, Spenser intimates that his poetry retains moral efficacy and can be part of productive time, a conviction conveyed in the doubled meaning of "delay." In drawing his comparison to Roman times, Spenser declares that "*Maro* oft did *Caesars* cares allay" and expresses the expectation that Hatton "With like delightes sometimes may eke delay, / The rugged brow of careful Policy" (lines 8, 11–12). "Delay" suggests interrupted process and so seemingly points Spenser's tacit admission that his "ydle rymes" remain outside productive time, offering an interlude merely in the march of state affairs – a reading of delay supported by his insistence that Roman leaders would "play" "with the sweet Lady Muses" (line 6). But "delay" can also mean "allay or assuage," an equally likely sense given the occurrence already in the poem of "allay" (line 8). According to this sense, Spenser cannot mean that poetry offers simply recreation to the political man. In fact, even "delay" as interrupted process, coupled with the nearly always opprobrious "policy," also points to poetry's efficacy – here its potential to interrupt merely politic schemes. By taking the time to read Spenser's poem – by "lend[ing] litle space" to his "rymes" (line 13) – the man of policy may be profitably delayed in pursuing "rugged" measures.

The insistently correlative structure of "To Hatton" – "So Ennius ... so Maro ... so you great Lord" – forges a series of equivalences: between Hatton and the Romans; between Spenser and Virgil; between English and Roman empires. These are precisely the easy parallels one might expect a less gifted, less searching, less moral poet to draw, especially in so conventional a form as the dedication. The equivocating and punning features of "To Hatton" unsettle these equations, however, to suggest that Spenser's understanding of his nation, its counsellors, and his role in empire-building admits unconventional effects.

"To Oxford" offers an especially deft instance of Spenser's finding accommodation within structures of authority by creating enabling distance from the court in the course of approaching courtly hierarchy. Addressed as the "Lord high Chamberlayne of England," Oxford holds an eminent position in Elizabeth's household and might well be expected to take definition from his title and position. Against the entitlements of this place, however, Spenser sets the imperatives and blandishments of Oxford's family dynasty, reasoning that it is incumbent upon Oxford to protect Spenser's poem from envy since "th'antique glory of thine auncestry / Under a shady vele is therein writ, / And eke thine owne long living memory, / Succeeding them in true nobility" (lines 6–9). "Glory" here attaches, not to Gloriana's court, but to Oxford's family, while "long living" and "succeeding" ascribe to this noble family the attributes fervently wished for the monarchy. To similar effect, the most intimate and sustaining relation holds, not between the chamberlain and his sovereign, but between Oxford and "th'*Heliconian* ymps." It "behoves" Oxford to "countenance" Spenser's poem "also for the love which thou doest beare / To th'*Heliconian* ymps, and they to thee, / They unto thee, and thou to them most deare" (lines 10–12). And this extra-courtly circuit of intimate exchange can expand to include Spenser, or at least his poem: "so love / That [he who or that which] loves and honours thee, as doth behove" (lines 13–14).

Moreover, the accommodation of Spenser (and/or his work) becomes the thing which can redeem Oxford from censurable self-love, a condition which frequently enough imperilled Elizabeth's courtiers. The echoic structure of the last five lines, which repeatedly ring on "thou," "thee," "thy," figures the danger of excessive self- (or family-) centredness. The danger appears especially imminent when the generative dyadic structure of affection between Oxford and the Heliconian ymps – so carefully established in the phrases "they to thee / They unto thee, and thou to them"– collapses into "Deare as thou art unto thy selfe." At the end of the line, however, Spenser effects Oxford's rescue from such entrapment, by extending the correlative structure and making Oxford's self-love the pattern from which to derive other love: "Deare as thou art unto thy selfe, so love / That loves and honours thee, as doth behove."

In keeping with his redeeming of Oxford, Spenser moves in this sonnet from humble supplicant, asking Oxford to "receive … the unrype fruit of an unready wit" (lines 1–2), to someone who admonishes Oxford and who will receive tribute from Oxford. Indeed, by the end of the first line, "Receive most noble Lord in gentle gree," Spenser's supplication has modulated into admonishement: punning on "gree" as both rank (degree) and favour or good will, Spenser implies that Oxford can show his high degree by exercising good will toward Spenser.

Another measure of the confidence in Spenser's negotiating of the courtly hierarchy is the panache with which he effects social adjustments, a manœuvre represented perhaps most adroitly in Spenser's addressing of women. Spenser's addressing all the "Ladies in the court" generates a particularly serviceable court dynamic, one able to convert marginal positions to points of power. As I remarked in the previous chapter, Spenser in this sonnet imagines himself to have been granted the right of entrée; the consequent implication is that the Ladies broker considerable political power. He also represents in the relationship among Ladies, Queen, and poet the formation of an alternative "body politic" to counter what he considers to be the most egregious costs, to the corporate subject, of participation in the state. A look back at the sonnets to Burghley and Hatton helps point the matter. In those sonnets, the imagery of "heads," "brows," and "shoulders" designates councillorship as a fragmentation of self. In contrast, "To all the Ladies" represents participation in Elizabeth's court, not as a means of diminishment, but as a generative process. Through their graces, their "ornament[s]" (line 8), the Ladies help to fashion Elizabeth, but with no consequent loss to themselves: "lesse [they] have not lefte" (line 14). Indeed, their ornaments are increased, since the poet's praise makes them known to the world. Moreover, the poet's role in fashioning the "body politic" is greatly amplified: it is he who "draw[s] the semblant trew" of Elizabeth, "the worlds sole wonderment" (lines 5–6), by "steal[ing]" with "cunning theft" some "part of ornament" from each "sundry beautie" (lines 13, 7). The poet, finally, is the one able to draw an image of Elizabeth because he is a "con-ning (knowing) artist." In a political system which relied heavily on, and controlled, images of the sovereign, such claims are large ones.

It comes as no surprise that a poet who begins his major work by declaring that "fierce warres" shall "moralize" (*Faerie Queene*, 1 proem 1.9) his song should advance militaristic themes in the dedicatory sequence. This feature of the sequence, apparent in the first state, more pronounced in the second, argues for Spenser's continued alliance with militant Protestantism. Such alliance is signalled on the one hand by Spenser's promotion in the sequence of the Leicester-Essex faction and on the other hand by his handling of Irish matters.

Spenser advertises his allegiance by adding sonnets to Walsingham – long connected with militant Protestantism – and the Countess of Pembroke, a move which lets Spenser refer at length to the late Philip Sidney, who remained a rallying figure for militant Protestant ambitions. Spenser demonstrates his allegiance further and most daringly in the sonnet to Essex, which, while not an added sonnet, does gain pointedness from the heightened military ethos of the second state. Indeed, this heightened context explains the scanting of praise in this sonnet where very little particularized praise is offered. Spenser's point is precisely that Essex's heroism has remained trammelled by a Queen famously reluctant to allow her favourite courtiers to practise arms. It is Spenser's hope, obliquely expressed, that Elizabeth will grow more militant, a change in policy which would permit Essex's playing of "Heroicke partes" (line 12). A militant ethos whould not only grant scope to Essex's heroic potential, but would also earn the "Faery Queene" her "last" – that is, ultimate and lasting – praises (line 10).

While Spenser thus unmistakably flags his continued allegiance to the increasingly decimated Leicester-Essex faction, signalling in this way his considerable independence of political mind, it is with connection to Ireland that he stakes his ground most firmly.

Several of the dedicatees bear, with varying degrees of directness, connection to Ireland: Hatton, Grey, Ralegh, Ormond, Burghley, Essex. The sonnets to Ormond and Grey can especially help us to define the contours of Spenser's Irish tenure, assumptions, and loyalties, largely because these two sonnets – sufficiently parallel in theme, vocabulary, and groundplot to invite pointed comparison – offer alternative imagined Irelands.[24]

Spenser's choosing to address Ormond is unremarkable: Thomas Butler, tenth Earl of Ormond and Ossory, was the Queen's kinsman, enemy of the rebel Desmonds, and arguably one of the key figures in the plans for Munster. Nor is it surprising that Spenser should address Lord Grey, under whose auspices Spenser assumed his Irish career. What is remarkable (although my emphasis on Spenser's audacity should temper surprise) is the extent to which Spenser censures Ormond, always countenanced by Elizabeth, and praises Grey, recalled from Ireland in disgrace and subsequently the object of Europe-wide animadversion.

Spenser's unwavering loyalty to Grey emerges eloquently in the intimacy of tone and in the impression that Spenser weaves his sense of himself from the ties binding him to Grey. Spenser's declaration at line 5 – "I now doe live" – is embedded within a larger sentence whose principal clause addresses Grey: "Most noble Lord ... Vouchsafe ... this small gift to receave" (lines 1–8). More specifically, the sonnet, which begins with an apostrophe and two appositives establishing Spenser's dependency upon Grey, brackets Spenser's self-proclaiming "I now doe live" with phrases (two adverbial and one adjectival) which articulate the nature and extent – in time and space – of Grey's continuing patronage of Spenser.

"To Ormond" does not claim any personal ties between Spenser and the addressee; indeed, most of the dedicatory sonnets do not. But this fact is worth remarking as a point of contrast between two poems so clearly counterpoised in their plotting of Irish grounds. Both poems claim that Spenser's work emerges from Ireland's "sauadge soyle" ("saluage" in "To Ormond"). But the sonnet to Grey tempers the uncouthness by imagining the poet and patron working together in a feudalized landscape informed by cultivation and industry, with Grey exercising the imperatives of *noblesse oblige* in exchange for Spenser's "vassalage" (line 5) –

here imaged as industrious "weaving" and the exact keeping of accounts (lines 11, 10). As the estate manager, so to speak, Spenser will sustain Grey's state with his "accounting," a pledge made in the syntactically ambiguous last line of the sonnet, a line which not only asks Grey to "vouchsafe" his favourable judgment to Spenser's work but also promises that Spenser's "rude rimes" "vouchsafe" a "favourable doom" to Grey. Spenser's "account," that is, redeems Grey from the charge of relying on cruel and savage means to subdue Ireland.

Moreover, against the overt theme of Irish wastes, the vocabulary of the Grey sonnet proffers plenitude, promise, and community: "large bountie," "rife," "first season," "redeeme," "vouchsafe," "pledge," and "all the rest" project a landscape redeemed from savageness. Time here is also redeemed, in a fantasy of benign teleology which presents as paradigmatic Spenser's growth from "pupillage" (line 2) to trusted and valued "vassalage" (line 5), from "feebleness" (line 4) to implicit strength. Similarly, from Spenser's "small gift" (of the 1590 *Faerie Queene*) will follow "all the rest," and from Grey's initial patronage will follow his "favourable doom." By implied analogy, just as Spenser and his poetry were and will be fostered in Ireland, so will English plans for cultivating Ireland reach fruition.

Quite in contrast, the sonnet to Ormond plots Ireland as irredeemably split between wastelands and pockets of culture. This "salvage soyle," says Spenser, "through long wars left almost waste," is "with brutish barbarisme ... overspredd"; and

> in so faire a land, as may be redd,
> Not one *Parnassus,* nor one *Helicone*
> Left for the sweet Muses to be harboured,
> But where thy selfe hast thy brave mansione.

Coming at line 8 of the sonnet, after seven lines describing the void that is Ireland, Ormond's home seems merely a last resort for culture, a *locus amoenus,* to be sure, but an unproductive one:

> There in deede dwel faire Graces many one.
>   And gentle Nymphes, delights of learned wits,
>   And in thy person without Paragone

> All goodly bountie and true honour sits,
> Such therefore, as that wasted soyl doth yield,
>   Receive dear Lord in worth, the fruit of barren field. (lines 10–14)

The firmly end-stopped lines (8–10) and the verb "sits" (line 12) imply enclosure rather than beneficent outward flow. Ormond's "goodly bountie and true honour" generate no fruitful exchange, in contrast to Grey's "large bountie" ("To Grey," line 13), whose generative effects we have noted already and whose abundance is even suggested in the accumulated open vowel sounds of the line. Unlike Grey's, Ormond's presence does not transform the landscape; the poem begins and ends with a wasteland. Correspondingly, the poet's relation with Ormond, again, unlike that with Grey, remains mutually unproductive: Spenser remains without promise, his field still barren.

Spenser's remaining exiled from Ormond's *locus amoenus* may also bear more pointed relevance to the question of Spenser's assuming a role as Ireland's poet of English empire. Despite his Oxford education and his much-touted loyalty to his Tudor sovereign, Ormond's "ethnic identity" remained decidedly "ambivalent," at least partly because of his fluency in Gaelic and his patronage of Irish bards.[25] Always a flash-point for cultural conflicts, language and its uses frequently exercised commentators on Ireland, including Spenser, who labels "barbaric" the speaking of Irish among the Anglo-Irish. In the *View*, Irenius complains that it is "unnatural" that any people should love another's language more than their own, and that such wantonness of tongue is "very inconvenient and the cause of many other evils," for "the speech being Irish, the heart must needs be Irish" (67–8). Spenser reserves particular animus for the Irish "bards and rhymers" who "for little reward or a share of a stolen cow" praise and encourage young minds in "lewd deeds." What must be especially galling, given that Spenser's avowed aim in *The Faerie Queene* is to "fashion a gentleman or noble person in vertuous and gentle discipline" (Letter to Ralegh, 737), is the bardic appropriation of "praises which are proper unto virtue itself."[26] This nexus of concerns about language and its abuses, especially in poetry, adds a very damning charge to the implicit criticism in "To Ormond." Spenser's lament that Ireland is "overspredd" with "brutish barbarisme" points the matter: "overspredd" implies that the barbarism is laid over an originally cultured land, while "barbarisme," with its customary etymological association with language, suggests that the root of Irish evils is the Irish language. Thus, rather than standing opposed, like Grey, to the wasteland, Ormond with his Gaelic and his countenancing of bards contributes to the spreading barbarism. Spenser's only very tepid plea for patronage from Ormond makes more sense in this context: Ormond's is an Ireland that Spenser would not wish to effect in his poetry.

Behind Spenser's reserve may also lie the new-English suspicion that Ormond remained remiss in his duties as loyal Tudor subject – particularly in the performance of military responsibilities and the punishment of rebels.[27] The two sonnets between those to Ormond and to Grey stress military themes, celebrating the defeat of threats to the security of the English nation-state. While the sonnet to Grey, which concludes this grouping of four, does not address explicitly military themes, its addressing of Grey as a "valiant knight of the noble order of the garter," its vocabulary of feudal loyalties, and its subtle attunement to criticism of Grey's actions at Smerwick keep operable the military ethos asserted so strenuously in the middle sonnets of the group. Moreover, the Ormond sonnet is immediately preceded by "To Essex," which, as we have seen, anticipates Essex's performance of "heroicke partes" in furtherance of Tudor militancy.

Spenser's advocacy of "heroicke partes" is, arguably, the definitive feature of his vision for Ireland. The group of four sonnets (two of which were added) that follows the poem to Grey aligns Spenser's reformist vision and imperial poetics squarely with a militant ethos – extolling Captain John Norris as exemplary, censuring Ralegh for mistakenly (in Spenser's view) articulating Petrarchan rather than heroic poetics, and situating Spenser's own epic poem within broadly imperial contexts. The grouping begins with the little-remarked added sonnet "To Buckhurst," a poem which draws on Buckhurst's reputation as a courtier poet, contributing author of *Mirror for Magistrates*, and author of *Gorboduc* – his reputation, in other words, as a poet of state and sovereign matters. As so often happens in the dedicatory sequence, Spenser's praise of Buckhurst turns readily to admonition, in this case to Spenser's suggestion that this poet and courtier would do better (is "much more fit," line 5) to direct his skill as poet and his authority in the Privy Council to promoting heroic, imperialist poetry and politics rather than to rehearsing *de casibus* tales of princes. Your "learned Muse," Spenser acknowledges, "hath writ her owne record, / In golden verse, worthy immortal fame," but

> Thou much more fit (were leasure to the same)
>   The gracious soverain praises to compile,
>   And her *imperiall* Maiestie to frame,
>   In loftie numbers and heroicke stile. (lines 3–8; my emphasis)

To "frame" Elizabeth in and to "heroicke stile" would add to (compile) the praises of Elizabeth which would proceed from her sponsoring of imperial designs. As does "To Oxford," "To Buckhurst" calculates nicely the function of self-love in court dynamics and courtier poetry, insinuating that in writing "her owne record, / In golden verse, worthy immortal fame," Buckhurst's muse elaborated the poetics of self rather than of state and sovereign. (A similar charge underwrites much of Spenser's treatment of Ralegh in *The Faerie Queene* and its apparatus, as we shall see.) With respect to Buckhurst, Spenser cunningly appeals to that same narcissism to encourage Buckhurst's turning to heroic poetry and politics, by promising in the syntactically ambiguous line 6 that framing imperial majesty would earn Buckhurst his Queen's praise.

Spenser extends the imperial context of his project in the next sonnet by likening Walsingham to Mecenas and so himself and his poem to Virgil and his *Aeneid*. As "To Walsingham" shows, the arts of empire are twofold, exercised by those (poets included) who "civil artes professe" as well as those who "are inspired with Martial rage" (lines 10–11). In this, an added sonnet, Spenser implies that Walsingham's patronage will help to promote not just English emulation of, but more significantly English overgoing of the poetry and politics of the Roman empire. The first line of the sonnet – "That Manutuane Poetes incompared spirit" – establishes comparative structure as integral to the logic of the sonnet even while seeming to assert that Virgil is incomparable: the Spenserian coinage "incompared" suggests that Virgil remains incomparable only because no one worthy of compare has yet emerged. This reading of "incompared" is reinforced by Spenser's subsequent claims that, following Virgil, he "learns like steps to trace" and that Walsingham is positioned to offer "aid" "like" that afforded Virgil by Mecenas (lines 7, 8). With the dynamics of comparison thus firmly established by the middle of the sonnet, the comparative "bigger" in the closing lines – Walsingham's patronage may "rayse" Spenser's muse to sing in "bigger tunes" – predicts not just Spenser's overgoing of his own initial "lowly" efforts, but also his bettering of Virgil.

The next sonnet in the group, that addressed "To the right noble Lord and most Valiaunt Captaine, John Norris knight, Lord president of Mounster," extends imperial matters specifically to Ireland and suggests the co-dependency of political and armed authority. That such controls must be coterminous is first implied in the very heading, with its doubled and chiasmic linking of political titles ("Lord"; "Lord president") and military epithets ("valiaunt Captaine"; "knight"), and then elaborated in the poem with its ascription to Norris of perfectly balanced chivalric and administrative merits: Spenser extols Norris as someone whose "warlike prowesse and manly courage" are "Tempered with reason and advizement sage" (lines 8–9). Norris is at once the "president" of Munster and the "Precedent of all that armes ensue" (line 7), a coincidence of terms which confirms the importance of matching administrative with armed strength. By listing the various scenes of Norris's military service – "sad Belgicke," "*France* and *Ireland*," "Lusitanian soile" (lines 10–12) – Spenser sketches a vision of an extensive English Protestant empire which stakes Irish ground as well.

Both the militant ethos and the imperial geography of "To Norris" stand instructively in contrast to the socio-political landscape which Spenser considers to be the product of his patron Ralegh's Petrarchan poetics and political vision. It is a landscape which, for all its seemingly secured pastoral pleasures, always threatens to become the land of the dispossessed and disenfranchised. One of Spenser's strongest criticisms of Petrarchism is that, because of its perpetually unbalanced relations of power, precariousness becomes the permanent condition of the supplicant. "To Ralegh" figures this condition with the imagery of summer nesting in Spenser's addressing of Ralegh as "the sommers Nightingale/ ... / In whose high thoughts Pleasure hath built her bowre" (lines 1, 6). As a man not for all seasons but only for the summer, Ralegh remains susceptible to the first wintry blast of disfavour. With characteristic "secret" wit, Spenser inscribes such threat when he wonders why he sends to Ralegh, "the sommers Nightingale," his own "rusticke madrigale" (lines 1, 3): in "nightingale" and "madrigale" (the latter word occurring just this once in Spenser's canon), puns on "gale" as "song or speech" and as "strong sea wind" suggest not only the vulnerability of Ralegh's position but also the tension between Ralegh's and Spenser's poetics.[28]

Spenser further points the precariousness of Ralegh's position with Elizabeth in the movement from the declaration that Ralegh is "the sommers Nightingale" who is Elizabeth's "most deare delight" to the claim that Ralegh is one "in whose high thoughts Pleasure [like a bird] hath built her bowre" (lines 1-2, 6). The attenuation figured here– from Ralegh's *being* Elizabeth's "most deare delight" to his being the *site* for what Elizabeth treasures – draws Ralegh away from Elizabeth's regard. To pursue the logic of Spenser's metaphors a little further, Ralegh's being merely the site for pleasure, not the treasured thing itself, means that the pleasaunce he provides is repeatable, by others. And reiteration is surely part of the dynamic of court flattery. In Spenser's view, Petrarchan courtier verse turns its practitioners into mere flatterers, a risk implied when he says that in Ralegh's thoughts "dainty love [has] learned sweetly to endite" (line 7). Modified by "sweetly," "endite" here can only mean compose and not, as it frequently does in Spenser, censure. As well, the characteristically adroit sentence structure makes available the reading that "Pleasure" has taught Ralegh's love for Elizabeth to compose only sweet notes. That is, Ralegh's desire to retain or regain his sovereign's pleasure, or favour, encourages his composing of only flattery. At the same time, since "dainty love" can mean "love which holds its object in high esteem" and since "dainty love" can grammatically be read as "Elizabeth's love for courtiers," Spenser again implies with his richly dense language that Elizabeth's granting of (or threat to withhold) esteem elicits from courtiers only flattering tributes. Spenser turns very elastic sentence structure to similar point when he suggests that Elizabeth's praise of, esteem for, Ralegh produces reciprocating praise from him – a circuit which again seems indistinguishable from the workings of flattery.

Spenser remains outside this courtly exchange, his madrigal "rusticke," his "rimes" "unsavory and sowre," his praises of Cynthia "rude" (lines 3, 8). By implication, Spenser's verses do not flatter, but rather endite, in the senses of compose and censure. Spenser thus implicitly opposes his own poetics to Ralegh's courtly pastoral and Petrarchan verse. Since Spenser's is Irish rustication, the extrapolation is that Ireland needs Spenser's, not Ralegh's, brand of poetics – a poetics which is not only more fully moral, but also more militant. Spenser's most trenchant admonishment of Ralegh is that he is "Fitter to thonder martiall stowre" (line 11) than "sweetly to endite."

In closing, we should note Spenser's implication that Ralegh's Petrarchism not only imperils him and taxes him with the charge of flatterer, but also exacts a price on the nation. As the "sommers Nightingale," Ralegh is his "soveraine Goddesses *most deare* delight" (line 2; my emphasis). The cost, suggested by "deare" as highly priced, to monarch and nation of Petrarchan sovereign relations is high, as we can surmise from the differences in landscape between "To Norris," with its extensions through time and space, and "To Ralegh," with its reductive insularity. The cost, in Spenser's view, could well be Ireland.

5 Ralegh in *The Faerie Queene* III

Not mere puffs, the dedicatory sonnets issue from the political, moral, and imaginative imperatives of Spenser's art of empire, as we have seen. In this chapter, I wish to examine the effects of these imperatives on Spenser's epic project at the point where patronal pressures and Irish exigencies merge: the story of Timias in Book 3.[1] Through this story, Spenser offers a reformative mirror of his patron's poetics and Irish career. Spenser's fiction, I will argue, reflects particularly the damaging effects of Ralegh's Petrarchism on the heroic form and energy needed to refashion Ireland.

The proem to Book 3 signals the close interdependence, in Spenser's mind and art, of sexual politics and Irish reformist designs, and so prepares us to understand Ralegh's Petrarchan poses as having political implications.[2] The project announced (and as announced) in the first line of Book 3 – "It falls me here to write of Chastity" – is weighted with unusually high stakes. To undertake to portray chastity is to take up a definitive feature of Elizabethan iconography, since Elizabeth's self-representations over the decades of her rule worked variations on her virginal status. To compound matters, Elizabeth in 1590 was fifty-seven years old, and certainly starting to show her age, a fact to which she reacted with characteristic determination by promoting fictions of her virginal youth. Little wonder that Spenser considers it his "lucklesse lot" to be "constrain[ed]" to represent Elizabeth's chastity, or that he claims that "living art" – in one sense, the art which attempts the living Elizabeth – cannot approximate her (*Faerie Queene* 3 proem 3.4; 2.1).[3]

In what I would argue is a localizing detail, Spenser's "it falls me *here*" (emphasis mine) inflects these matters with the still more urgent concerns not only of representing Elizabeth generally in Ireland (a matter discussed in the previous chapter) but of representing chastity in a land whose "unruliness" was regularly and particularly associated with female wantonness.[4] Offering a portrait of chastity "to all the Ladies" of Ireland who "profess" chastity amounts to a lesson in good government – not only of sexual economies, but of political ones as well. In his "Epithalamion," Spenser envisions the reformation of the young Anglo-Irish women of Munster as both sign of, and prerequisite to, general Irish reformation, in particular imagining the former as the movement of the young women from the "labyrinth" to the "temple."[5] Spenser's reference in the proem to a "daedale" hand (3 proem 2.4) forges a subtle, but nonetheless strong, connection between the reformist visions of the two poems: Daedalus's career featured his escape from a labyrinth to Athens where he built a temple to Apollo. Because religious reform was felt by many (including Spenser's patron, Lord Grey) to be a necessary if not sufficient precursor for wholesale political reform in Ireland, recusancy was regarded as a serious setback. And to judge by reports out of Cork in 1595, recusancy – which became increasingly widespread after 1593 – was especially prevalent amongst Anglo-Irish women.[6] In Spenser's reformist vision, women need literally to re-enter the temple, that is, the English Church, headed by Elizabeth, to help re-create Ireland in the image of England. They need also, and this bears more directly upon the issues in proem 3, to enter the figurative temple of chastity in order to secure English hegemony in Ireland. To the English, the success of the "plantation" of Ireland depended largely upon the burgeoning of all-English families; articles for the Plantation of Munster include stipulations regarding marriage and the passing on of estates. Since, moreover, the proem tells us that chastity is "shrined" in Elizabeth's breast, to "profess" chastity assumes political valence: it is to profess Elizabeth, that is, to acknowledge her sovereignty (3 proem 1.5–7). For Spenser, the political stakes of writing the Legend of Chastity "here," in Ireland, are therefore considerable.

Once alerted to the localizing pressure registered by Spenser's "here" in the first line, we can see that other details of the proem similarly point to Ireland, as the ground upon which Spenser figures his writing of Chastity, and as grounds not only for problems in the representation of Elizabeth but also for differences with his patron Ralegh. When in stanza 3 Spenser laments that his "lucklesse lott" constrains him "Hereto perforce" (3 proem 3.4–5), we can understand this as a reference, not only (as it most immediately is) to his being constrained to portray Elizabeth's heart, but also to its being his lot to be constrained "to this place," that is, Ireland. In *Colin Clouts*, the phrase "lucklesse lot" occurs in the course of Colin's relating how the Shepherd of the Ocean (Ralegh) persuaded him to leave Ireland, at least temporarily, for Cynthia's court:

> He gan to cast great lyking to my lore,
> And great dislyking to my lucklesse lot:
> That banisht had my selfe, like wight forlore,
> Into that waste, where I was quite forgot.
> The which to leave, thenceforth he counseled mee,
> Unmeet for man, in whom is ought regardfull,
> And wend with him, his *Cynthia* to see. (lines 180–6)

In both poems, the lucklessness of Spenser's lot – his being in Ireland – seems to reside particularly in his being thus prevented from seeing his sovereign: Elizabeth's royal progresses never took her to Ireland; by the fall of 1589 Spenser had been in Ireland for nearly a decade. Formally, stanza 3 of Spenser's proem approximates the gap between poet and sovereign in the strong caesura – the strongest in the proem – of line 5: "my luckless lot doth me constrayne / Hereto perforce. But, O dredd Soverayne!" When Spenser continues his apostrophe with "Thus *far-forth* pardon" (3 proem 3.6; my emphasis), his phrasing once again tropes the physical distance between court and Ireland. "Far-forth" also effectively raises the issue of just how far Elizabeth's authority can efficiently extend. The lines of communication between court and Ireland were sufficiently vexed by distance and weather to permit the Crown's deputies in Ireland to initiate actions.

As is so often the case in Spenser, with distance from the royal court comes agency and authority, as we can surmise from the ways in which in the proem he distinguishes his poetic project from that of Ralegh. In its political scope, aims, and assumption of agency, Spenser's undertaking opposes that of his patron Ralegh, whose own representations of Elizabeth as "Cynthia" would, initially, seem to coincide so thoroughly with Spenser's project. In his Letter to Ralegh, Spenser certainly implies a coincidence of aim and purpose when he claims to have derived "Belphoebe" from Ralegh's "own excellent conceit" (Letter, 737). But the proem registers telling differences. While Spenser's (published) poem offers a mirror "to all Ladies" (1.7), Ralegh's (unpublished) one offers a mirror to Elizabeth (if "your selfe you covet to see" [4.2]); while Spenser's horizons extend from the court to Ireland, Ralegh's contract to Elizabeth's Privy Chamber (the room in which she might look into a mirror); while Spenser's poem characteristically relies on the proliferation of figures, persons, heroes (fitting "praises unto present persons" [3.9]), Ralegh's is all about Cynthia. Moreover, Spenser insists that while his poem limns Elizabeth's sovereignty – and so therefore also the corporate subject – Ralegh's poem pictures only Elizabeth's "self," that is, her personhood, her (private) body natural, and so eschews questions about the corporate subject's relationship to monarchy.

Anna Beer has recently demonstrated just how fully Ralegh attempted throughout his career to inscribe his relationship with Elizabeth as private and personal, as outside the bonds linking monarch and subject.[7] Ralegh relies nearly exclusively on Petrarchan tropes to figure, and to manoeuvre within, his relationship with the Queen. Spenser certainly recognizes, and regrets, this feature of his patron's career and poetics. Always concerned to construct a position of authority for himself as poet and for the corporate subject generally, Spenser sees clearly that Ralegh's Petrarchism vitiates agency and autonomy, not least because it locks Ralegh into solipsism. Spenser describes Ralegh's poem as "that sweete verse, with Nectar sprinckeled, / In which a gracious servant pictured / His Cynthia, his heavens fayrest light" (3 proem 4.4–6). "Pictured" here sustains two readings, one suggesting that Ralegh has (actively) portrayed Elizabeth in his verse, the other subverting this agency by suggesting that Ralegh (passively) sees his Cynthia in his own verse. The occurrence of "pictured" three lines earlier as a predicate adjective (3 proem 4.2) prepares us to detect the passivity in Ralegh's picturing, prepares us, more precisely, to understand Ralegh as the reader, rather than the writer, of his own verse. In thus figuring Ralegh's verse as a mirror, not of Elizabeth, but of his own mind, Spenser reveals the narcissism which underwrites Ralegh's Petrarchan posture.

Extending his critique of Ralegh's self-mirroring, Spenser implies that it's a mirror trick that, finally, doesn't work. Spenser points the lack of authorial agency in Ralegh's poem by declining to name Ralegh as the author of "that sweete Verse." At the spot where, grammatically, we would expect to find Ralegh's name or an identifying epithet, we find Ralegh's "verse" instead: "But if in living colours, and right hew," Spenser advises Elizabeth, "Thy selfe thou covet to see pictured, / Who can it doe more lively, or more trew, / Then that sweete verse" (3 proem 4.1–4). One might speculate further and conclude that Spenser wryly leaves the personal pronoun "who" without antecedent to reserve that space for himself. Indeed, given the slippage between pronoun and antecedent in these lines, it is possible to construe Spenser's question about the truest "picturing" of Elizabeth in an entirely different way: not as a seemingly rhetorical question promoting Ralegh's verse ("No one can do it more lively and true than can Ralegh"), but as a question asking seriously, "Who can picture Elizabeth in ways more lively and true than Ralegh's?" We have our answer a stanza later when Spenser urges Ralegh's Cynthia not to "refuse / In mirrours more than one her selfe to see" (3 proem 5.5–6) and offers her not the alternatives of Ralegh's mirror and his own, as might be expected, but the different mirrors proffered in the *Faerie Queene*: "But either Gloriana let her chuse, / Or in Belphoebe fashioned to bee" (3 proem 5.7–8).

Nowhere in the proem, in fact, does Spenser actually imagine Elizabeth as reader of Ralegh's poem. He seems to do so, to be sure, with the line "That with his melting sweetnes ravished" (3 proem 4.7), a line imaging the effects of Ralegh's verse. This line, which seems grammatically to depend on Spenser's earlier addressing of Elizabeth (3 proem 4.2), leads us strongly to expect that "thou" (Elizabeth) will be the grammatical subject of the clause to follow, the clause which will identify the "ravished" object of Ralegh's sweetness. In a startling displacement, however, Spenser makes his own "senses," not Elizabeth, the grammatical suject of the clause:

> That with his melting sweetnes ravished,
> And with the wonder of her beames bright,
> My sences lulled are in slomber of delight. (3 proem 5.7–9)

Spenser's displacement of Elizabeth as reader of Ralegh's verse serves a number of interrelated functions in Spenser's subtle (and earnest) art of self-promotion. In short-circuiting the connection between Elizabeth and Ralegh's poem, Spenser leaves Elizabeth suspended – a reader with nothing (yet) to read. Spenser's *Faerie Queene*, as I've already suggested, can nicely fill that void. More daringly, in supplanting Elizabeth as reader, Spenser effects the Queen's rescue – from ravishment – thus casting himself as the Knight in service of Chastity. Spenser not only interrupts the circuit between Elizabeth and Ralegh's poetry; he also attenuates his own vocational connection with Ralegh, while at the same time hinting at the larger debilitating influences of Ralegh's Petrarchism His wording in line 9, his making "my sences" rather than "I" the grammatical subject of the clause, suggests a powerful, yet finally only partial, engagement with Ralegh's poem and poetic vision: his patron's poem can entrance his senses, but not his wit. We have, of course, just witnessed in the proem a Spenser who very ably keeps his wits about him as he establishes, within the potentially constricting parameters of both royal iconography and patronage, his own agency, authority, and pre-eminence. Although he modestly asks his patron Ralegh, "that same delitious Poet," to "lend / a little leave unto a rusticke Muse / To sing his mistesse prayse," his subsequent petition, "and let him mend / If ought amis her liking may abuse" (3 proem 5.1–4), can be taken to mean, not only "let Ralegh mend my mistakes," but also (just as easily and perhaps primarily) "let Ralegh learn from my song to correct what is wrong in his own portrait of Elizabeth."

Just what is wrong with Ralegh's portrait? I have suggested already that Spenser objects to Ralegh's Petrarchism, on the grounds that it remains solipsistic, even narcissitic.[8] Spenser's imagery of ravishment and slumbering delight points to still other objections, on grounds which are epistemological, philosophical, political, poetic, and Irish – objections adumbrated here in the proem and worked out in the fiction of Timias and Belphoebe. For Spenser, we will see, what is most damaging in Petrarchism's poses – particularly with respect to Ireland – is the vitiation of heroic agency and energy. But also, as the imagery of ravishing, melting sweetness implies, Ralegh's Petrarchan poses and poetry subsume an unacknowledged carnal charge, conveyed especially in the image of ravishment and pointed in the proem by the startling (and saving) displacement of Elizabeth as object of Ralegh's ravishing verse. In Book 3 proper, in the fiction of Timias and Belphoebe, Spenser will again point the unacknowledged carnality of Ralegh's service-discourse, this time by having Timias repeatedly return to the idea of dying without ever picking up on the ubiquitous Renaissance pun on dying as orgasm. At the same time, and as suggested also by the word "ravish," Spenser intimates that Ralegh's Petrarchism fails to acknowledge Elizabeth as incarnate and fails to mirror that aspect to Elizabeth. One meaning of "to ravish" is to transport spiritually, to leave the body behind. In a proem which specifically flags, as we have seen, Elizabeth's aging, corporeal body, "ravish" insinuates that Ralegh's verse elides corporeal lineaments. Idealizing is certainly no new feature of Elizabethan portraiture, or of early modern love discourse, or of the service-discourse which developed in Elizabeth's court, but Ralegh's wish to have his relationship with Elizabeth viewed as personal and private – as outside courtiership – makes *his* eschewing of Elizabeth's corporeal self seem like an attempt to have it both ways. Such eschewing of corporeality, moreover, resolves readily (once again) into solipsism. Ironically, Ralegh's mirroring not only fails to reflect the Elizabeth that he claims to court, but – turned back on himself – fails, and spectacularly so, to lead him to self-knowledge. For Spenser, whose own exquisite erotic vision culminates in knowledge of self and other, Ralegh's Petrarchism must seem short-sighted indeed.

Spenser thus figures Ralegh's Petrarchism as a poetics which neither registers the object it claims to reflect nor promotes self-knowledge, a poetics which cannot, in other words, foster reformation of the self or the other. Ralegh's poetics thus remains ill fitted to the related tasks of forming the corporate subject and reforming Ireland. Spenser's declaration in the dedicatory sonnet to Ralegh that his patron is perhaps "fitter to thonder martial stower" (line 11) than to remain the "sommers Nightingale" (line 1) exactly reverses the emphases of Ralegh's first commendatory sonnet, with its foregrounding of Petrarchan poetics and virtual elision of martial poetics. Spenser thus implies both that Ralegh has misread *The Faerie Queene*, mistaken its allegory for extended Petrarchan conceit, and that Ralegh has misread – and mis-written – his own position in relationship to the Queen. In his fiction of Timias and Belphoebe, Spenser will offer a reformative mirror.

That Spenser's fiction of Timias is centrally concerned with Timias's subject formation is indicated by the fact that Timias is so named for the first time at the moment he sets off in pursuit of the forester who is menacing Florimell. That the grounds for Timias's emergence as subject are Irish ones becomes apparent soon after this fact – Timias's battle with the foresters takes place in recognizably Irish woodlands. And that these grounds are heroic rather than erotic seems more evident than most commentators allow. Timias's formative adventures begin in what proves for him mirror scene manqué, when Florimell appears out of the woods with a face "as cleare as Christall stone," a face, that is, designed to reveal the propensities, or predict the destinies, of those who behold her flight (3.1.15.4).[9] (That Florimell engages onlookers in ways which clarify, at least for us, their complex erotic motives is suggested by the fact that the "evil" feared by Florimell [3.1.16] materializes as a lustful forester directly as a result of the onlookers' gaze: "So as they gazed after her a while, / Lo where a griesly Foster forth did rush" [3.1.17.1–2].) Although he is presumably one of the lookers-on, Timias is named only as he sets off after the forester, implying that, unlike those of Guyon and Arthur, his are not at this point erotic motives. Indeed, when Spenser takes up Timias's story again, in canto 5, he detaches Timias's pursuit of the forester from its originating context of allegorized lust. The "griesly foster" who sought to "defile" Florimell eludes Timias, by escaping into the woods and out of the frame and time of this moral allegory. Punishment awaits him, but it is meted out over an extended period of time, and not by Timias, but by syphilis; the forester reaps "dew reward / Of his bad deedes, which daily he increast, / Ne ceased not, till him oppressed hard / The heavie plague that for such leachours is prepared" (3.5.14.6–9).

When Spenser returns in the next stanza to the narrative thread and time of Timias's pursuit, the grounds of contention between Timias and the (now three) foresters have shifted to the topical allegory of the Desmond rebellion.[10] James Bednarz in "Ralegh in Spenser's Historical Allegory" has demonstrated convincingly that Timias's battle in the ford, which in fact conflates two separate incidents, recalls Ralegh's role in the crushing of that rebellion. The recounting of Timias's battle, however, engages even more particularly than Bednarz suggests questions of jurisprudence in Ireland – questions of considerable moment for Spenser, who, in the late 1580s, was securing his status as undertaker and his title to Kilcolman, an endeavour wholly contingent upon confiscated lands' remaining in Crown control.

Forbidding Timias's "passage through the ford," the foresters in effect demand a toll – "amends and full restore / For all the damage which [Timias] had ... doen [to the forester] afore" (3.5.18.8–9), a demand which makes sense only in terms of the confiscation of the "rebel" lands after the quelling of the Desmond uprising. The foresters' ambushing of Timias operates as what Charles Ross has analysed as a "foul custom of the castle," indicating that what is at stake in the ensuing battle is, immediately, possession of these woodlands, and, more broadly, the reformation of Ireland in a contest of sovereignties, polities, and cultures. Timias directs his efforts especially towards "seizing" the "high banke," something he needs to do, of course, in order to fight with full force; but the phrasing also reflects determination to possess the land. Spenser's emphasis becomes more pointed by comparison with Hooker's account of the ambush, according to which Ralegh, travelling with a small band strung out along the path, made it clear of the ford, but returned to help a companion whose horse had foundered in the water. Ralegh then remained in the ford, holding off, with his staff and pistol, the seneschal of Imokellie until his remaining companions caught up.[11]

More revealingly, Timias's dispatching of the foresters transforms the landscape – from a perilous Irish woodland to a secured, cultivated, "Englished" landscape. Immediately following his victory, Timias swoons into a landscape containing park and chase and nobility. Spenser insists that, "[i]n those *same* woods" which harboured the foresters, a "noble hunteresse did wonne" (3.5.27.5–6; my emphasis), who

> pursewd the chace
> Of some wild beast, which with her arrowes keene
> She wounded had, the same along did trace
> By tract of bloud, which she had freshly seene
> To have besprinckled all the grassy greene. (3.5.28.1–5)

Other features of Belphoebe's rural retreat help to configure this woodland specifically as a demesne: the herbal garden; the cultivated trees; the channelled brook; the principal house fit for "greatest Princes."[12] The landscape in which Timias adventures, then, bears an even more potent political charge than previous readings have measured, as we can understand more clearly when we note with Terence Reeves-Smyth that medieval and early modern Irish demesnes (even the Gaelic ones) closely resembled English ones. Demesnes thus not only demarcated separate social and economic areas, as Reeves-Smyth observes, but could also signal political inclinations. While demesnes would certainly not have been common in the Munster of the 1580s, the province having been wasted by the rebellion and its quelling, demesnes (and related ways of demarcating the landscape) do figure significantly in the plans for the Plantation of Munster. Repeated references to demesnes, seigniories, and castles envision Munster as recreated in the image of England. The reality fell far short of this dream of English hegemony, of course: broken castles, razed towns, and wasted ploughlands were the norm.

Spenser's 1590 episode of Timias and Belphoebe thus participates in a reformist vision of empire, a claim supported by the impression that Belphoebe's sovereignty extends into those very woods in which moments before the foresters exercised prerogatives of land title: we read that Belphoebe's dwelling is "farre" inside the forest and that Belphoebe, clearly without fear for their safety, sends her nymphs to fetch Timias's horse, "which was strayed / *Farre* into the woods" (3.5.38.6–7; my emphasis). What this dream of easy movement through Irish woods elides is the fact that in the 1580s Elizabethan sovereignty informed only intermittently the Irish landscape, producing a jurisdictional quagmire full of perils and inconvenience for the travelling new English. Spenser's own travels in Ireland must have made him all too aware that traversing this country could generate contests of loyalty. The *Calendar of State Papers, Ir. 1588–92*, for example, records the reprisals exacted against someone who gave Spenser shelter for a night as he was returning from assizes at Limerick (247).

More details, small but resonant, point to the envisioning of empire which underwrites the Timias episode. In mentioning the recovery of Timias's horse, for example, Spenser significantly revises Hooker's account, drawing from its welter of observations about the nitty-gritty of empire-building a detail which he transmutes into a vision of empire already achieved. Hooker notes that the horse of Ralegh's companion Henry Moile fled into the woods, where it was captured by the Irish.¹³ While this may seem to us at our remove a note of little consequence, the purloining of horses, and cattle, was a vital matter in Tudor Ireland, where livestock represented wealth, leverage, and tactical advantages.

As well as drawing on Hooker to seed his dream of empire, Spenser alludes to the *Aeneid* both to link Timias's heroism to empire-building and to glance at forces which thwart the English project in Ireland. One of the herbs Belphoebe seeks in ministering to Timias's wound is "panachea" (3.5.32.7), a herb provided by Venus to cure the deep-bleeding wound that Aeneas suffered in his empire-founding battle with Turnus. The immediate aftermath of the curing of Aeneas is equally instructive, for the lack of parallel with Timias's case. Aeneas's strength having returned, the ministering Iapyx shouts for the warrior's arms and Aeneas returns to battle.¹⁴ Timias, we recall, is "conveyed" from the battle site, smitten with Belphoebe, and rendered martially inert, a feature of his career which will concern us in detail later in the chapter. In the meantime, we should notice how the very wounding of Timias confirms Spenser's wish to connect Timias-Ralegh to heroic expansionism in so far as the wounding foregrounds more broadly allusive rather than strictly topical meanings. Ralegh was *not* wounded at the ford. Timias's wounding is thus "fictional," and what the fiction of his wounding establishes is not only the connection to Aeneas just noted but arguably also a link to Sidney's martial exploits in Zutphen, one of the fields of militant English Protestant expansionist activity on the continent. Sidney suffered an ultimately fatal thigh-wound, sustained, the story ran, because he threw off his leg armour in a gesture of defiance or magnanimity.¹⁵ Timias's is similarly a thigh-wound, similarly sustained in that this part alone of his body appears to be without armour. Spenser thus clearly places the reformation of Ireland under the aegis of militant Protestant expansionism and ascribes to Ralegh heroic agency.

Spenser's belief that Timias-Ralegh's subject position should be a heroic one (and that both Ralegh and the Queen should understand it this way) surfaces as well in two other features of the battle at the ford: its deploying matters of "shame" and "villeiny" and its imagining of *squire* Timias as, in effect, a knight. First, Timias's pursuit of the forester, we notice, implicates him in an economy of shame. When Spenser takes up Timias's story in canto 5, we read that

> [Timias] all this while full hardly was assayd
> Of deadly daunger, which to him betid;
> For whiles his Lord pursewed that noble Mayd,
> After that foster fowle he fiercely rid,
> To be avenged of the shame, he did
> To that faire Damizell: Him he chaced long
> Through that thicke woods, wherein he would have hid
> His shamefull head from his avengement strong,
> And oft him threatened death for his outrageous wrong. (3.5.13)

There is certainly enough shame to go around here: grammatically, and because of the characteristically Spenserian confusion of pronouns, "shame" attaches itself not only to the forester, but also to Arthur and even to Timias. Moreover, the ambiguous syntax leaves unanswerable the question of who threatens whom with "death for his outrageous wrong." The moral lineaments of the contest manifestly remain to be delineated.

Although the conflict between Timias and the forester does not constitute a full-fledged "custom of the castle" topos of the kind analysed recently by Ross, the contest raises similar moral and political issues. As Ross observes, the "castle topos" "can organize for our perception ... the moral problem created when the standards of one society or group clash with the customs of others."[16] The Tudor English project in Ireland inevitably generated much clashing of customs, laws, beliefs, as Ross himself notes in another Spenserian context. Given the Irish implications of Timias's pursuit of the forester, one could suppose their contest to be likewise inflected. Spenser, whose own undertaking in Munster embroiled him in land-title disputes and boycotts and whose *View* addresses the relativity of customs, must have experienced Ireland as constantly contested ground. Spenser's imagining of Ireland is seldom starkly imperialistic, however; frequently, even when he espouses the party line, his poetry accommodates competing claims for authority and sovereignty.[17] This is not for one moment to suggest that Spenser endorses the foresters or their designs against Timias. It is, though, to contend that, in the battle between Timias and the forester(s), rather than simply foreclosing the foresters' claims, Spenser adjudicates the opposing claimants' entitlement – entitlement to possess, not just these woods (and so Munster), but also the moral and social high ground. Indeed, moral and social pre-eminence comes to be the sign of "rightful" possession. To reduce this dynamic to its baldest statement: Spenser's narrative *makes the case* that the English, represented here by Timias, "deserve" Ireland because they are more "civil."

I have suggested already that Timias's battle is a fight to "seize" the land. We should also note that the battle deploys social values in a way which elevates Timias and degrades the foresters: gentility attaches to Timias as he moves from being a "squire unknowne" (3.5.17.5) to being a "squire [who] lives with renowne" (3.5.25.9), while shame attaches itself to the foresters, who behave not only villainously but also like villeins, status signalled by their weapons and logistics. The social disparity between Timias and the foresters is heightened by Spenser's implying that Timias behaves like a knight (an anachronistic assessment, since Ralegh was knighted in 1585, six years after the battle at the ford). Spenser's emphasis here on Timias's highly serviceable armour glances at Timias's elevation from squire to knight, the delivery of arms being closely associated in chivalric literature with the conferring of knighthood. More revealingly, Timias's victory wins him "honour" and "renown," long-established chivalric values, while the victory is specifically trumpeted as a victory over "treason bad." Ramon Lull's widely disseminated *Libre del ordre de cavayleria* identifies "treason" as a particular vice to be eschewed by knights, something Timias manages to do, while the foresters (historically, men of rank and distinction) do not.[18] Spenser's "conferring" of knighthood on Timias-Ralegh necessarily remains oblique, not only because of its being anachronistic, but also because it signals much presumption – both in its implicit message that Ralegh should be distinguished by his martial exploits rather than by Elizabeth's wish to keep Ralegh near her and in Spenser's arrogation of the sovereign authority to fashion a knight.

Spenser's ascription of social difference (and so his adjudication of political prerogative) extends to the more fundamental matter of assigning differential values to the bodies of the combatants. The foresters appear irredeemably carnal, a quality signalled repeatedly in the details of the episode, from the ambiguous word order, which implies that the foresters are themselves "with thicke woods over growne" (3.5.17.7), to the graphically physical descriptions of their "gnashing teeth" (3.5.22.1), split heads (3.5.23.5–6), and grovelling carcasses (3.5.23.7). His evidently superior strength and prowess notwithstanding, Timias, by contrast, seems less exclusively corporeal, more inspired, a distinction marked especially by the detail of his wounding: the "wicked steele"

> did light
> In his left thigh, and deepely did it thrill:
> Exceeding griefe that wound in him empight,
> But more that with his foes he could not come to fight. (3.5.20.6–9)

Although it later bleeds copiously, an issue to which I shall return, here Timias's wound produces affliction felt in spirit and mind rather than flesh.

The inextricableness with which Spenser's rendering of bodies is bound up with matters of propietorship and jurisdiction can be surmised from his punning introduction of the foresters, an introduction which marks the shift from the moral allegory of lust to the topical allegory of the Desmond rebellion. Spenser writes that the three were "ungracious children of one gracelesse syre" (3.5.15.6). Spenser's "ungracious" and "gracelesse" not only convey the irredeemable carnality of the foresters but are also densely packed with allusions to definitive conflicts in Munster, to the fact, for example, that the Earl of Desmond was labelled a rebel and so forfeited the Queen's "grace," and to the fact that the Pope, surely from the Protestant point of view a "gracelesse syre," countenanced the band of invaders who landed at Dingle Bay in 1579. Because the three foresters are triply "ungracious" – in body, in politics, and in religion – they do not "deserve" to possess the Irish landscape. Spenser thus maps onto the bodies of the foresters and Timias differential social and political values in such a way that their bodies then act as signs or guarantors of social and political standing.

Such distinctions between the combatants prove all the more important to draw given the extent to which the battle at the ford threatens to collapse these distinctions. Timias's pursuit of the forester, we recall, places him in an economy of shame – or better, a hall of mirrors – where distinctions among Arthur, the forester, and Timias are grammatically hard to maintain. Timias's riding "fiercely" "[a]fter that fowle foster" (3.5.13.4) thus permits the idea that he rides fiercely *in the manner of* the forester. Once embroiled in battle, Timias "takes after" the foresters more closely still, like them adding to his force "wrath and vengeance" as well as their weapon of choice, the boar-spear (3.5.21.1; 20.1). The conclusion of the battle sees Timias's nearest and most perilous approach to merging with the foresters. His defeat of the foresters *seems* to utterly distinguish him from them, for "[T]hey three be dead with shame, the squire lives with renown" (3.5.25.9). Indeed, Spenser's antithetical scheme creates carefully balanced moral discriminations. To take the first clause first: the death of the foresters proves their shamefulness (they died so they must have been shameful) as well as tainting them with shame (they died in a shamefull manner); at the same time, it was their shameful conduct toward Timias that prosecuted their deaths. Such a spiralling of cause and effect marks the foresters' fate as both ineluctable and deserved. According to this logic, Timias is the instrument through which their self-sealed fate is effected, not someone implicated in a contest from which no one can emerge without shame. Indeed, as the "squire [who] lives with renown," Timias now stands outside the circulation of shame. These carefully established moral discriminations collapse with the very next lines, however, when we read that the wounded Timias

> lives, but takes small joy of his renowne;
> For of that cruell wound he bled so sore,
> That from his steed he fell in deadly swowne.
> Yet still the blood forth gusht in so great store,
> That he lay wallowd all in his owne gore. (3.5.26.1–5)

There seems little now to distinguish Timias from the foresters, and still less to distinguish "shame" from "renowne," since renown obviously cannot preclude a "deadly" swoon, as the rhyming of "renowne" and "swowne" confirms. What is in danger of collapsing, in other words, is the system of differential values by which Spenser and others justified the Tudor English conquest of Ireland.

That Spenser's fiction of Timias verges on this particular precipice testifies, I think, to the ampleness and flexibility of Spenser's moral vision, to his willingness to subject to scrutiny and threat of dismantlemant his own "official" political line as undertaker and administrator in Tudor Ireland. While wishing to stress the heroic and moral lineaments of Timias's victory, Spenser nevertheless recognizes the difficulty of – and indeed the artifice involved in – maintaining distinctions between Irish and English. Spenser's own day-to-day life in Ireland must have repeatedly blurred the lines separating English from Irish and Anglo-Irish, while widening the gap between "official" Tudor English designs for Ireland and the reality of the lived experience of the new English in Ireland. His assocation with Thomas Norris, for example, whose heading of a second commission to hear land-title suits resulted in some redistribution of confiscated lands to Irish and Anglo-Irish claimants, must have helped to clarify Spenser's fairness of vision.[19]

Timias's bleeding wound offers an especially provocative instance of the subtlety with which Spenser anatomizes Ralegh's Irish career. Gail Paster has demonstrated the ways in which bleeding wounds can register issues of agency and dependency. Certainly, Timias's wound reinscribes his heroic, martial body as both vulnerable and difficult to distinguish from the bodies of the shameful foresters, since, as Paster notes, a "bleeding body" can be a "shameful token of uncontrol ... a failure of physical self-mastery."[20] Accordingly, Timias's wound marks a shift in his subject position, from a masculine position of agency to a feminine position of dependency. Timias's lapse into unconsciousness, his evacuating the seat of reason, so to speak, further confirms his now feminized position. David Miller in *The Poem's Two Bodies* has argued convincingly that Timias's thigh-wound marks him as subject to lust; at this crucial point of the narrative, then, the moral allegory of lust is conjoined to the topical allegory of the Desmond rebellion. That Timias's wound conscripts him into the allegory of lust thus marks an intersecting of heroic and erotic, Virgilian and Petrarchan, poetics, an intersection which in fact mirrors the career of Ralegh, whose military service in Ireland inaugurated his association with Queen, court, and courtiership. His abjection is not as thoroughgoing as it might initially seem, however. Paradoxically, his bleeding wound also provides evidence of his self-control – he seemingly does not bleed until after he had done with the foresters – and of his youthfulness and manly vigour – attested to by his "great store" of blood.[21]

To account for the ambivalence of Timias's bleeding wound we need to return to its cause – a "cruell shaft, headed with deadly ill, / And fethered with an unlucky quill" (3.5.20.4–5) – and surmise that, as is so often the case, "quill" refers secondarily to "pen," and so points us to discursive fields. The massacre at Smerwick, in which Ralegh played a prominent part, stirred controversy across Europe, a fact registered obliquely by Spenser's describing the wounded Timias as "with bloud deformed" (3.5.29.2) as well as by the fact that, in pursuing the forester, Timias-Ralegh enters a realm rife with possibilities for slander.[22] The animus of the foresters is represented in terms specifically appropriate to slander, as defined legally and as imaged by Spenser in Book 4 of *The Faerie Queene*. Indeed, the foresters bear a striking resemblance to Sclaunder: Sclaunder is "stuft with rancour and despight / Up to the throat, that oft with bitternesses / It forth would breake" (4.8.24.3–5), while, regarding the foresters, we read that "Vile rancour their rude harts had fild with ... despight" (3.5.16.9). Both Sclaunder and the foresters harbour malice and both Sclaunder and the foresters inflict wounds which cause grief. Further, as Lindsay Kaplan has recently documented, both malice and despight are defamatory motives.[23]

This implied link between slander and Timias's wound testifies to the precariousness of heroic agency in Tudor colonial Ireland, where, in the absence of a concerted and sustained policy regading the "pacifying" of Ireland, any one individual's actions were subject to varying constructions. This context helps to explain the efficacy of Belphoebe's ministering. Belphoebe's palliatives have long been recognized as referring to the offices and remuneration which came Ralegh's way. In a society in which reputation *really* counted, the Queen's material favour could well obviate the effects of slander.

I would contend further that, as well as insinuating the effects of slander, Spenser's "cruel shaft ... fethered with an unlucky quill" targets – proleptically – Ralegh's participation in the Petrarchan dynamics of courtiership. This context helps to explain, in turn, the *inefficacy* of Belphoebe's ministrations. Although helped materially – his flesh wound knits up – Timias suffers the immaterial and wasting wound of the Petrarchan lover. Spenser's phrasing in describing the curing of Timias's flesh wound advances a finely tuned critique of Petrarchan courtiership as a dynamic which produces epistemological confusion, as well as (and therefore) the vitiation of the heroic energy and agency needed to continue the reformation of Ireland. To consider the former first, when Spenser writes that with the appliction of Belphoebe's salves Timias's "foule sore [was] reduced to faire plight" (3.5.41.8), the equivocal "reduced," which suggests a shrinking of both the wound and of possibilities, encourages us to understand Timias's plight as a diminishment of endeavour. More specifically, while "reduced" as straitened circumstances leads us to read Timias's plight, despite the adjective "faire," as unfortunate (an unstable reading fixed by the next line, "[the sore] she reduced, but himselfe destroyed quight"), the conjoining of "faire" to "plight" taps the reservoir of Petrarchan vocabulary and gesture, directing us to understand Timias's Petrarchan posture as the reduction. That Timias's wound "did gather, and grow hole" (3.5.43.1), not "whole," suggests more powerfully that, positioned in Petrarchan discourse, the Timias whose martial exploits gave him form has become a cipher, a naught.

The vitiation of Timias's heroic agency and energy is signalled as well in the continuing play of allusion to the *Aeneid*, wryly counterpointed by a simultaneous intratextual allusion to Spenser's locus classicus of masculine enervation. When Timias regains consciousness and sees Belphoebe, "The goodly Maide, ful of divinities / ... / Her bow and gilden quiver lying him beside" (3.5.34.7–9), like Aeneas meeting the similarly clad Venus (*Aeneid*, 1.307–39), Timias wonders how to address her: "Angell, or Goddesse doe I call thee right?" (3.5.35.5). Aeneas's meeting with Venus, however, punctuates Jupiter's prophecy of the Roman imperium and Aeneas's role in its founding. Timias's meeting with Belphoebe forecloses his heroic career, as is underscored by his reference to the "bower of bliss," known to Spenser's readers as the place where Verdant reclines, careless of honour, his nobility "defaced" because his "warlike Armes ... [hang] upon a tree" (2.12.79–80). Given Spenser's habit of overdetermining his allegorical meanings, one might be tempted to find also in Timias's "distressed" state an allusion to the shorn and emasculated Samson.

Through his representation of Timias's meeting with Belphoebe, Spenser suggests that Petrarchism trammels heroic energy because it locks the hero into an idolatrous dynamic in which material cause is mistaken for final cause.[24] Spenser introduces Belphoebe into Timias's story by speaking of "Providence heavenly [which] passeth living thought" (3.5.27.1) and thus instructing us to regard Belphoebe as an instrument of divine design. Timias proves to be a less astute reader, as his immediate responses to Belphoebe demonstrate:

> By this he had sweet life recur'd agayne,
> And, groning inly deepe, at last his eies,
> His watry eies drizling like deawy rayne,
> He gan lifte toward the azure skies,
> From whence descend all hopelesse remedies:
> Therewith he sigh'd; and, turning him aside,
> The goodly Maide, ful of divinities
> And gifts of heavenly grace, he by him spide,
> Her bow and gilden quiver lying him besidie.
>
> "Mercy, deare Lord!" (said he) "what grace is this
> That thou has shewed to me sinfull wight,
> To send thine Angell from her bowre of blis
> To comfort me in my distressed plight.
> Angell, or Goddesse do I call thee right?
> What service may I doe unto thee meete,
> That hast from darkenes me returnd to light,
> And with thy hevenly salves and med'cines sweete
> Hast drest my sinfull wounds? I kisse thy blessed feete. (3.5.34, 35)

These stanzas bear close scrutiny. Notably, the sovereign-subject relationship is here constituted as a loss of faith: when Timias turns from the sky "whence descend all hopelesse remedies," "hopelesse" slides from its original task (of modifying remedies-for-situations-seemingly-without-hope) to modify as well Timias's specific frame of mind. His "turning aside" thus becomes errancy. *The Faerie Queene* is certainly a book of errancies, many of which, as Linda Gregerson has recently demonstrated so deftly, open up space for reformation and self-fashioning.[25] But Timias's error here will prove, not generative, but delimiting.

Timias makes two related, cardinal, mistakes in his construing of Belphoebe, errors which show that he does not "read aright." First, as the paratactic construction of lines 8 and 9 of stanza 34 implies, Timias seems not to see Belphoebe's "bow and quiver" and so does not read her either as an avatar of Diana or as an allusion to the disguised Venus of the *Aeneid*'s imperial program. It may also be that Timias *does* see the bow and quiver and chooses to ignore their significance, showing himself thus to be a willful misreader of signs, a more damnable offence in Spenser's view. Either way, Timias-Ralegh's misreading distorts his own position as a corporate subject. Second, although his recognizing the "grace" in Belphoebe's presence and his wondering if she is an "angel" signify the ability to understand her providentially, his alluding to the bower of bliss undermines that potential by corrupting the providential figure with earthly designs. When Timias asks, "Angell, *or Goddesse* do I call thee right," his second term shifts the frame of reference from Christian eschatology to the secularized world of Petrarchism, without (as his first reading error indicates) incorporating the saving fiction of Belphoebe as providential, imperial, Venus. Thus, Timias's very elaboration of what Belphoebe might be leads him astray.

In other words, Timias slides into a kind of idolatry, with its consequent perils – not the least of which is the fact that love for the saviour-figure becomes an obstacle to be negotiated. Much of Timias's love lament will be taken up with trying without success to sublimate unseemly sensual love into a expression of spiritual service. Timias's failure to do so is signalled by his being inwardly consumed by the effort, his becoming a mere shell. Timias's "will," uninformed by grace, wins out, "ransacking" and "wasting" his "inward partes,"leaving him "dried up and blasted," just as "percing levin ... the inner part / Of everything consumes, and calcineth by art" (3.5.58). Spenser's "calcineth" is a reminder that Timias has fallen from the realm of grace and spirit to the stony world of exclusively material causes. Thus dispirited, Timias lacks heroic form and agency.

The dwindling of Timias's heroic form and agency is matched by a drastic narrowing of the field for action, a reduction which offers a trenchant critique of court structure and dynamics. Arguably, the conveyance (and note the negative implications of "steal") of Timias to the deepest recesses of Belphoebe's dwelling recalls in particular Ralegh's promotion in 1587 to Captain of the Guard, a position of peculiar ambivalence when the monarch is female. Traditionally, that is, when the monarch is male, the Captain of the Guard is a squire of the king's body and is thus afforded an intimacy of contact not possible when the sovereign is female. To be Captain of the Guard for a queen is in many ways an untenable position with little scope for really intimate service. Into this void, Spenser's argument runs, fits Petrarchan discourse, with its terms and postures of pseudo-intimacy.

Timias's three-stanza Petrarchan lament (3.5.45–7), with its ever-narrowing circles of logic, spurious binaries, and closing-off of possibilities, figures the particular entrapments in Petrarchan courtiership as he talks, or perhaps writes, himself into silent abjection. The lament effects an insidious appropriation of heroic energy and agency, as Timias moves from possessing sufficient autonomy to at at least imagine dying for his own honour to regarding his life and death as *only* for Belphoebe. One might counter that such complete subordination of courtier to sovereign constitutes an ideal sovereign-subject relationship. But in practice and even in theory – and certainly in Spenser's view – courtiers retained some autonomy and presided in relatively independent spheres of action. Utter subordination of the kind posed by Petrarchan courtiership produces inertia or simply the illusion of movement. Witness Timias's becoming "calcified" (3.5.48.9) or his ending his lament with the same conclusion with which he begins. Witness, too, the fact that in his lament "service" can mean *only* death ("dying do her serve / … / Dye rather, dye, then ever from her service swerve" [3.5.46.6–9]) and so death becomes the only alternative to "disloyalty." The intense focus in stanza 46 on "serve" – a term which reverberates through "deserve," "ever," and "swerve" – mimes an obsessively turned frame of mind, one which cannot admit or imagine alternative subject positions.

Petrarchan quarters and service seem constraining indeed, particularly when set alongside the meanings signalled by "service" in Hooker's Irish chronicle. In Hooker's rehearsal of Ralegh's activities around the time of the ambush at the ford, the word "service[s]" (which appears twelve times in a passage of about 2100 words) always means martial service. Moreover, Captain Ralegh is represented as someone with sufficient position, command, and initiative to implement measures to redress the "outrages, bodrages and villanies daily practised by Barrie, Condon, and others upon the good subjects [of Munster] and her maiesties garrisons," to win from the Lord Deputy of Ireland and his council a "commission unto himselfe, to seize and enter upon the castell and house of Barrie court," and to be appointed one of three interim governors of Munster. Fashioned by Hooker as a knight errant riding through Munster and challenging "rebels" and "villeins," Ralegh emerges as someone able, independently of the Crown, to subject Ireland to English rule.[26] Hooker's rendition of Ralegh's Irish career provides a further model of service to contest Petrarchan courtiership. Through the counterpointed actions of two of Ralegh's servants, one an Irishman who villeinously abandons Ralegh to his own devices at the ford and one a Yorkshireman who directs an Irishman to save a beleaguered Ralegh during another skirmish, Hooker draws the "good servant" as someone whose immediate loyalty is owed to his captain. The military ethos celebrated by Hooker forms the alter-ideal against which Spenser plots the shortcomings of Petrarchan courtiership, something signalled not only by the diminishments which, we have seen, attend Timias's movement into Belphoebe's landscape, or by the military metaphors which play ironically through the description of Timias's Petrarchan posture, but also by the fact that, in plighting himself to Belphoebe, Timias proves a disloyal servant to Arthur, whose squire he is.

In closing this consideration of Spenser's reformative mirroring of Ralegh's career and poetics, I would like to return briefly to Irish land matters, a feature of Spenser's narrative whose sustained importance is signalled by Timias's referring to Belphoebe's "gracious *deed*" (3.5.45.3) and by the occurrence in both the proem (3 proem 3.4) and the lead-in to Timias's lament of the phrase "lucklesse *lot*" (3.5.44.9; my emphasis). What Spenser's narrative seems designed, on one level, to do is to remind his readers – preeminently, Ralegh and the Queen – that it was the heroic, military actions of captains such as Ralegh that established England's "Ireland," a point made with characteristically Spenserian wryness when Belphoebe enters the woods of Timias's story as a "hunteresse [who] did *wonne*" (3.5.27.6; my emphasis) immediately following Timias's "winning" of the woods from the foresters. Again in typically Spenserian fashion, Spenser gives to Timias title for these lands when in "The Ruines of Time" he refers (*not* inadvertently,

I would argue) to "a pleasant Paradize, / ... / which *Merlin* by his Magicke slights / Made for the gentle squire, to entertaine / His fayre *Belphoebe*" (lines 519–24). Spenser and Merlin – revisionists both – allot to Timias-Ralegh what his Petrarchan courtiership leaves him unable to claim for himself. Spenser deftly points the difference between his and his patron's poetics and postures by demonstrating that, while the "lucklesse lot" of his position in Ireland finally enables both reformative vision and *real* estate, Timias-Ralegh's "lucklesse lot" in Petrarchan discourse – a position which obscures his formative Irish experiences – diminishes his state.

6 Conclusion

I began this study by reading Spenser's 1590 dedicatory sonnet to Lady Carew as an index to the complexity and suppleness of his patronal relations. Through the course of the book, we have seen that, within the potential confinements of patronage, Spenser finds means to amplify his sense of agency as well as room for the amplitude of his moral, political, and poetic imagination. In closing, I will turn to Spenser's 1596 fictional treatment, in Book 4 of *The Faerie Queene*, of his patron Ralegh's clandestine marriage to Elizabeth Throckmorton, the event that occasioned Ralegh's most serious fall from Queen Elizabeth's favour. This matter, which Spenser handles with a characteristic combination of delicacy and trenchancy, can furnish a final instance of Spenser's enabling engagements with patrons.

If in Book 3 Spenser dramatizes Timias-Ralegh's entrapment in Petrarchism, in Book 4 he effects Timias-Ralegh's rescue from that enthralment – but not before he rehearses once again the limitations of Petrarchan courtiership and poetics. The episode calculates the shortfall of Petrarchan courtiership by representing both Timias and Belphoebe as subject to perversions of will and insufficiencies of sight.[1]

When Spenser returns in Book 4 to Timias, the "gentle squire" (4.7.24.3) is hunting with Belphoebe and her nymphs. Separated from them in the course of the chase, Timias comes upon Amoret, who, having just escaped from Lust's cave, is fleeing in terror from her pursuing captor. Timias's reaction is prompt and impeccable:

> And that same gentle Squire arriv'd in place,
> Where this same cursed caytive did appeare,
> Pursuing that faire Lady full of feare,
> And now he her quite overtaken had;
> And now he her away with him did beare
> Under his arme, as seeming wondrous glad,
> That by his grenning laughter mote farre off be rad.
>
> Which drery sight the gentle Squire espying,
> Dost hast to crosse him by the nearest way,
> Led with that wofull Ladies piteous crying. (4.7.24.3–9; 25.1–3)

Our sense of the rightness of Timias's actions is sharpened by the contrast Spenser develops between the squire's solicitude and Belphoebe's self-sufficiency. When the narrator describes Amoret's flight, he observes that "Ne living aide for her on earth appeares, / But if the heavens helpe to redresse her wrong" (4.7.23.2–3). Belphoebe, elsewhere an agent of grace, enters the narrative:

> It fortuned *Belphebe* with her peares
> The woody Nimphs, and with that lovely boy,
> Was hunting then the Libbards and the Beares,
> In these wild woods, as was her wonted joy,
> To banish sloth, that oft doth noble mindes annoy. (4.7.23.5–9)

The rhetorical construction indicates not only that companionship, for Belphoebe, remains subordinated to the activity of hunting – the references to companions occur in prepositional phrases – but also that, in her wish to banish sloth, she serves primarily her own interests. She emerges from this stanza as noble and self-sufficient, certainly, but also as self-contained.

In Spenser's moral world, self-containment shades easily into a self-absorption that precludes the beneficent outward movement so crucial, in his view, to the sustaining of life. One might think of the sixth of the *Mutabilitie Cantos* where Diana, another virgin huntress and avatar of Queen Elizabeth, withdraws and retreats from the Arlo landscape, turning what was once a flourishing resort fit for the gods into a wasteland. More immediately, one might recall the circumstances of Amoret's conception and fostering in Book 3 to realize how centrally Spenser imagines the world, physical, moral, and spiritual, to depend upon beneficent outward movement. Chrysogone's impregnation by the rays of the sun – which generates Amoret and Belphoebe – tropes this movement as the influence of divine grace (3.6.5–7); the unceasing flow of things from the Garden of Adonis – where Amoret is fostered by Venus – figures it as natural generation (3.6.30–8); the mount of Venus in the Garden figures it as sexual love (3.6.43–50). All three are analogous, just as in sonnet 68 of Spenser's *Amoretti*, "Most glorious lord of life," divine and human love are analogous.

Given how absolutely central to Spenser's vision is this notion of restorative outward movement, movement out of self-containment – in other words, love – we are surely to approve Timias's attempt to help Amoret. We might note that his effort is always marked by concern for Amoret. Throughout the fight with Lust, Timias remains aware of what his blows might do to her (stanzas 26, 27). Significantly, he is moved to help Amoret, not by the "grenning laughter" of Lust that "mote farre off be rad" (4.7.24.9), but by Amoret's "piteous crying" (4.25.3); thus, he fulfils the narrative injunction that "Moved with pity of her plenteous teares," "heavens helpe to redresse her wrong" (4.7.23.4,3). Timias, then, emerges as the instrument of grace, a distinction reflected in the same rhetorical construction that sketches Belphoebe's self-containment as she hunts "with her peares / The woody nimphs, and with that lovely boy" (4.7.23.5–6): the caesura and the lack of the expected parallelism between the prepositional phrases direct attention to the boy, Timias.

Spenser thus encourages the reader to understand Timias's rescuing of Amoret as laudable, though not unambiguously so – for Timias does wound Amoret in the process (4.7.27.5–9; 35.9). At least part of the point here is, simply enough, that it is difficult to sort through human impulses, desires, and designs, to say "this is love," "this is lust," "this is self-interest," and so on. Spenser makes this point also in his descriptions of the various pursuits in the episode: when Amoret escapes from Lust's cave, we read that "after her fully lightly he uprose, / And her pursu'd as fast as she did flie" (4.7.21.6–7); when Lust flees from Belphoebe, we read that "she speedily poursewed / With winged feete, as nimble as the winde" (4.7.30.1–2); when Belphoebe turns from Timias, we read that he "arose up light, / ... / And follow'd fast" (4.7.37.1–3). In this episode, as elsewhere in his poetry, Spenser presents a world in which it is absolutely imperative to maintain fine moral distinctions, but almost impossible to do so. Almost, but not entirely. We can make the necessary distinctions, provided we attend closely to detail, to context, to history.

Spenser implies as much, not only in the rehearsing of Timias's dealings with Amoret, but also in the recounting of Amoret's exhanges with Amylia. Amoret's express sympathy for Amylia – who is likewise captive in Lust's den – elides distinctions between them: "what are you," asks Amoret, "whom like unlucky lot / Hath linckt with me in the same chaine attone?" (4.7.14.6–7). Amoret's "attone," catching at more than coincidences of time and place, posits identity between the two victims. Amoret's question elicits from Amylia her history, the recounting of which prompts Amoret to identify her case even more fully with that of her fellow sufferer: "Thy ruefull plight I pitty as mine owne," laments Amoret. Amylia's history, however, establishes distinctions between the two cases, and the two characters, despite Amylia's construing their two plights as "like haplesse." To begin with, Amylia does not share Amoret's readiness to empathize: "Ah wretched wight," Amylia remonstrates,

> That seekes to know anothers griefe in vaine,
> Unweeting of thine owne like haplesse plight:
> Selfe to forget to mind another, is oversight. (4.7.10.6–9)

In counselling Amoret to think only of herself, Amylia remains true to form. Her own love affair with the "squire of low degree" proceeded in wilful disregard of family and friends, as her recounting demonstrates. Amylia recalls that, although she was reproved often by her father for her choice,

> nothing could my fixed mind remove,
> But whether willed or nilled friend or foe,
> I me resolv'd the utmost end to prove,
> And rather then my love abandon so,
> Both sire, and friends, and all for ever to forgo.
> Thenceforth I sought by secret meanes to worke

Time to my will, and from his wrathfull sight
To hide th'intent, which in my heart did lurke. (4.7.16.5–9; 17.1–2)

Elsewhere, Spenser certainly praises constancy in love. Amylia's determination seems like just wilfulness, however, as is suggested not only by the guilefulness of her conduct – gauged exactly in that "lurke" – but also by the facts that Amylia's love for the squire was premised on her "faining eye" (4.7.15.9) (always potentially treacherous grounds in Spenser); that her love was exclusively physical as well as fuelled by female rivalry (this "Leman" was "meet" to "have lain" by "any Ladies side [4.7.15.8, 9]); and, most tellingly, that Amylia now seems to have quite forgotten her squire (she never once laments his absence) and to regret most the social fall occasioned by her tryst ("what I was, it irkes me to rehearse; / Daughter unto a Lord of high degree" [4.7.15.1–2]). The last point clinches the matter by retroactively rendering completely hollow Amylia's declaration of her willingness "for ever to forgo" her "sire, and friends" rather than "abandon" her "love" (4.7.16.8–9).

Despite Amoret's perception that her case is like Amylia's, this is not so, either in the fiction – unlike Amylia, Amoret scarcely seems blameable for her plight – or in the topical allegory: Elizabeth Throckmorton did not have in Ralegh a "squire of low degree"; moreover, by all accounts their marriage was a loving one. I may be seeming to quibble here; Spenser's allegorical method does not always require exact, detailed correspondence between historical particulars and allegorical designs. But this episode foregrounds the importance of attending closely to detail and context, the importance of drawing distinctions between seemingly like cases.

In so doing, the episode highlights what for Spenser is a damaging limitation in the Petrarchan courtiership performed by his patron Ralegh: the neglect of history and context. In Spenser's estimation, Petrarchan courtiership, with its hardened categories, remains insufficiently circumstantial. Belphoebe's discountenancing of Timias when she finds him tending to the wounded Amoret – "she turned her face, and fled away for evermore" (4.7.36.9) – follows from her apprehending the two of them "with sodaine glauncing eye" (4.7.36.1), with a look which, uninformed by the history and context understood by the reader, sees only a compromised Timias. So seeing, Belphoebe can only respond with "disdain" and "indignity" (4.7.36.3). We have seen that Timias's case, fully considered, demands more nuanced responses. Belphoebe's inability, or unwillingness, to recognize mitigating factors is underscored by her "gazing" a long time at the defeated figure of Lust and noting his "monstrous shape" and "mighty limbs" (4.7.32.6–8) without being moved to realize that he must have proved a formidable foe to Timias and that Timias must have at least held his own in their encounter. That the problem, for Spenser, lies in the incompleteness of Belphoebe's judgment, not in its quickness, is signalled by his calling her eye "sodaine." Historically, the Queen did not react quickly to the news of Ralegh's marriage, waiting at least several weeks before sending the Raleghs to the Tower. Accordingly, the suddeness of Belphoebe's view must trope the Queen's reaction as insufficient in scope and understanding.

Utterly in keeping with the dynamics of Petrarchan courtiership, Timias reacts to Belphoebe's discountenancing of him with anguish and abjection. Having long followed the indignant Belphoebe with "no ease of griefe, nor hope of grace" (4.7.38.1–2), Timias

> Unto those woods ... turned backe againe,
> Full of sad anguish, and in heavy case:
> And finding there fit solitary place
> For wofull wight, chose out a gloomy glade,
> Where hardly eye mote see bright heavens face,
> For mossy trees, which covered all with shade
> And sad melancholy: there he his cabin made. (4.7.38.3–9)

In choosing a glade where "hardly eye mote see bright heavens face," Timias replicates the very distance now separating him from Belphoebe – a sign, surely, of the intransigence of Petrarchan postures. And it is tempting to find in the phrasing "eye mote" a wry Spenserian glance at the inadequacies of Petrarchan seeing. Moreover, Timias's calculated withdrawal into melancholy amounts to a perversion of the will, as the narrator repeatedly insists in emphasizing that Timias *chooses* to "wast his wretched daies in wofull plight" (4.7.39.8); that he "wilfully did cut and shape anew" his garment, to reflect his woe (4.7.40.2, 1); that he "let to grow and griesly to concrew" his "faire locks" (4.7.40.5, 3,); that he is "consumed quight" through "wilfull penury" (4.7.41.3). Spenser underlines the artifice in Timias's response, intimating that Timias's "wofull plight" (4.7.39.8) – his situation – results from his continuing in "carefull plight" (4.7.41.1) – his continuing to commit himself to this posture and role. That a Petrarchan role has exacted a continued commitment from Ralegh is underscored by the fact that so much of the description of the woebegone Timias derives from Ralegh's own poem "Like to a Hermit poore," written in response to his 1592 fall from favour and published anonymously in *The Phoenix Nest* (1593).[2] Timias is transformed, that is, into an image previously fashioned by Ralegh.

Spenser emphasizes the perverseness of Timias's choices by recording Arthur's surmises about the "cabin" that Timias makes and about Timias himself. Spying the cabin as he "strays" through these woods in search of adventures, Arthur approaches it "[w]eening therein some holy Hermit lay, / That did resort of sinfull people shonne; / Or else some woodman shrowded there from scorching sunne" (4.7.42.7–9). Arthur's imagining that there "some holy Hermit lay" both confirms the allusion to Ralegh's poem (or "lay") and provides, along with the reference to the woodsman, circumstances against which to measure the legitimacy of Timias's withdrawal. Unlike a hermit or woodsman, Timias has no good reason, spiritual or pragmatic, to retreat into isolation and obscurity.

Attempting to construe Timias from the "secret signes of manlinesse, / Which close appeared in that rude brutishness" (4.7.45.4–5), Arthur surmises

> That he whilome some gentle swaine had beene,
> Trained up in feats of armes and knightlinesse;
> Which he observ'd, by that he him had seene
> To weld his naked sword, and try the edges keene.
>
> And eke by that he saw on every tree,
> How he the name of one engraven had,
> Which likly was his liefest love to be,
> For whom he now so sorely was bestad;
> Which was by him BELPHEBE rightly rad.
>
> Yet who was that *Belphebe*, he ne wist;
> Yet saw he often how he wexed glad,
> When he it heard, and how the ground he kist,
> Wherein it written was, and how himselfe he blist: (4.7.45.6–9; 46)

As I have suggested, this episode is integrally about making distinctions, and Arthur's reading of Timias's inscriptions invites us to distinguish between Timias's writing of Belphoebe and Spenser's, – to compare, finally, Ralegh's *Book of the Ocean to Cynthia* and Spenser's *The Faerie Queene*. Arthur remains baffled by Timias's "BELPHEBE" not because of any deficiency in him – he "rightly" reads the name – but because Timias's writing provides no context, no history, no story for his figure. Timias's Belphoebe consequently remains inert, unable to exert any explicatory or reformative force – quite unlike Spenser's *storied* Belphoebe, whose appearances in *The Faerie Queene* produce effects, both in other characters and, potentially, in readers, who can learn from Belphoebe the strengths and limitations of her virtue. In Spenser's poem, too, history becomes intelligible and providential, becomes, that is, mythology. Like Timias's writing of BELPHEBE, Ralegh's fragmentary poem of Queen Elizabeth, *The Ocean to Cynthia*, assumes only lyrical, not narrative, epic, or didactic force. It is obscure, elliptical, even incoherent, in its articulation of Ralegh's regret over his banishment. It is, moreover, a poem in which the rehearsing of Ralegh's frustrated desire for Queen Elizabeth also records the collapsing of mythology – of intelligible history – into mere flux, and locates this failure in the solipsism of Ralegh's conceit of Elizabeth.[3]

Having dramatized the failures of will and sight that enthral both Timias and Belphoebe, Spenser moves to effect their rescue from such confinement; in the process, he again advances his poetics as reformative. When Arthur finds that he is unable to help Timias – "Ne ought mote make him change his wonted tenor, / Ne ought mote ease or mitigate his paine" (4.7.47.3–4) – he leaves him "there in languor to remaine, / Till time for him should remedy provide, / And him restore to former grace againe" (4.7.47.5–7). In the event, it is not time but a Dove that restores Timias. A turtle Dove, who "likewise late had lost her dearest love" (4.8.3.4), happens upon Timias "as in his wonted wise / His doole he made" (4.8.3.1–2), and begins to "mone his undeserved smart / And with her dolefull accents beare with him a part" (4.8.3.8–9). The Dove continues to "repaire" to Timias and "to recomfort [him] in his greatest care" (4.8.5.2, 4); a greatly solaced Timias rewards her by placing round her neck on a ribbon a "Ruby of right perfect hew, / Shaped like a heart, yet bleeding of the wound, / And with a litle golden chaine about it bond" (4.8.6.6–9) – a jewel once given to Timias by Belphoebe. Almost immediately, the Dove flies to Belphoebe, who recognizes the ruby, reaches for it, and so is led by the bird (who stays just out of reach) to Timias. Belphoebe, moved to pity the unrecognized Timias, asks him his story, and, eventually, "receive[s] [him] againe to former favours state" (4.8.17.9).

In the most important treatment to date of the Dove allegory, Patrick Cheney, in a densely reasoned argument, demonstrates the ways in which the Dove episode provides a "mimetic model of Spenserian epic."[4] Drawing on Renaissance theology and poetic practice and theory, Cheney finds that, because the Dove represents divine grace and epic aspiration as well as figuring Spenser as a national poet, the episode presents Spenser "as a Protestant poet functioning as an agent of grace in the providential fashioning of an ideal power structure ordering the English commonwealth."[5] Spenser's use of the Dove "instructs Elizabeth and Ralegh in the providential relation between divine and sovereign grace," and "defend[s] the divine authority of the epic poet to re-establish the ideal of chastity and friendship in the commonwealth," while the ruby carried by the Dove becomes "a trope … for [both] the grace and glory of [the poet's] eloquence … [and] the grace and glory of imperial power" and so points to a process of reciprocal fashioning between poet and sovereign.[6]

Cheney's claims are large, and largely unassailable, if a little schematic. I would, however, add to his already multilayered and widely informed reading still another level of analyis, one that directs our attention more immediately to the surface details of the story to find there the salutary workings of Spenser's poetics of patronage. We need to register the fact that the Dove, however informed with the theological, vocational, and political dimensions adduced by Cheney, effects her restoration in the terms of the episode. Thus, for example, Timias's placing the ruby on the Dove makes her into a figure informed with at least some of the history of Timias's plight. We have seen that, for Spenser, poetry needs to be so informed. And accordingly, it is only when the Dove assumes the weight of this circumstance that she seeks out Belphoebe. Similarly, the Dove becomes a figure for poetry which remains flexibly circumstantial. Spenser's Dove is able to bring together Belphoebe and Timias because she adapts herself so readily to the positions – predicated and occupied – of each. With Timias, she becomes a mirror of his woe – a feature of her comforting of him reflected in the vocabulary of recursiveness: she "re-pairs" to him to "re-comfort him"(4.8.3.2, 4). With Belphoebe, she becomes prey to be pursued (4.8.11.4). In each case, the Dove is attuned to the very tendencies which have hardened into attitudes precluding restorative exchanges. In each case, she figures those tendencies in prelude to drawing both Belphoebe and Timias from that entrapment.

Spenser's claims for poetry, for his poetry, are large ones. This claim about Spenser is not new. But the discovery that he stakes his ground so consistently, so creatively, and so engagingly within the confinements of patronage maps new territory in Spenser studies, perhaps especially in conjoining new historicist themes, materialist assumptions and contexts, and close reading. Spenser's own ampleness turns all such ranging into excursion.

Notes

CHAPTER ONE

1 Edmund Spenser, "To ... Lady Carew," *The Faerie Queene*, ed. A.C. Hamilton, 743.
2 Lady Carew was Elizabeth Spencer, one of the Spencers of Althorp, with whom Spenser claimed kinship. See Judson, *The Life of Edmund Spenser*, 1–7, as well as entries in the *Dictionary of National Biography* (hereafter DNB) on the Spencers of Althorp and on George Carey.
3 On Lady Carew's relative obscurity, see Long, "Spenser and Lady Cary." While she was not prominent among court ladies, she was married to George Carey (Carew), son of Lord Hunsdon, cousin to the Queen and addressee of another of the dedicatory sonnets. Lord Hunsdon was also Lord Chamberlain and in that capacity was responsible for the Maids-of-Honour. On Spenser's careful observance of heraldic precedence, see Stillman, "Politics, Precedence, and the Order of the Dedicatory Sonnets in *The Faerie Queene*." For recent treatments of "national" as a still-emerging category in early modern England, see Helgerson, *Forms*, who investigates the new sense of nationhood emerging in such varied disciplines as literature, law, and choreography; Hadfield, *Literature, Politics, and National Identity,* who observes that "the problem of national identity required urgent attention in the sixteenth

century" (9); McEachern, *The Poetics of Nationhood*, who argues that "English nationhood is a sixteenth-century phenomenon" and that "this nation is founded in and by the religious culture and ideology of Elizabethan England" (5); Baker, *Between Nations*, who sees "early modern Britain" as "a nexus ... of relations of alterity among 'England' and 'Scotland' and 'Wales' and 'Ireland'" (10).

4 Waller, *Edmund Spenser*, calls Spenser "the first and most prominent poet of British imperialism" (20); Fox, "The Decline of Literary Patronage in the 1590s," calls *The Faerie Queene* "a stupendous achievement – a client's flattery of the queen to excel all flatteries" (236).

5 On the feudalism of *The Faerie Queene*, see Helgerson, *Forms*, 48–59.

6 Among recent critics, Berry, *Of Chastity and Power*, and Bates, *The Rhetoric of Courtship*, have examined in minute detail the dynamics of Petrarchan courtiership with a view to emphasizing how courtiers turned the cult of courtly love to advantage. Both Bates and Berry recognize, however, that the practices and vocabulary of courtly, Petrarchan love masked anxiety about subordination to a female monarch. Frye, *Elizabeth I*, and Levin, *"The Heart and Stomach of a King,"* shift the emphasis to Elizabeth's own strategies of self-representation and to her control of courtly politics.

7 Bates, "Poetry, Patronage, and the Court," 97.

8 The role of patronage in fostering literary production has long been recognized in criticism of the early modern period. Sheavyn, *The Literary Profession in the Elizabethan Age* (1909; rpt. 1964), observed that patronage, though a "dying system" in the sixteenth century, was "hoped for, struggled after all the more feverishly" (11). Thomson, "The Literature of Patronage" (1952), concluded that, increasingly in the sixteenth century, poets "strove to cater to the tastes of individual patrons" (275); Edwin H. Miller, *The Professional Writer in Elizabethan England* (1959), examined the "economics of publication," concluding that literature "could not become a respected profession until it achieved freedom from patronage" and finding particularly objectionable what he considered the poet's self-abasement (136); Rosenberg, in her 1955 study of the Earl of Leicester's exercising of patronage, argued that patronage served in "the dissemination of what we today call propaganda" (xiii).

More recent critics do not limit the importance of patronage to propagandistic purposes; nor do they define patronage as exclusively economic or as always asymmetrical in its influences. For example, influential essays by Marotti ("John Donne and the Rewards of Patronage") and Tennenhouse ("Sir Walter Ralegh and the Literature of Clientage"), both published in *Patronage in the Renaissance* (1981), edited by Lytle and Orgel, encouraged a new generation of critics to read literature as encoding and enacting what Tennenhouse terms the "social dynamics and political realities" of patronage (235–6). Essays by Marotti, Burnett, Lewalski, Donnelly, and Lindenbaum in part 1 of *Patronage, Politics, and Literary Traditions in England* (1991), edited by Brown, examine patronage in the much wider contexts provided by print culture, apprentice culture, gender relation, religious life, and republicanism, for example. Essays by White, McKluskie, Heinemann, and Payne, in part 2 of that collection, focus in particular on the various roles and kinds of patronage in the drama of the period.

9 In early modern usage, "citizen" refers to someone, usually a man and member of a guild, who has been "made free" of the city and so is able to trade and is eligible to serve in civic office. I am using "citizen" loosely, and interchangeably with "corporate subject," to mean simply "member of a polity."

10 Questions about power and agency – about subject position – remain very much in the forefront of studies of early modern political and literary culture. My phrasing of the issue points in several critical directions: to broad-ranging questions about authority and resistance in various political structures and to narrower questions about relations between writer and state, as well as to more fundamental questions about early modern subjectivity. For recent analysis of manœuvrability within structures of authority, readers can consult *The Experience of Authority*, edited by Griffiths et al., a collection of essays which emphasizes that early modern authority was "contingent upon context" and "process," and that the "majority of the people ... possessed some degree of agency in constructing the terms of their inferiority" (4–5). Recent examinations of relations between writers and state include Patterson, *Censorship*; Clare, *Art Made*; Dutton, *Mastering*; Burt, *Licensed*; Kaplan, *Culture*; Tylus, *Writing*. The last two decades have produced notable studies of the early modern subject, a topic which lends itself to divergent, sometimes conflicting, lines of inquiry. These investigations take as starting points conceptual models ranging from Foucault's understanding of the subject as produced by power structures to Bakhtin's notions of the festive and freeing, from Lacanian tenets

to rhetorical theories, from social to devotional tracts; they adduce in evidence sources ranging from literary to medical to legal to religious documents, discourses, and practices; they differ in the degree to which historicizing underpins their aims; they differ in the degree to which they imagine the subject to possess agency; and they differ in their willingness to posit the existence of a "self," then or now. The following list (which is not exhaustive, since my study is not primarily a foray into the history of the subject) can direct readers to the range of current approaches and emphases: Ferry, *Inward*; Barker, *Tremulous*; Belsey, *Subject*; Maus, *Inwardness*; Kaufman, *Prayer*; Bloom, *Shakespeare*; Hanson, *Discovering*; Schoenfeldt, *Bodies*.

My study both investigates Spenser's construction, particularly in the *Calender*, of inwardness and privacy (which I treat largely as a rhetorical effect, and function of the dialogue between text and paratext – but an effect with extratextual ramifications) and, more extensively, explores Spenser's deployment of socio-political and creative autonomy.

11 Bisham, located up the Thames just past Marlow, was the home of Lady Elizabeth Russell, daughter of Sir Anthony Cooke, widow of Thomas Hoby and of John Russell, second son of Francis second Earl of Bedford. In his "Ruines of Time," Spenser includes the Russell family among those he celebrates and eulogizes. Rycote, in Oxfordshire, was the home of Lord Norris, whose sons John and Thomas served as captains and administrators in Munster when Spenser was the Clerk of the Council of Munster. For the texts of the entertainments, see John Nichols, *The Progresses and Public Processions of Queen Elizabeth*. Parenthetical citations are to this book.
12 Richard Wilson, "'Like the old Robin Hood,'" reads the Bisham and Rycote entertainments as primarily designed to reassure Elizabeth of continued aristocratic loyalty in the face of possible insurgence from "woodland commoners and squatters" (2).
13 Jean Wilson, *Entertainments for Elizabeth I*, 149n106.
14 Wilson, *Entertainments*, 47; 149n108.
15 For details of Ralegh's marriage and its fallout, readers can consult Lacey, *Sir Walter Ralegh*; Winton, *Sir Walter Ralegh*; and Rowse, *Ralegh and the Throckmortons*. Lady Russell may have had an inside track on the matter and so been able to direct the author of the entertainment, John Lyly, to develop the theme of chastity. She was

an aunt to Robert Cecil, who was likely among the first to get wind of Ralegh's secret and to whom Ralegh, in an apparently bald-faced lie, flatly denied rumours of his marriage.
16 Leslie, "'Something Nasty,'" discusses Elizabeth's occasional avoidance and recriminatory tactics at entertainments.
17 Rowse, *The English Past*, 39. For an abbreviated version of Lady Russell's account of the wrangling over Donnington Castle, see *Calendar of State Papers, Domestic. 1591–94*, 379. On Lady Russell, readers can consult, in addition to Rowse and the pertinent entries on the Russells, Hobys, and Cookes in DNB, Violet Wilson, *Society Women*; du Maurier, *Golden Lads*; and Strong, *The Cult of Elizabeth*.
18 In his *View of the Present State of Ireland*, Spenser's Irenius castigates those English in Ireland who speak Irish, remarking that "the speech being Irish, the heart must needs be Irish" (68).
19 On the services and offices of the Norris sons, see DNB and Wallace MacCaffrey, *Elizabeth I*, 152–83 passim.
20 On post-Armada anxieties, see, for example, Rowse, *The Expansion of Elizabethan England*, chap. 8; Wallace MacCaffrey, *Elizabeth I*, part 2.
21 The comment is cited in the DNB entry for Henry Norris, 568.
22 For a review of this social model, see Scott Wilson, *Cultural Materialism*, 12, 62–3, 150.
23 For examinations of aristocratic autonomy, see McCoy, *The Rites*, passim; and Breight, "Realpolitik," 34–7. Leslie, "'Something Nasty,'" discussing Kenilworth, Wanstead, and Elvetham, emphasizes the extent to which "landscape drama," in contrast to masques and civic entertainments, destabilizes the monarch's control: "using the fluidity of the landscape setting, these entertainments could indeed enter into a debate with the monarch about where the centre lay and who should occupy that position" (62).
24 Cole, *The Portable Queen*, 4.
25 Mulcaster, *Positions*, 37. Subsequent references to this text are indicated by parenthetical page numbers.
26 In discussing punishment of students, for example, Mulcaster remarks that the "*rod* may no more be spared in schools than the *sword* may in the prince's hand" (253). Elsewhere, he compares the lot of the "poor teacher" to that of the sun, the divine, and the prince, observing that the "poor teacher must be subject to as much as ... the prince is, who neither for reward nor penalty can have general obedience" (261).

27 For information on Mulcaster, I am especially indebted to conversations with Natalie Johnson and to her research and unpublished work, "Merchant Taylors' School."
28 On schooling in Tudor England, readers can consult Cressy, *Education*; O'Day, *Education*; Simon, *Education*. The differences in purposes, curricula, and student bodies between petty and grammar schools are not sufficient to account for the different socio-political charge I describe.
29 Clement, *Petie*, 59; 53; 72. Subsequent references to this work are indicated parenthetically.
30 Manwood, *A Treatise of the Lawes of the Forest*, Preface. Subsequent references to this work are indicated parenthetically. On forest law, readers can consult Cox, *The Royal Forests of England*; Hart, *The Royal Forest*; Pettit, *The Royal Forests of Northamptonshire*; Young, *The Royal Forests of Medieval England*.
31 The recorded verses about William the Conqueror's forest law include the following lines: "He made great protection for the game / And imposed laws for the same, / That who so slew hart or hind / Should be made blind / ... Powerful men complained of it and poor men lamented it, / But so fierce was he that he cared not for the rancour of them all, / But they had to follow out the king's will entirely / If they wished to live or hold their land" (*Anglo-Saxon Chronicle*, 165).
32 Helgerson, *Forms*, 67.
33 Helgerson, *Forms*, 69–70.
34 Pettit, *Royal Forests*, 65.
35 On legendary outlaws, readers can consult Keen, *The Outlaws of Medieval Legend*; Harrison, *Forests*; Marienstras (trans. Janet Lloyd), *New Perspectives on the Shakespearean World*. For an account that balances the pervasiveness and endurance of legendary outlawry against the harsh realities of outlawry, see Wood's chapter on Robin Hood in *In Search of England*. Among other works and authors, Wood cites *The Gest of Robin Hood*, May-day revels, and Shakespeare in evidence of the popularity of the Robin Hood legend (71–2).
36 Harrison, *Forests*; Montrose, "The Place of a Brother"; Richard Wilson, "Like the old Robin Hood."
37 On the critical deployment of feudal values, see McCoy, *Rites*; Breight, "Realpolitik"; Berry, *Of Chastity and Power*.
38 Holahan, "Wyatt, the Heart's Forest," 66; 65.

39 Heale, *Wyatt, Surrey*, 96.
40 There is a widespread assumption, derived from near-contemporary sources and from Wyatt's poetry, that Wyatt had a relationship with Anne Boleyn before she became the King's mistress and then wife. See, for example, Ives, *Anne Boleyn*; Carolly Erickson, *Mistress Anne*. However, Antonia Fraser, *The Wives of Henry VIII*, calls the "premarital relationship" a "nebulous affair" and concludes that it was a "flirtation along the accepted lines of courtly love" (127); and Warnicke, *The Rise and Fall of Anne Boleyn*, discredits the "assertion that Anne had a love affair with Thomas Wyatt," noting that any "attempt to establish a close relationship between Wyatt and Anne must rely on a speculative reading of the evidence" (64; 67). My reading of "The long love" does not require the assumption that Wyatt and Anne had an affair; the poem's rhetorical assertions retain their force and point without such grounding.
41 Crewe, *Trials of Authorship*, 27.
42 Greene, *The Light in Troy*, 252.
43 Crewe, *Trials*, 37–45.
44 Holahan "Wyatt, the Heart's Forest," 50.
45 This issue is addressed, from different perspectives, by such critics as Helgerson, *The Elizabethan Prodigals*; Brennan, *Literary Patronage*; Wall, *The Imprint of Gender*; Pask, *The Emergence of the English Author*.
46 On Ponsonby, see McKerrow, ed., *A Dictionary of Printers and Booksellers*, 217–18.
47 Citations are to *The Yale Edition of the Shorter Poems of Edmund Spenser*, ed. Oram et al., and are indicated parenthetically in the text.
48 Corbett and Lightbrown, *The Comely Frontispiece*, have demonstrated that frontispieces were frequently chosen for their emblematic qualities. It seems highly likely, therefore, that the title-page to *Complaints* was selected to foreground a particular intersection of authorial and cultural agency. This seems all the more likely in view of the title-page that Ponsonby used in publishing Sidney's *Arcadia* in 1593; its design is closely connected to the characters and motifs of that work, which suggests that Ponsonby was someone alert to the emblematic value of title-pages. While it is true, of course, that devices and borders were reused and assigned to a variety of works, it seems also true that Moses and David, who appear in the *Complaints* title-page, figure often in frontispieces of

devotional works (see McKerrow and Ferguson, *Title-Page Borders*); in his preface to the reader, Ponsonby stresses that the poems in the volume bear an unworldly tenor.

49 For the probable dates of Spenser's sojourns in England, see Maley, *A Spenser Chronology*.
50 Marotti, *Manuscript, Print*, passim.
51 On Ponsonby's acquiring the Sidney line, see Loewenstein, "Spenser's Retrography."
52 Marotti, *Manuscript, Print*, 25, 49.
53 On the Spencer sisters and their husbands, see Judson, *The Life of Edmund Spencer*, and DNB.
54 Schleiner, *Tudor and Stuart Women Writers*, passim.
55 Marx's comment occurs in his *Ethnographical Notebooks*, 305, and concerns Spenser's Irish tenure. The comment is quoted recently by Hadfield, "Introduction," 13.
56 Helgerson, *Forms*, 54.
57 On Verlame's ungodliness, see especially Rasmussen, "'How Weak Be the Passions of Woefulness.'"
58 On the "remembrance" as a literary form, see Gutierrez, "The Remembrance."
59 See Derek Wilson, *Sweet Robin*, chap. 16.
60 Quoted by Hager, "The Exemplary Mirage," 7.
61 Lacey, *Robert, Earl of Essex*, 89.
62 Brink, "Spenser's Political Patronage," 24–5.

CHAPTER TWO

1 See Waldman, "Spenser's Pseudonym 'E.K.'" It makes little difference to my argument whether E.K. is Spenser or not; E.K. assumes a role and position against which Spenser defines his vocation.
2 Patterson, "Re-opening the Green Cabinet," and Tylus, " Spenser, Virgil, and the Politics of Poetic Labor," have looked provocatively at patronage in the *Calender*, but without gauging immediately felt pressures of patronage at the interpretive level of language and image, on the one hand, or looking in detail at specific patronly relations, on the other hand.
3 For arguments regarding Spenser's creation of vocational identity, see especially Helgerson, *Self-Crowned Laureates*; Montrose, "'The perfecte paterne of a Poete'"; David Miller, "Authorship, Anonymity."

Helgerson argues that the "New Poet seems less securely set on his way than E.K. would have us think" (75), largely because as yet there exists no clearly defined role of poet laureate. Helgerson sees Colin's history as Spenser's "forceful critique of the conventional poet-as-lover, revealing that poetry written under such a guise is solipsistic, self-indulgent, and fruitless" (72). Unlike Helgerson, Montrose believes that Spenser has his poetic goals firmly in focus and intends to follow successfully the Virgilian progression. But, Montrose argues, intimations of failure remain very much a part of the *Calender* and designedly so, for Spenser "readies for his greater flight by apprising himself of its hazards" (37). Colin's career "projects a poetic vocation of the kind upon which Spenser himself is ambitiously embarking – but one which runs its course toward that failure which the aspiring minds of Elizabethan society are forever being warned to expect" (37). Miller concludes that Colin's career "describes a negative *Bildungsroman* from which Spenser dissociates himself emphatically" (233). My own argument differs from these three in defining Colin's relationship to Spenser more positively. Craig, in "The Queen, Her Handmaid," finds a "clear distinction, amounting to alienation, between the persona [Colin] and the narrator, whose perspective unequivocally assumes and expresses the official values of authority and power" (256). My reading of Spenser's interaction with E.K. suggests that Spenser in fact interrogates "official values." In a book-length study of the *Calender*, Lynn Staley Johnson finds that Spenser "employs Colin to dramatize the effects of allowing personal appetites and desires to master the self, particularly the poetic self ... As Spenser most powerfully suggests through Colin, the most deadly trap is the self" (8). My argument leads to virtually the opposite conclusion.

Hamilton, "The Argument of Spenser's *Shepheardes Calender*," sees in Colin a rejection of the pastoral life for the active life of heroic poetry. Cullen, *Spenser, Marvell, and Renaissance Pastoral*, 76–98, argues that Colin fails through frailty to realize his vocation as a great poet in the pastoral world. Influential treatments of Colin, which focus on the ways the *Calender* enacts conflicts between body and spirit, eternity and temporality, include Durr, "Spenser's Calendar of Christian Time"; Heninger, "The Implications of Form for *The Shepheardes Calender*"; and Isabel MacCaffrey, "Allegory and Pastoral in *The Shepheardes Calender*."

4 Letter from Spenser to Harvey, *Spenser: Poetical Works*, ed. Smith and de Selincourt, 635. Subsequent citations to the letter are to this text.
5 Duncan-Jones, *Sir Philip Sidney*, 140.
6 Spenser, "To His Booke," *The Shepheardes Calender*, in *The Yale Edition of the Shorter Poems. Calender* citations are to this text, and are indicated parenthetically by line numbers (for the poetry) and by page number (for the paratextual matter).
7 On the Protestantism of the *Calender* see Hume, *Edmund Spenser*, especially chaps. 1, 2, and 3; and Norbrook, *Poetry and Politics*, chap. 3.
8 As commentators frequently remark, Spenser's large claims in the envoy play off against the expression of humility in the dedicatory poem to Sidney. Bernard finds in this dialectic evidence of the ambivalence in Spenser's "claim to public recognition" (*Ceremonies*, 76). He sees this ambivalence as arising from the "implicit contest of authorities going on in the *Calender* between the desired patron, behind which figure stands the entire power structure in Spenser's society, and the Vergilian precursor, i.e. between political context and intertextuality" (49). "Spenser," concludes Bernard, "combines plenitude and emptiness: he is filled with the legacy of his pastoral forebears and yet avers a need for material sustenance" (50). Although it usefully highlights the importance of patronage in shaping Spenser's debut, Bernard's equation omits Spenser's own calculated withdrawal from any exchange which would figure his work as currency. Spenser's poetic "plenitude" does not depend solely upon his "filiation to the line" of Virgilian poets (*Ceremonies*, 49); as my reading of the envoys suggests, his plenitude – his fecundity and his moral autonomy – results, in the first instance, from his redefining of patronly relations, from, specifically, his abandonment of whatever civic identity he had established in the service of Rochester and Leicester.
9 "Unknowe" occurs in Chaucer's *Troilus and Criseyde*, 1.809.
10 The book to which E.K. refers is Thomas Smith's *De Republica Anglorum*. Bradbrook, "No Room at the Top," notes that Smith was a "famous Greek scholar, friend of Cheke and Ascham, Regius Professor of Civil Law," that "he rose to be Secretary of State, Privy Councillor and Ambassador to France," and that he remains the "most notable Elizabethan example of pure scholar turned successful politician" (95). Stern, *Gabriel Harvey*, observes that Harvey's

letters to Smith refer to Smith's "orienting Harvey toward a life of service to the state" (13).

11 Goldberg, "Colin to Hobbinol," observes that "[w]hat the eclogues structure as denial and refusal, the surrounding context figures as the acceptance of a special friendship" (117). He argues that Colin's refusal of [Hobbinol's] advances ... signals his frustrated attempts to pass beyond pastoral" (117). My own argument focuses the matter quite differently, to suggest that Colin's rejection of Hobbinol implies his reluctance to enter fully into public vocation, whether as pastoral or as epic poet.

12 Bernard finds that "we are invited to view Colin's difficulties in terms of a wholly private grief barring him from an advancement that otherwise awaits his bidding," citing "June," in particular, where "Colin's assertion of the metarecreative motif of self-delight in the face of Hobbinoll's exhortation to pursue his Muse underscores the private/public antinomy in the poem and connects the idiosyncratic choice of the private sphere with the aberrant Colin's wasteful love" (*Ceremonies*, 74). Bernard, concerned to show how Spenser uses pastoral to assert balance, views Hobbinol as a corrective to Colin. My argument regarding their relationship reverses this view.

13 Rix, in *Rhetoric in Spenser's Poetry*, says of "Januarye" that "in no other of Spenser's poems of equal length – save the 'Doleful Lay of Clorinda' – is the underlying structure so predominantly rhetorical as in the first eclogue of the *Shepheardes Calender*" (65). Evidence from outside the *Calender* supports such a reading of "gifts." Letters which passed between the two men at about the time of the *Calender* refer repeatedly to their exchanging of poems, their criticizing of one another's work, and their strategies for securing preferment by means of literary skill. Within the fiction of the eclogue, the listing of "early fruit" (58) as one of the gifts Hobbinol offers works against our taking these gifts literally, as tokens of "the conditions of rural life." This phrase is from Shore, *Spenser and the Poetics of Pastoral*, who uses it in the course of arguing that pastoral love complaint insists "on objective setting and the consequent evocation of an image of pastoral contentment" (71). The fruit would have to be early indeed to be available for giving in January. A metaphoric meaning seems more likely and the metaphor that seems most likely is that of literary work as fruit.

14 Berger, in "The Mirror Stage of Colin Clout," finds this rhetorical play especially incriminating in his case to convict Colin, generally, of narcissism and, particularly, of a confusion of poetic and erotic motives. "Perhaps," says Berger, "to speculate idly, this confusion of literary and erotic motives informed the poetry addressed to Rosalind and affected her adverse reaction; perhaps she questioned the poet-lover's sincerity as well as his taste" (341). Berger's criticism obscures the dynamics of this particular rhetorical turn. The point is not so much that Colin confuses poetic and erotic motives as that, unlike E.K., he aligns poetic-rhetorical motives with his private affairs, with the matter of love.

15 Berger, "The Mirror Stage of Colin Clout," 342, makes a similar observation, but does not distinguish E.K's reading from Colin's use of the pun.

16 See Ferry, *The Art of Naming*, on the "relative syntactical looseness of English" in the sixteenth century (64).

17 In his introduction to "Januarye," Cain makes a similar point (28); Chaudhuri, *Renaissance Pastoral*, remarks that the "controlling image of the seasonal cycle contradicts Colin's gloom" (145).

18 Sedgwick, *Between Men*, 39.

19 In the sixth book of *The Faerie Queene*, published fifteen years or so later, Spenser presents Colin's dance of the graces in terms and images which recall expressly the April lay. In that later dance, the "jolly Shepheards lasse" is placed "in the midst" (*Faerie Queen*, 6.10.16.1; 15.7). There, private desire and public obligation are distinctly at odds. Donald Cheney, "Spenser's Fortieth Birthday," draws as two extremes "the explicit celebration of the queen as the fourth grace in the *Calender*, Aprill, and the equally explicit celebration of Colin's mistress as the fourth grace in *The Faerie Queene* VI.x" (8), suggesting that he finds no reference to private matters in the April lay.

Bernard, *Ceremonies*, also reads "my lady" as a reference to Rosalind (72). Several features of the lay support this reading. In the two stanzas immediately preceding this one, Colin refers to Elisa as his "Goddesse." Since the poem's progress has been one of rising to this identification, it seems unlikely that the poet would now descend to call Elisa "my Lady." Moreover, the stanza which follows this one makes a clear distinction between the "bevie of Ladies bright," the "Ladyes of the lake," and Elisa, the "Princesse," suggesting again the unlikelihood that "my Lady" refers to Elisa.

We should observe as well that, throughout the paean, Elisa remains the cynosure, the focus of celebration and adornment, but passive: she sits, she shows herself, she shines. Only at the end of the poem does Colin assign to her an action, saying "Now ryse up *Elisa*." Her joining the other graces "to make the daunce even" would be out of keeping with this characterization.

20 Colin's term "homely" is aptly expressive in its implication that poetry should concern itself with matters close to home, with love and with shepherding.

21 See Helgerson, *The Elizabethan Prodigals* and *Self-Crowned Laureates*, on the cultural paradigm of the prodigal poet returned to civic uses.

22 The phrase "kingdome of oure owne language" (*Poetical Works*, ed. Smith and de Selincourt, 611) is Spenser's in a letter to Harvey dated April 1580. Helgerson, *Forms*, begins his analysis of nation-writing with a meditation on this phrase.

23 E.K.'s phrasing, "be they witnesse which are *privie* to his *study*" (my emphasis), bears testimony to his apparent inability or refusal to let the private remain private: those who are "privie" to the inner space – mental and physical – of Spenser's "study" publicize what they find there. E.K.'s phrasing thus relates revealingly to his earlier "December" gloss of "cabinet" as a "diminutive" and to Patterson's illuminating discussion, in "Re-opening the Green Cabinet," of the polysemous "cabinet." Patterson cites the several available meanings of "cabinet" "to show how exclusive was E.K.'s gloss" of "cabinet" as a diminutive in the course of demonstrating "a plausible collocation of meanings in which pastoral already had a special interest," meanings pertaining to "the human mental cabinet," as well as meanings suggesting "artfulness, privacy or secrecy" (46–7). What E.K.'s gloss excludes is precisely the privacy which Colin assumes, a point not made by Patterson. On private rooms in early modern homes, see Summerson, *Architecture in Britain*; Lawrence and Jeanne Fawtier Stone, *An Open Elite?*; Girouard, *Life in the English Country House*; Friedman, *House and Household*.

24 Tylus, "Spenser, Virgil, and the Politics of Poetic Labor," articulates the linkage between husbandry metaphors and poetry which is publicly oriented by focusing on the ways in which the georgic "naturalizes – and thereby institutionalizes – not only the process of poetic creation, but the process of an empire's creation" (55).

25 For Spenser's debt to Marot, see, besides Patterson's important article "Re-opening the Green Cabinet," Shore, *Spenser and the*

Poetics of Pastoral, who argues that Spenser "drastically altered the direction and emphasis of Marot's poem," saying that Spenser "makes no request for material assistance comparable to that made by Marot's 'petit Robinet'" (91).

CHAPTER THREE

1. Hadfield, "Introduction," *Literature, Politics, and National Identity*.
2. Wayne Erickson, "Spenser and His Friends," treats the commendatory poems at some length, reading them as part of the "ironic play ... at work in the 1590 *Faerie Queene*'s ancillary texts" (16) – play which he views as scripted by Spenser and friends in a bid for patronage. My argument finds a wider range of assumptions and more far-reaching political import in the verses. See Genette, "Introduction to the Paratext," on paratextual matter (which includes such things as commendatory and dedicatory poems) as a "zone ... of *transaction*" (261).
3. On anti-poetic, and anti-poet, sentiment, see Russell Fraser, *The War against Poetry*; Helgerson, *The Elizabethan Prodigals*; Spingarn, *A History of Literary Criticism in the Renaissance*; Nelson, *Fact or Fiction*; Herman, *Squitter-Wits and Muse-Haters*. Citations to the commendatory verses, the dedicatory sonnets, and *The Faerie Queene* are to *The Faerie Queene*, ed. A.C. Hamilton, and are indicated parenthetically by line numbers.
4. Saunders, "The Stigma of Print," remains the classic statement about the stigmatizing effects of print.
5. Spenser, *Colin Clouts Come Home Again*, lines 330–1. Citations to this poem are to the *Yale Shorter Poems*, and are indicated parenthetically by line number.
6. David Miller, *Poem's Two Bodies*, 57, 61–2; Carol Stillman, "Politics, Precedence."
7. Peck, *Northampton*, passim.
8. Wright, "A Change in Direction," 159, 161.
9. Wright, "A Change in Direction," 160, notes an instance when even Elizabeth's long-time favourite, Robert Dudley, Earl of Leicester, was denied admittance.
10. Montrose, "'The perfect paterne of a Poete,'" 34.
11. Bednarz, "The Collaborator as Thief," assumes that Spenser is humble in the face of hierarchy. See Wayne Erickson, "Spenser and His Friends," for a critique of Bednarz's position.

12 On the Harvey-Nashe quarrel, see McKerrow, ed., *The Works of Thomas Nashe*, 5:65–109.
13 The Queen's stay at Audley End turned out inauspiciously for Harvey. He took part in a debate not attended by the Queen, who – the day being hot and she being tired – retired to her rooms after the welcoming address. Burghley, who chaired the debate, limited repetitions and lengths of speeches. Harvey presented Burghley with Latin verses in his own hand, dedicated to the Queen, Burghley, Leicester, and Hatton, among others; Harvey subsequently published the verses and dedications. See Nichols, *Progresses*, 3:109–14; Dovey, *An Elizabethan Progress*, 31–6; Stern, *Gabriel Harvey*, 39–45.
14 Spenser, *Works*, ed. Greenlaw et al., 3.307, 306.
15 Waller, *Edmund Spenser*, 20.
16 For a study of Elizabethan courtier verse as flattering and self-promotional, see May, *The Elizabethan Courtier Poets*.
17 Frye, *Elizabeth I*, chap. 1.
18 On the import/export market of early modern London, see, in addition to Frye, Rappaport, *Worlds within Worlds*, Beier and Finlay, eds., *London*, part 2; Porter, *London*, chap. 3
19 The city does figure prominently in critical discussion of Elizabethan and Jacobean city comedy. See, for example, Paster, *The Idea of the City*; Leggatt, *Jacobean Public Theatre*. Manley's *Literature and Culture* provides a thoroughgoing analysis of the ways in which the city figures in several literary kinds, including Spenser's epic poem.
20 Recent critical study of civic pageantry includes Bergeron, *English Civic Pageantry* and Bergeron, ed., *Pageantry*; Lobanov-Rostovsky, "The Triumphes of Gold."
21 For Dekker's text, see *The Dramatic Works of Thomas Dekker*, ed. Bowers.
22 Manley, *Literature and Culture*, 209, notes R.S.'s celebration of the city.
23 In this regard, R.S. anticipates (or recognizes) a feature of Spenser's epideictic practice. Typically, Spenser resists the singularity of, say, Ralegh's vision of Cynthia/Elizabeth, preferring to multiply exemplary figures.
24 See Helgerson, "The Land Speaks," in *Forms*, on "a cartographically and chorographically shaped consciousness of national power" (108).
25 On the dynamics of gift-giving, see Mauss, *The Gift*; and see Fumerton's application of gift-rings to Tudor English and Irish customs of fosterage, in "Exchanging Gifts."

26 See Nichols, *Progresses*; Jean Wilson, *Entertainments*.
27 Frye, *Elizabeth I*, 41–2, 47.
28 See Radcliffe, *Edmund Spenser*; Heffner, *Spenser Allusions*.
29 Radcliffe, *Edmund Spenser*, 9; Webbe, *Discourse*, 35, 56; Puttenham, *Arte*, 63; Fraunce, *Arcadian Rhetoricke*, passim.
30 Radcliffe, *Edmund Spenser*, 10.
31 On Spenser's Irish acquisitions and offices, see Henley, *Spenser in Ireland*; Rambuss, *Spenser's Secret Career*; Maley, *A Spenser Chronology*.
32 On "English" and "British," see Hadfield, "From English to British Literature."
33 Highley, "The Royal Image," 63.
34 Carroll, "Representations of Women."
35 On Lord Deputies Arthur Grey and John Perrot, both of whom were recalled from Ireland, see Berleth, *The Twilight Lords*, 190–9; 237–40. For a recent dissenting view regarding Grey's "disgrace," see Canino, "Reconstructing Lord Grey's Reputation."
36 For a recent examination of anti-Elizabeth sentiment and propaganda, see Walker, ed., *Dissing Elizabeth*; see also Levin, "The Heart and Stomach of a King," chaps. 4–5.
37 On English representations of the Irish as barbarous, see Leerssen, *Mere Irish*.
38 See Highley, "The Royal Image."
39 See Highley, "The Royal Image," 67–71, and *Shakespeare, Spenser*, 110–11; Levin, "Heart and Stomach," 115.
40 *Calendar of State Papers, Ireland, 1588–92*, 142–3.
41 See Highley, *Shakespeare, Spenser*, who concludes that "Ireland offered the New English émigrés an arena conducive to unfettered exhibition of male prowess ... Certainly the arts most practiced in Ireland are the 'masculine' ones of warfare and domination" (111–12). See his chap. 5, passim.

CHAPTER FOUR

1 See, for example, Cain, *Praise*; Wells, *Spenser's "Faerie Queen."*
2 Francis R. Johnson, *A Critical Bibliography*, 11, notes John Wolfe's device on the title-page.
3 Loewenstein, "Spenser's Retrography."
4 Plant, *The English Book Trade*, 89–90, discusses the speed of work in the typical Elizabethan print shop. My estimate of twelve weeks

may be generous. In the years 1589–91, Wolfe was far and away the busiest printer in London. In a three-month period around the time *The Faerie Queene* was entered for publication, *The Stationers' Register* lists fifty-two titles entered to twenty-seven different printers; of those fifty-two titles, thirteen were entered to Wolfe's name. Plant, notes that at a time when few printers exceeded six works per year, Wolfe issued twenty works in 1589, eighteen works in 1590, and seventeen works in 1591 (89).

5 On Wolfe's career, especially his role in the printers' revolt, see Huffman, *Elizabethan Impressions*, 1–3, 12–13; Plant, *English Book Trade*, 105–9; Bennett, *English Books and Readers*, 68–73; Greg, *Companion to Arber*, 22–3, 24, 26, 27–8, 118–19; Judge, *Elizabethan Book-Pirates*, chap. 3; McKerrow, *Dictionary of Printers and Booksellers*, 296–8; Loewenstein, "For a History of Literary Property." Readers can follow the dispute in Arber, *A Transcript*, 2:773, 777–82.
6 Quoted in Huffman, *Elizabethan Impressions*, 12.
7 Huffman, *Elizabethan Impressions*, 13.
8 On Wolfe's part in the Marprelate controversy, see Huffman, *Elizabethan Impressions*, chap. 2.
9 On the salary increase, see Greg and Boswell, eds., *Records of the Court*, 38, cited by Judge, *Elizabethan Book-Pirates*, 41.
10 Wolfe also engaged in surreptitious printing under the auspices of Lord Burghley,
11 The complaints by the Stationers about Wolfe included his gathering "disorderly" people to the cause and his inciting "common talke in Alehouses, taverns, and such like places, whereupon insued dangerous and undutifull speaches of her Majesties most gracious government" (Arber, *A Transcript*, 2:781–2).
12 Huffman, *Elizabethan Impressions*, 21.
13 See Francis R. Johnson, *A Critical Bibliography*, 15–16, on the various states of the dedicatory sonnets.
14 Nashe, *Pierce Penilesse*, 135, 136.
15 On title-pages posted by publishers, see Plant, *The English Book Trade*, 248.
16 Wallace MacCaffrey, *Elizabeth I*, observes that the plethora of dedicatees shows Spenser's recognition of the "metamorphosis from pastoral and dynastic monarchy to monarchal state" (77).
17 Citations to the commendatory verses, the dedicatory sonnets, and *The Faerie Queene* are to *The Faerie Queene*, ed. A.C. Hamilton, and are indicated parenthetically by line numbers.

18 On the rebellion of the northern earls, see Wallace MacCaffrey, *The Shaping of the Elizabethan Regime*, chap. 13.
19 See Greg, *Licensers for the Press*, on Walsingham, Howard, Burghley, Essex, and Hunsdon.
20 For the Star Chamber decree arising from the printers' revolt, see Arber, *A Transcript*, 2:807–12.
21 See Arber, *A Transcript*, for the months following the November 1569 uprising.
22 See Rasmussen, "How Weak Be the Passions of Woefulness."
23 Brooks, *Sir Christopher Hatton*, concludes that "there is good evidence that Hatton had been brought up a Catholic and ... had Catholic sympathies" (17–18).
24 Hadfield, *Edmund Spenser's Irish Experience*, reads the sonnets to Ormond and Grey as providing evidence of "the fracturing of Englishness in Ireland" (6), but finds that Spenser uncritically praises both men. Highley, *Shakespeare, Spenser, and the Crisis in Ireland*, reads "To Ormond" as Spenser's "most overt bid for the protection and patronage of Ormond" (25).
25 Highley, *Shakespeare*, 24.
26 Spenser, *A View of the Present State of Ireland*, 68.
27 On accusations of remissness against Ormond, see Bagwell, *Ireland under the Tudors*, vols. 2 and 3, passim; Falls, "Black Tom of Ormonde"; Moody et al., eds., *A New History of Ireland*, 108; Berleth, *The Twilight Lords*, 178, 179–80, 182.
28 Oram, "What Did Spenser Really Think of Sir Walter Ralegh," examines Spenser's independence and criticism of his great patron's poetics. My thanks to the author for giving me a copy of his paper.

CHAPTER FIVE

1 On the historical allegory of Timias-Ralegh and Belphoebe-Elizabeth, see Gilbert, "Belphoebe's Misdeeming of Timias"; English, "Spenser's Accommodation of Allegory to History"; O'Connell, *Mirror and Veil*; Bednarz, "Ralegh in Spenser's Historical Allegory"; Oram, "Elizabethan Fact and Spenserian Fiction" and "Spenser's Raleghs"; David Miller, *The Poem's Two Bodies*, 225–34.
2 On Spenser's setting forth problems of representation in the proem to book 3, see Anderson, "In living colours"; DeNeef, *Spenser and the Motives of Metaphor*, 111–17; David Miller, *The Poem's Two Bodies*, 149–53; Wofford, "Gendering Allegory."

Citations to Spenser's *Faerie Queene* are to the edition by A.C. Hamilton.

3 On the aging Elizabeth's strategies of self-representation, see Frye, *Elizabeth I*, 98–104; Hibbert, *The Virgin Queen*, 101–2. Portraiture of Elizabeth was a matter of concern throughout her reign: a proclamation of 1563 prohibits portraits of the Queen and declares that "some cunning person" will be appointed to make a portrait from which a pattern can be derived for use by other artists; editors Hughes and Larkin, citing *Acts of the Privy Council*, note that "as late as 1596, the Privy Council found it necessary to order all officers to seek out and deface 'unseemly portraits of the Queen'" (*Tudor Royal Proclamations* 240–1).
4 See Cavanagh, "The fatal destiny," 122–5; Carroll, "Representations of Women."
5 On the reformist designs of Spenser's *Epithalamion*, see my "The Poetics of Accommodation in Spenser's *Epithalamion*."
6 On the rise of recusancy, see Ford, *The Protestant Reformation in Ireland*, 26; Edwards, *Church and State*, chaps. 19 and 21; Rowse, *The Expansion of Elizabethan England*, 24–5.
7 Beer, *Sir Walter Ralegh*, passim.
8 For a recent examination of the "problematics of Petrarchism," see Dubrow, *Echoes of Desire*, chap. 2.
9 On the discovery and increasing use in the sixteenth and early seventeenth centuries of clear, "crystal" glass mirrors, see Shuger, "The 'I' of the Beholder," 21.
10 On the Desmond rebellion, see the *Calender of State Papers, Ireland* for the relevant years (c.1578–83); Bagwell, *Ireland under the Tudors*, vol. 3; Rowse, *The Expansion of Elizabethan England*; Berleth, *The Twilight Lords*; Wallace MacCaffrey, *Elizabeth I*.
11 Ross, *The Custom of the Castle*; Hooker, *Chronicles*, 441–2.
12 For these features, see *Faerie Queene* 3.5.39–41. On early modern Irish demesnes, see Reeves-Smyth, "The Natural History of Demesnes" and my "Professing Ireland in the Woods of *Mutabilitie*."
13 Hooker, *Chronicles*, 441.
14 Virgil, *Aeneid*, 12.418–50.
15 Hamilton, *Sir Philip Sidney*, repeats the story that Sidney discarded his thigh-armour when he saw a fellow knight not wearing his (5); Duncan-Jones, *Sir Philip Sidney*, writes that Sidney "in too much of a hurry, left off his thigh-armour" (294).
16 Ross, *Custom*, xiv.

17 See my "Poetics of Accommodation" and "Professing Ireland."
18 Keen, *Chivalry*, notes that according to Lull the knight must especially eschew treason (10).
19 On the administration of Thomas Norris, see Maccarthy-Morrogh, *The Munster Plantation*.
20 See Paster, *The Body Embarrassed*, 92 and chap. 2.
21 See Paster, *The Body Embarrassed*, who notes the accepted link between blood volume and youthfulness and strength (70).
22 Berleth, *The Twilight Lords*, notes that "Raleigh's troops [and presumably Ralegh himself] ... came out of the abbatoir [the fort] dazed and blood-spattered ... The whole of the next day they spent ... scrubbing their gear" (174).
23 Kaplan, *The Culture of Slander*, passim.
24 For a different, but related, reading of Petrarchan entrapments in Spenser, see Dasenbrock, *Imitating the Italians*, chap. 3.
25 Gregerson, *The Reformation of the Subject*, passim.
26 Hooker, *Chronicles*, 440, 441, 442–3.

CHAPTER SIX

1 Treatments of this usually neglected episode include those by Roche, *The Kindly Flame*, who privileges the moral, rather than historical, allegory; O'Connell, *Mirror*, who addresses the topical allegory; Goldberg, *Endlesse*, who emphasizes the episode's vocational allegory; Oram, "Spenser's Raleghs," who emphasizes Spenser's championing of Ralegh's choosing marriage over courtiership; and Patrick Cheney, *Spenser's Famous Flight*, whose argument I will address in more detail in this chapter.
2 Printed in *The Poems of Sir Walter Ralegh*, ed. Latham, 11–12.
3 For a reading of Ralegh's poem that stresses similar features in the context of pursuing the argument that the poem records the collapse of a symbolic vocabulary, see Robert Stillman, "'Words cannot knytt.'"
4 Cheney, *Spenser's Famous Flight*, 112.
5 Cheney, *Spenser's Famous Flight*, 114.
6 Cheney, *Spenser's Famous Flight*, 133, 145.

Works Cited

Anderson, Judith. "'In living colours and right hew': The Queen of Spenser's Central Books." *Poetic Traditions of the Renaissance*. Ed. Maynard Mack and George DeForest Lord. New Haven: Yale Univ. Press, 1982. 47–66.

Anglo-Saxon Chronicle. Revised translation. Ed. Dorothy Whitelock, David Douglas, and Susie Tucker. London: Eyre and Spottiswoode, 1961.

Arber, E. *A Transcript of the Register of the Company of Stationers of London, 1554–1640*. 5 vols. London, 1875–94.

Bagwell, Richard. *Ireland under the Tudors, with a Succinct Account of the Earlier History*. 3 vols. London: Holland Press, 1963.

Baker, David. *Between Nations: Shakespeare, Spenser, Marvell, and the Question of Britain*. Stanford: Stanford Univ. Press, 1997.

Barker, Francis. *The Tremulous Private Body: Essays on Subjection*. London: Methuen, 1985.

Bates, Catherine. "Poetry, Patronage, and the Court." *The Cambridge Companion to English Literature, 1500–1600*. Ed. Arthur Kinney. Cambridge: Cambridge Univ. Press, 2000.

– *The Rhetoric of Courtship in Elizabethan Language and Literature*. Cambridge: Cambridge Univ. Press, 1992.

Bednarz, James. "The Collaborator as Thief: Ralegh's (Re)Vision of *The Faerie Queene*." ELH 63 (1996): 279–307.

– "Ralegh in Spenser's Historical Allegory." *Spenser Studies* 4 (1983): 49–70.

Beer, Anna. *Sir Walter Ralegh and His Readers in the Seventeenth Century*. London: Macmillan, 1997.

Beier, A.L., and Roger Finlay, eds. *London, 1500–1700*. London: Longman, 1986.

Belsey, Catherine. *The Subject of Tragedy.* London: Methuen, 1985.

Bennett, H.S. *English Books and Readers 1558–1603*. Cambridge: Cambridge Univ. Press, 1965.

Berger, Harry. "The Mirror Stage of Colin Clout: A Reading of Spenser's *Januarye* Eclogue." *Helios* 10 (1983): 139–60. Rpt. in his *Revisionary Play: Studies in the Spenserian Dynamics*. Intro. Louis Montrose. Berkeley: Univ. of California Press, 1988. 325–46.

Bergeron, David. *English Civic Pageantry, 1558–1642*. London: Edward Arnold, 1971,

Bergeron, David, ed. *Pageantry in the Shakespearean Theatre*. Athens: Univ. of Georgia Press, 1975.

Berleth, Richard. *The Twilight Lords: An Irish Chronicle*. New York: Alfred Knopf, 1978.

Bernard, John. *Ceremonies of Innocence: Pastoralism in the Poetry of Edmund Spenser*. Cambridge: Cambridge Univ. Press, 1989.

Berry, Philippa. *Of Chastity and Power: Elizabethan Literature and the Unmarried Queen*. London: Routledge, 1994.

Bloom, Harold. *Shakespeare: The Invention of the Human*. New York: Riverhead Books, 1995.

Bradbrook, Muriel. "No Room at the Top: Spenser's Pursuit of Fame." *Stratford-Upon-Avon Studies* 2. Elizabethan Poetry. London: Edward Arnold, 1960. 91–109.

Breight, Curt. "Realpolitik and Elizabethan Ceremony: The Earl of Hertford's Entertainment of Elizabeth at Elvetham, 1591." *Renaissance Quarterly* 45.1 (Spring 1992): 20–48.

Brennan, Michael. *Literary Patronage in the English Renaissance: The Pembroke Family*. London: Routledge, 1988.

Brink, Jean. "Spenser's Political Patronage." Sixteenth-Century Studies Conference, Toronto, 22–5 October 1998. Abstracted in *Spenser Newsletter* 30.1 (Winter 1998): 24–5.

Brooks, Eric St John. *Sir Christopher Hatton: Queen Elizabeth's Favourite*. London: Jonathan Cape, 1946.

Brown, Cedric, ed. *Patronage, Politics, and Literary Traditions in England, 1558–1658*. Detroit: Wayne State Univ. Press, 1991.

Burt, Richard. *Licensed by Authority: Ben Jonson and the Discourses of Censorship*. Ithaca: Cornell Univ. Press, 1993.

Cain, Thomas. *Praise in "The Faerie Queene."* Lincoln: Univ. of Nebraska Press, 1978.

Calendar of State Papers, Domestic Series, of the Reigns of Edward VI, Mary, Elizabeth, 1547- 1625. Liechtenstein: Kraus Reprint, 1971.

Calendar of State Papers Relating to Ireland, of the Reigns of Edward VIII, Edward VI, Mary, and Elizabeth I. Ed. Hans Claude Hamilton et al. 11 vols. London, 1860–1912.

Canino, Catherine G. "Reconstructing Lord Grey's Reputation: A New View of the *View*." *Sixteenth Century Journal* 29.1 (Spring 1998): 3–18.

Carroll, Clare. "Representations of Women in Some Early Modern English Tracts on the Colonization of Ireland." *Albion* 25.3 (Fall 1993): 379–93.

Cavanagh, Sheila. "'The fatal destiny of that land': Elizabethan Views of Ireland." *Representing Ireland*. Ed. Brendan Bradshaw, Andrew Hadfield, and Willy Maley. Cambridge: Cambridge Univ. Press, 1993. 116–31.

Chaudhuri, Sukanta. *Renaissance Pastoral and Its English Developments*. Oxford: Clarendon Press, 1989.

Cheney, Donald. "Spenser's Fortieth Birthday and Related Fictions." *Spenser Studies* 4 (1983): 3–31.

Cheney, Patrick. *Spenser's Famous Flight: A Renaissance Idea of a Literary Career*. Toronto: Univ. of Toronto Press, 1993.

Clare, Janet. *"Art Made Tongue-Tied by Authority": Elizabethan and Jacobean Dramatic Censorship*. Manchester: Manchester Univ. Press, 1990.

Clement, Francis. *The Petie Schole* (1587). *Four Tudor Books on Education*. Ed. Robert Pepper. Gainesville: Scholars' Facsimilies and Reprints, 1966.

Cole, Mary Hill. *The Portable Queen: Elizabeth I and the Politics of Ceremony*. Amherst: Univ. of Massachusetts Press, 1999.

Corbett, Margery, and Ronald Lightbrown. *The Comely Frontispiece: The Emblematic Title-Page in England, 1550–1660*. London: Routledge and Kegan Paul, 1979.

Cox, J. Charles. *The Royal Forests of England*. London: Methuen, 1905.

Craig, Joanne. "The Queen, Her Handmaid, and Spenser's Career." *English Studies in Canada* 12.3 (Sept. 1986): 255–68.

Cressy, David. *Education in Tudor and Stuart England*. London: E. Arnold, 1975.

Crewe, Jonathan. *Trials of Authorship: Anterior Forms and Poetic Reconstruction from Wyatt to Shakespeare*. Berkeley: Univ. of California Press, 1990.

Cullen, Patrick. *Spenser, Marvell, and Renaissance Pastoral*. Cambridge, Mass.: Harvard Univ. Press, 1970.

Dasenbrock, Reed Way. *Imitating the Italians: Wyatt, Spenser, Synge, Pound, Joyce*. Baltimore: Johns Hopkins Univ. Press, 1991.

Dekker, Thomas. *The Dramatic Works of Thomas Dekker*. Ed. Fredson Bowers. New York: Cambridge Univ. Press, 1980.
DeNeef, A. Leigh. *Spenser and the Motives of Metaphor*. Durham: Duke Univ. Press, 1982.
Dictionary of National Biography. 22 vols. Ed. Leslie Stephen and Sidney Lee. Oxford: Oxford Univ. Press, 1917.
Dovey, Zillah. *An Elizabethan Progress: The Queen's Journey into East Anglia, 1578*. Foreword by David Laodes. Madison: Fairleigh Dickinson Univ. Press.
Dubrow, Heather. *Echoes of Desire: English Petrarchism and Its Counterdiscourses*. Ithaca: Cornell Univ. Press, 1995.
Du Maurier, Daphne. *Golden Lads: Sir Francis Bacon, Antlory Bacon, and Their Friends*. Garden City, NY: Doubleday, 1975.
Duncan-Jones, Katherine. *Sir Philip Sidney: Courtier Poet*. New Haven: Yale Univ. Press, 1991.
Durr, Robert. "Spenser's Calendar of Christian Time." ELH 24 (1957): 269–95.
Dutton, Richard. *Mastering the Revels: The Regulation and Censorship of English Renaissance Drama*. Iowa City: Univ. of Iowa Press, 1991.
Edwards, R.D. *Church and State in Tudor Ireland*. New York: Russell and Russell, 1935; rpt. 1972.
English, H.M. "Spenser's Accommodation of Allegory to History in the Story of Timias and Belphoebe." JEGP 59 (1960): 417–29.
Erickson, Carolly. *Mistress Anne*. Summit Books, 1984.
Erickson, Wayne. "Spenser and His Friends Stage a Publishing Event: Praise, Play, and Warning in the Commendatory Verses to the 1590 *Faerie Queene*." *Renaissance Papers*. Columbia, SC: Camden House, 1997.
Falls, Cyril. "Black Tom of Ormonde." *Irish Sword* 5 (1961–2): 10–22.
Ferry, Anne. *The Art of Naming*. Chicago: Univ. of Chicago Press, 1988.
– *The "Inward" Language: Sonnets of Wyatt, Sidney, Shakespeare, and Donne*. Chicago: Univ. of Chicago Press, 1983.
Ford, Alan. *The Protestant Reformation in Ireland, 1590–1641*. Frankfurt am Main and New York: P. Lang, 1987.
Fox, Alistair. "The Decline of Literary Patronage in the 1590s." *The Reign of Elizabeth I: Court and Culture in the Last Decade*. Ed. John Guy. Cambridge: Cambridge Univ. Press, 1995. 229–57.
Fraser, Antonia. *The Wives of Henry VIII*. New York: Knopf, 1992.
Fraser, Russell. *The War against Poetry*. Princeton: Princeton Univ. Press, 1970.
Fraunce, Abraham. *The Arcadian Rhetoricke*. Ed. Ethel Seaton. Oxford: Basil Blackwell, 1950.

Friedman, Alice. *House and Household in Elizabethan England*. Chicago: Univ. of Chicago Press, 1989.
Frye, Susan. *Elizabeth I: The Competition for Representation*. New York: Oxford Univ. Press, 1993.
Fumerton, Patricia. "Exchanging Gifts: The Elizabethan Currency of Children and Poetry." ELH 53.1 (1986): 241-78.
Genette, Gerard. "Introduction to the Paratext." *New Literary History* 22 (Spring 1991): 261-79.
Gilbert, Allan. "Belphoebe's Misdeeming of Timias." PMLA 62 (1947): 622-43.
Girouard, Mark. *Life in the English Country House: A Social and Architectural History*. New Haven: Yale Univ. Press, 1978.
Goldberg, Jonathan. "Colin to Hobbinol: Spenser's Familiar Letters." *South Atlantic Quarterly* 88.1 (Winter 1989): 107-26.
– *Endlesse Worke: Spenser and the Structures of Discourse*. Baltimore: Johns Hopkins Univ. Press, 1981.
Greene, Thomas. *The Light in Troy: Imitation and Discovery in Renaissance Poetry*. New Haven: Yale Univ. Press, 1982.
Greg, W.W., ed. *A Companion to Arber. Being a Calendar of Documents in Edward Arber's Transcript of the Register of the Company of Stationers of London, 1554-1640*. Oxford: Clarendon Press, 1967.
– *Licensers for the Press, etc., to 1640: A Biographical Index*. Oxford: Oxford Bibliographical Society, 1962.
Greg, W.W., and E. Boswell, eds. *Records of the Court of the Stationers Company*. London, 1930.
Gregerson, Linda. *The Reformation of the Subject: Spenser, Milton, and the Renaissance Protestant Epic*. Cambridge: Cambridge Univ. Press, 1995.
Griffiths, Paul, Adam Fox, and Steve Hindle, eds. *The Experience of Authority in Early Modern England*. New York: St Martin's Press, 1996.
Gutierrez, Nancy. "The Remembrance: A Form of Renaissance Verse Biography." *Selected Papers from the West Virginia Shakespeare and Renaissance Association* 7.2 (Spring 1982): 54-9.
Hadfield, Andrew. *Edmund Spenser's Irish Experience: Wilde Fruit and Salvage Soyl*. Oxford: Clarendon Press, 1997.
– "From English to British Literature: John Lyly's *Euphues* and Edmund Spenser's *The Faerie Queene*." *British Consciousness and Identity*. Ed. Brendan Bradshaw and Peter Roberts. Cambridge: Cambridge Univ. Press, 1998. 140-58.
– "Introduction." *Edmund Spenser*. Ed. Andrew Hadfield. London: Longman, 1996.

– *Literature, Politics, and National Identity: Reformation to Renaissance.* Cambridge: Cambridge Univ. Press, 1994.

Hager, Alan. "The Exemplary Mirage: Fabrication of Sir Philip Sidney's Biographical Image and the Sidney Reader." ELH 48 (1981): 1–16.

Hamilton, A.C. "The Argument of Spenser's *Shepheardes Calender*." ELH 23 (1956): 171–83.

– *Sir Philip Sidney: A Study of His Life and Work.* Cambridge: Cambridge Univ. Press, 1977.

Hanson, Elizabeth. *Discovering the Subject in Renaissance England.* Cambridge: Cambridge Univ. Press, 1998.

Harrison, Robert. *Forests: The Shadow of Civilization.* Chicago: Chicago Univ. Press, 1992.

Hart, Cyril. *The Royal Forest.* Oxford: Oxford Univ. Press, 1966.

Heale, Elizabeth. *Wyatt, Surrey, and Early Tudor Poetry.* London: Longman, 1998.

Heffner, Ray. *Spenser Allusions in the Sixteenth and Seventeenth Centuries.* Chapel Hill: Univ. of North Carolina Press, 1972.

Helgerson, Richard. *The Elizabethan Prodigals.* Berkeley: Univ. of California Press, 1976.

– *Forms of Nationhood: The Elizabethan Writing of England.* Chicago: Univ. of Chicago Press, 1992.

– *Self-Crowned Laureates: Spenser, Jonson, Milton, and the Literary System.* Berkeley: Univ. of California Press, 1983.

Heninger, S.K. "The Implications of Form for *The Shepheardes Calender*." *Studies in the Renaissance* 9 (1962): 309–21.

Henley, Pauline. *Spenser in Ireland.* Dublin: Cork Univ. Press, 1928.

Herman, Peter. *Squitter-Wits and Muse-Haters: Sidney, Spenser, Milton, and Anti-Poetic Sentiment.* Detroit: Wayne State Univ. Press, 1996.

Hibbert, Christopher. *The Virgin Queen: The Personal History of Elizabeth I.* Harmondsworth: Penguin Books, 1990.

Highley, Christopher. "The Royal Image in Elizabethan Ireland." *Dissing Elizabeth: Negative Representations of Gloriana.* Ed. Julia Walker. Durham: Duke Univ. Press, 1998.

– *Shakespeare, Spenser, and the Crisis in Ireland.* Cambridge: Cambridge Univ. Press, 1997.

Holahan, Michael. "Wyatt, the Heart's Forest, and Ancient Savings." ELR 23.1 (1993): 46–80.

Hooker, John. *Chronicles of Ireland.* In *Holinshed's Chronicles of England, Scotland, and Ireland.* 6 vols. London: J. Johnson, 1807–8.

Huffman, Clifford. *Elizabethan Impressions*. New York: AMS Press, 1988.
Hume, Anthea. *Edmund Spenser: Protestant Poet*. Cambridge: Cambridge Univ. Press, 1984.
Ives, E.W. *Anne Boleyn*. Oxford: Blackwell, 1986.
Johnson, Natalie. "Merchant Taylors' School: A Social Analysis, 1562–1640." Unpublished.
Johnson, Francis R. *A Critical Bibliography of the Works of Edmund Spenser Printed before 1700*. Baltimore: Johns Hopkins Univ. Press, 1933.
Johnson, Lynn Staley. *The Shepheardes Calender: An Introduction*. University Park: Pennsylvania State Univ. Press, 1990.
Judge, C.B. *Elizabethan Book-Pirates*. Cambridge, Mass.: Harvard Univ. Press, 1934.
Judson, Alexander. *The Life of Edmund Spenser. The Works of Edmund Spenser: A Variorum Edition*. Ed. Edwin Greenlaw et al. Vol. 11. Baltimore: Johns Hopkins Univ. Press, 1945.
Kaplan, Lindsay M. *The Culture of Slander in Early Modern England*. Cambridge: Cambridge Univ. Press, 1997.
Kaufman, Peter. *Prayer, Despair, and Drama: Elizabethan Introspection*. Urbana: Univ. of Illinois Press, 1966.
Keen, Maurice. *Chivalry*. New Haven: Yale Univ. Press, 1984.
– *The Outlaws of Medieval Legend*. London: Routledge and Kegan Paul, 1961.
Lacey, Robert. *Robert, Earl of Essex*. New York: Atheneum, 1971.
– *Sir Walter Ralegh*. London: Weidenfeld and Nicolson, 1973.
Leerssen, Joseph Th. *Mere Irish and Fíor-Ghael: Studies in the Idea of Irish Nationality, Its Development and Literary Expression Prior to the Nineteenth Century*. Philadelphia: John Benjamins, 1986.
Leggatt, Alexander. *Jacobean Public Theatre*. London: Routledge, 1992.
Leslie, Michael. "'Something Nasty in the Wilderness': Entertaining Queen Elizabeth on Her Progresses." *Medieval and Renaissance Drama in England*. Ed. John Pitcher. London: Associated Univ. Presses. Vol. 10 (1998): 47–72.
Levin, Carole. *"The Heart and Stomach of a King": Elizabeth I and the Politics of Sex and Power*. Philadelphia: Univ. of Pennsylvania Press, 1994.
Lobanov-Rostovsky, Sergei. "*The Triumphes of Gold*: Economic Authority in the Jacobean Lord Mayor's Show." ELH 60 (1993): 879–98.
Loewenstein, Joseph. "For a History of Literary Property: John Wolfe's Reformation." ELR 18.3 (1988): 389–412.

– "Spenser's Retrography: Two Episodes in Post-Petrarchan Bibliography." *Spenser's Life and the Subject of Biography.* Ed. Judith Anderson et al. Amherst: Univ. of Massachusetts Press, 1996.
Long, Percy. "Spenser and Lady Cary." MLR 3 (1907–8): 257–67.
Lytle, Guy Fitch, and Stephen Orgel, eds. *Patronage in the Renaissance.* Princeton: Princeton Univ. Press, 1981.
MacCaffrey, Isabel. "Allegory and Pastoral in *The Shepheardes Calender.*" ELH 36 (1969): 88–109.
MacCaffrey, Wallace. *Elizabeth I: War and Politics.* Princeton: Princeton Univ. Press, 1992.
– *The Shaping of the Elizabethan Regime.* Princeton: Princeton Univ. Press, 1968.
Maccarthy-Morrogh, Michael. *The Munster Plantation: English Migration to Southern Ireland, 1583–1641.* Oxford: Clarendon Press, 1986.
Maley, Willy. *A Spenser Chronology.* London: Macmillan, 1994.
Manley, Lawrence. *Literature and Culture in Early Modern London.* Cambridge: Cambridge Univ. Press, 1995.
Manwood, John. *A Treatise of the Lawes of the Forest.* (1598). The English Experience. No. 184. Norwood, NJ: Walter J. Johnson, 1976.
Marienstras, Richard. *New Perspectives on the Shakespearean World.* Trans. Janet Lloyd. Cambridge: Cambridge Univ. Press, 1985.
Marotti, Arthur. *Manuscript, Print, and the English Renaissance Lyric.* Ithaca: Cornell Univ. Press, 1995.
Marx, Karl. *Ethnographical Notebooks.* Ed. L. Krader. Assen: Van Gorcum, 1974.
Maus, Katharine. *Inwardness and Theatre in the English Renaissance.* Chicago: Univ. of Chicago Press, 1995.
Mauss, Marcel. *The Gift: The Form and Reason for Exchange in Archaic Societies.* London: Routledge, 1990.
May, Steven W. *The Elizabethan Courtier Poets: The Poems and Their Contexts.* Columbia: Univ. of Missouri Press, 1991.
McCoy, Richard. *The Rites of Knighthood: The Literature and Politics of Elizabethan Chivalry.* Berkeley: Univ. of California Press, 1989.
McEachern, Claire. *The Poetics of English Nationhood.* Cambridge: Cambridge Univ. Press, 1996.
McKerrow, R.B. *A Dictionary of Printers and Booksellers in England, Scotland, and Ireland, and of Foreign Printers of English Books 1557–1640.* Bibliographical Society, 1910. Rpt. 1968.
McKerrow, R.B., ed. *The Works of Thomas Nashe.* 5 vols. Rpt. ed. F.P. Wilson. Oxford: Blackwell, 1958.
McKerrow, R.B., and F.S. Ferguson. *Title-Page Borders Used in England and Scotland 1485–1640.* London: Bibliographical Society, 1932.

Miller, David. "Authorship, Anonymity, and *The Shepheardes Calender*." *MLQ* 40 (1979): 219–36.
- *The Poem's Two Bodies: The Poetics of the 1590 "Faerie Queene.*" Princeton: Princeton Univ. Press, 1988.

Miller, Edwin H. *The Professional Writer in Elizabethan England: A Study in Nondramatic Literature*. Cambridge: Harvard Univ. Press, 1959.

Montrose, Louis. "'The perfecte paterne of a Poete': The Poetics of Courtship in *The Shepheardes Calender*." *TSLL* 21.1 (Spring 1979): 34–87.
- "The Place of a Brother in *As You Like It*: Social Process and Comic Form." *Shakespeare Quarterly* 32.1 (1981): 28–54.

Moody, T.W., F.X. Martin, and F.J. Byrne, eds. *A New History of Ireland*. Vol. 3: Early Modern Ireland, 1534–1691. Oxford: Clarendon Press, 1976.

Mulcaster, Richard. *Positions* (1581). Abridged and ed. Richard L. DeMolen. New York: Teachers College Press, 1971.

Nashe, Thomas. *Pierce Penilesse, His Supplication to the Divell*. Ed. G.B. Harrison. Edinburgh: Edinburgh Univ. Press, 1966.

Nelson, William. *Fact or Fiction: The Dilemma of the Renaissance Storyteller*. Cambridge, Mass.: Harvard Univ. Press, 1973.

Nichols, John. *The Progresses and Public Processions of Queen Elizabeth*. Vols. 2 and 3. New York: Burt Franklin, 1823.

Norbrook, David. *Poetry and Politics in the English Renaissance*. London: Routledge and Kegan Paul, 1984.

O'Connell, Michael. *Mirror and Veil: The Historical Dimension of Spenser's "Faerie Queene."* Chapel Hill: Univ. of North Carolina Press, 1977.

O'Day, Rosemary. *Education and Society, 1500–1800: The Social Foundation of Education in Early Modern Britain*. London: Longman, 1982.

Oram, William. "Elizabethan Fact and Spenserian Fiction." *Spenser Studies* 4 (1983): 33–47.
- "Spenser's Raleghs." *Studies in Philology* 87.3 (Summer 1990): 341–62.
- "What Did Spenser Really Think of Sir Walter Ralegh When He Published the 1590 *Faerie Queene*?" Sixteenth-Century Studies Conference, Toronto, 22–5 October 1998. Abstract in *Spenser Newsletter* 30.1 (Winter 1999): 20–1.

Owens, Judith. "The Poetics of Accommodation in Spenser's *Epithalamion*." *SEL* 40.1 (Winter 2000): 41–62.
- "Professing Ireland in the Woods of *Mutabilitie*." World Medieval Congress, Kalamazoo, 6–9 May 1999.

Pask, Kevin. *The Emergence of the English Author*. Cambridge: Cambridge Univ. Press, 1996.

Paster, Gail Kern. *The Body Embarrassed: Drama and the Discipline of Shame in Early Modern England*. Ithaca: Cornell Univ. Press, 1993.

– *The Idea of the City in the Age of Shakespeare*. Athens: Univ. of Georgia Press, 1985.

Patterson, Annabel. *Censorship and Interpretation: The Conditions of Writing and Reading in Early Modern England*. Madison: Univ. of Wisconsin Press, 1984.

– "Re-opening the Green Cabinet: Clement Marot and Edmund Spenser." *ELR* 16.1 (Winter 1986): 44–70.

Peck, Linda Levy. *Northampton: Patronage and Policy at the Court of James I*. London: George Allen and Unwin, 1982.

Pettit, Philip A.J. *The Royal Forests of Northamptonshire: A Study in their Economy, 1558–1714*. Gateshead (Co. Durham): Northamptonshire Record Society, 1968.

Plant, Marjorie. *The English Book Trade: An Economic History of the Making and Sale of Books*. 3rd edition. London: George Allen and Unwin, 1974.

Porter, Roy. *London: A Social History*. Cambridge, Mass.: Harvard Univ. Press, 1995.

Puttenham, George. *The Arte of English Poesie*. Ed. Gladys Willock and Alice Walker. Cambridge: Cambridge Univ. Press, 1936.

Radcliffe, David. *Edmund Spenser: A Reception History*. Columbia, SC: Camden House, 1996.

Ralegh, Walter. *The Poems of Sir Walter Ralegh*. Ed. Agnes Latham. Cambridge: Harvard Univ. Press, 1951.

Rambuss, Richard. *Spenser's Secret Career*. Cambridge: Cambridge Univ. Press, 1993.

Rappaport, Steven. *Worlds within Worlds: Structures of Life in Sixteenth-Century London*. Cambridge: Cambridge Univ. Press, 1989.

Rasmussen, Carl. "'How Weak Be the Passions of Woefulness': Spenser's *Ruines of Time*." *Spenser Studies* 2 (1981): 159–81.

Reeves-Smyth, Terence. "The Natural History of Demesnes." *Nature in Ireland*. Ed. John Foster. Dublin: Lilliput Press, 1997. 549–72.

Rix, Herbert. *Rhetoric in Spenser's Poetry*. State College: Pennsylvania State College Press, 1940.

Roche, Thomas. *The Kindly Flame: A Study of "The Faerie Queene III and IV."* Princeton: Princeton Univ. Press, 1964.

Rosenberg, Eleanor. *Leicester, Patron of Letters*. New York: Columbia Univ. Press, 1955.

Ross, Charles Stanley. *The Custom of the Castle: From Malory to Macbeth*. Berkeley: Univ. of California Press, 1997.

Rowse, A.L. *The English Past*. London: Macmillan, 1951.

– *The Expansion of Elizabethan England*. New York: Charles Scribners' Sons, 1955.
– *Ralegh and the Throckmortons*. London: Macmillan, 1962.
Saunders, J.W. "The Stigma of Print: A Note on the Social Bases of Tudor Poetry." *Essays in Criticism* 1 (1951): 139–64.
Schleiner, Louise. *Tudor and Stuart Women Writers*. Bloomington: Indiana Univ. Press, 1994.
Schoenfeldt, Michael. *Bodies and Selves in Early Modern England*. Cambridge: Cambridge Univ. Press, 1999.
Sedgwick, Eve Kosofsky. *Between Men: English Literature and Male Homosocial Desire*. New York: Columbia Univ. Press, 1985.
Shakespeare, William. *As You Like It* and *Henry IV, Part 1. The Complete Works of Shakespeare*. Rev. edition. Ed. Hardin Craig and David Bevington. Glenview, Ill.: Scott, Foresman and Company, 1973.
Sheavyn, Phoebe. *The Literary Profession in the Elizabethan Age*. Manchester: Manchester Univ. Press, 1909. Rpt. New York: Haskell House, 1964.
Shore, David. *Spenser and the Poetics of Pastoral: A Study of the World of Colin Clout*. Montreal and Kingston: McGill-Queen's Univ. Press, 1985.
Shuger, Debora. "The 'I' of the Beholder: Renaissance Mirrors and the Reflexive Mind." *Renaissance Culture and the Everyday*. Ed. Patricia Fumerton and Simon Hunt. Pittsburgh: Univ. of Pennsylvania Press, 1999.
Simon, Joan. *Education and Society in Tudor England*. Cambridge: Cambridge Univ. Press, 1966.
Smith, Thomas. *De Republica Anglorum*. London, 1583. Menston, England: Scolar Press, 1970.
Spenser, Edmund. *The Faerie Queene*. Ed. A.C. Hamilton. London: Longman, 1977.
– *The Poetical Works of Edmund Spenser*. Ed. J.C. Smith and E. de Selincourt. 1 volume edition, with the Spenser-Harvey correspondence. 1912. Rpt. New York: Oxford Paperbacks, 1979.
– *The Shepheardes Calender, Complaints, Colin Clouts Come Home Againe*. In *The Yale Edition of the Shorter Poems of Edmund Spenser*. Ed. William Oram et al. New Haven: Yale Univ. Press, 1989.
– *A View of the Present State of Ireland*. Ed. W.L. Renwick. Oxford: Clarendon Press, 1970.
– *The Works of Edmund Spenser*. A Variorum Edition. 11 vols. Ed. Edwin Greenlaw et al. Baltimore: Johns Hopkins Univ. Press, 1945.
Spingarn, Joel. *A History of Literary Criticism in the Renaissance*. 2nd edition. New York: Columbia Univ. Press, 1912.

Stern, Virginia. *Gabriel Harvey: His Life, Marginalia, and Library.* Oxford: Clarendon Press, 1979.

Stillman, Carol. "Politics, Precedence, and the Order of the Dedicatory Sonnets in *The Faerie Queene.*" *Spenser Studies* 5 (1984): 143-8.

Stillman, Robert. "'Words cannot knytt': Language and Desire in Ralegh's *The Ocean to Cynthia.*" SEL 27 (1987): 35-51.

Stone, Lawrence, and Jeanne Fawtier Stone. *An Open Elite?: England, 1540-1880.* Oxford: Clarendon Press, 1984.

Strong, Roy. *The Cult of Elizabeth: Elizabethan Portraiture and Pageantry.* London: Thames and Hudson, 1977.

Summerson, John. *Architecture in Britain, 1530-1830.* Harmondsworth: Penguin Books, 1970.

Thomson, Patricia. "The Literature of Patronage." *Essays in Criticism* 2 (1952): 267-85.

Tudor Royal Proclamations. Vol. 2. The Later Tudors (1553-1587). Ed. Paul Hughes and James F. Larkin. New Haven: Yale Univ. Press, 1969.

Tylus, Jane. "Spenser, Virgil, and the Politics of Poetic Labor." ELH 55.1 (Spring 1988): 53-77.

– *Writing and Vulnerability in the Late Renaissance.* Stanford: Stanford Univ. Press, 1993.

Virgil. *Aeneid.* Trans. W.F. Jackson Kight. Harmondsworth: Penguin Books, 1958.

Waldman, Louis. "Spenser's Pseudonym 'E.K.' and Humanist Self-Naming." *Spenser Studies* 9 (1991): 21-31.

Walker, Julia, ed. *Dissing Elizabeth: Negative Representations of Gloriana.* Durham: Duke Univ. Press, 1998.

Wall, Wendy. *The Imprint of Gender: Authorship and Publication in the English Renaissance.* Ithaca: Cornell Univ. Press, 1993.

Waller, Gary. *Edmund Spenser: A Literary Life.* New York: St Martin's Press, [1994].

Warnicke, Retha. *The Rise and Fall of Anne Boleyn: Family Politics at the Court of Henry VIII.* Cambridge: Cambridge Univ. Press, 1991.

Webbe, William. *A Discourse of English Poetrie.* Ed. Edward Arber. Westminster: A. Constable and Co., 1895.

Wells, Robin Headlam. *Spenser's "Faerie Queene" and the Cult of Elizabeth.* London: Croom Helm, 1983.

Wilson, Derek. *Sweet Robin: A Biography of Robert Dudley, Earl of Leicester 1533-88.* London, 1981.

Wilson, Jean. *Entertainments for Elizabeth I.* Totowa, NJ: D.S. Brewer, 1980.

Wilson, Richard. "'Like the old Robin Hood': *As You Like It* and the Enclosure Riots." *Shakespeare Quarterly* 43.1 (1992): 1–19.

Wilson, Scott. *Cultural Materialism: Theory and Practice.* Oxford: Blackwell, 1995.

Wilson, Violet. *Society Women of Shakespeare's Time.* New York: E.P. Dutton and Co., 1925.

Winton, John. *Sir Walter Ralegh.* New York: Coward, McCann, and Geoghegan, 1975.

Wofford, Susanne Lindgren. "Gendering Allegory: Spenser's Bold Reader and the Emergence of Character in *The Faerie Queene* III." *Criticism* 30.1 (Winter 1988): 1–21.

Wood, Michael. *In Search of England: Journeys into the Past.* Berkeley: Univ. of California Press, 1999.

Wright, Pam. "A Change in Direction: The Ramifications of a Female Household, 1588–1603." *The English Court: From the Wars of the Roses to the Civil War.* Ed. David Starkey et al. London: Longman, 1987.

Wyatt, Thomas. "The long love." *Collected Poems of Sir Thomas Wyatt.* Ed. Kenneth Muir. London: Routledge and Kegan Paul, 1949.

Young, Charles. *The Royal Forests of Medieval England.* Philadelphia: Univ. of Pennsylvania Press, 1979.

Index

Aeneid, 62, 120, 127
Anderson, Judith, 160n2
Anglo-Saxon Chronicle, 19, 148n31
Arber, E., 159n5
authority structures, 6, 7, 14, 15, 18, 73, 89–91; and authors, 30, 31, 34; challenges to, 6–30, 147n23; and subject positions, 38, 87, 113, 145n10

Bagwell, Richard, 160n27, 161n10
Baker, David, 144n3
Bakhtin, M., 145n10
Barker, Francis, 146n10
Bates, Catherine, 5, 144n6
Bednarz, James, 117, 156n11, 160n1
Beer, Anna, 113
Beier, A.L., 157n18
Belphoebe. *See* Spenser (*The Faerie Queene*)
Belsey, Catherine, 146n10
Bennett, H.S., 159n5
Berger, Harry, 154n14, n15
Bergeron, David, 157n20
Berleth, Richard, 158n35, 160n27, 161n10, 162n22
Bernard, John, 152n8, 153n12, 154n19
Berry, Philippa, 144n6, 148n37
Bisham: royal entertainments, 7–11, 146n15; and the Russells, 7, 146n11
Bloom, Harold, 146n10
Boswell, E. *See* Greg, W.W.
Bradbrook, Muriel, 152n10
Breight, Curtis, 147n23, 148n37
Brennan, Michael, 149n45
Brink, Jean, 38
Brooks, Eric St John, 160n23
Burnett, Mark, 145n8
Burt, Richard, 145n10
Byrne, F.J. *See* Moody, T.W.

Cain, Thomas, 154n17, 158n1
Calendar of State Papers, Domestic, 147n17
Calendar of State Papers, Ireland, 119, 161n10
Canino, Catherine, 158n35

Carew (Carey), Lady, 143n2, n3. *See also* Spencer sisters; Spenser (dedicatory sonnets)
Carroll, Clare, 83
Cavanagh, Sheila, 161n4
Chaucer, Geoffrey, 50, 63
Chaudhuri, Sukanta, 154n17
Cheney, Donald, 154n19
Cheney, Patrick, 141–2, 162n1
Clare, Janet, 145n10
Clement, Francis, 17–18
Cole, Mary Hill, 14
Colin Clout, 36–7, 41, 151n3, 153n11. *See also* Spenser (*Colin Clouts Come Home Againe* and *The Shepheardes Calender*)
Corbett, Margery, 149n48
Cox, J. Charles, 148n30
Craig, Joanne, 151n3
Cressy, David, 148n28
Crewe, Jonathan, 28, 30
Cullen, Patrick, 151n3
cultural commodification, 30–4

Dasenbrock, Reed Way, 162n24
Dekker, Thomas: *Troi-Nova Triumphans*, 78–9
DeNeef, A. Leigh, 160n2
Desmond rebellion, 117–18, 123. *See also* Ralegh; Spenser (*The Faerie Queene*)
Donnelly, M.L., 145n8
Dovey, Zillah, 157n13
Dubrow, Heather, 161n8
Du Maurier, Daphne, 147n17
Duncan-Jones, Katherine, 42, 161n15
Durr, Robert, 151n3
Dutton, Richard, 145n10

Edwards, R.D., 161n6
E.K., 38, 40, 150n1; and homosociality, 48–51; prefaces to *Shepheardes Calender*, 46–9. *See also* Spenser (*The Shepheardes Calender*)
Elizabeth I: and Anne Boleyn, 13; and Alençon, 45; criticized, 23; and Ireland, 85–6; and Lady Elizabeth Russell, 10–11; militancy, 37–8; and the Norrises, 13–14; and Ralegh, 71, 133, 138; and representations, 84–6, 110, 161n3; and royal entertainments, 7–14; and woodlands, 23. *See also* Ralegh; Spenser
English, H.M., 160n1
Erickson, Carolly, 149n40
Erickson, Wayne, 156n2, n11
Essex, Earl of, 38

Falls, Cyril, 160n27
Ferguson, R.S., 149–50n48
Ferry, Anne, 146n10, 154n16
feudal values, 4, 13, 25, 102. *See also* Rycote; Spenser (*Complaints*)
Finlay, Roger. *See* Beier, A.L.
Ford, Alan, 161n6
forests: in law, 6, 18–19, 24, 27; literary, 7, 23–30; and outlawry, 24, 27, 148n35
Foucault, Michel, 145n10
Fox, Adam. *See* Griffiths, Paul
Fox, Alistair, 144n4
Fraser, Antonia, 149n40
Fraser, Russell, 156n3
Fraunce, Abraham, 82
Friedman, Alice, 155n23
Frye, Susan, 77, 81, 144n6, 161n3
Fumerton, Patricia, 157n25

Genette, Gerard, 156n2
gift-giving, 81
Gilbert, Allan, 160n1
Girouard, Mark, 155n23
Goldberg, Jonathan, 153n11, 162n1
Greene, Thomas, 29
Greg, W.W., 159n5
Gregerson, Linda, 128
Griffiths, Paul, 145n10
Gutierrez, Nancy, 150n58

Hadfield, Andrew, 69, 143–4n3, 150n55, 158n32, 160n24
Hager, Alan, 150n60
Hamilton, A.C., 77, 151n3, 161n15
Hanson, Elizabeth, 146n10
Harrison, Robert, 24, 148n35
Hart, Cyril, 148n30
Harvey, Gabriel, 39, 40, 75–7, 79, 80, 83, 84, 157n13; and E.K., 46, 49–51. *See also* Spenser (commendatory poems and *The Shepheardes Calender*)
H.B.: commendatory poem, 81, 83–4, 87
Heale, Elizabeth, 27
Heffner, Ray, 158n28
Heinemann, Margot, 145n8
Helgerson, Richard, 20, 36, 40–1, 62–3, 143n3, 144n5, 149n45, 150–1n3, 155n21, n22, 156n3, 157n24
Heninger, S.K., 151n3
Henley, Pauline, 158n31
Herman, Peter, 156n3
Hibbert, Christopher, 161n3
Highley, Christopher, 83, 86, 104, 158n38, n39, n41, 160n24
Hindle, Steve. *See* Griffiths, Paul
Hobbinol, 40. *See also* Harvey, Gabriel; Spenser
Holahan, Michael, 26–7
Hooker, John: on Ralegh, 118, 119–20, 130–1
Huffman, Clifford, 91, 159n5
Hume, Anthea, 152n7

Ignoto: commendatory poem, 87. *See also* Spenser
Ireland, 12–13, 83; marriage in, 111; women in, 111; Smerwick, 162n22. *See also* Elizabeth I; Spenser
Ives, E.W., 149n40

Johnson, Francis, 158n2, 159n13
Johnson, Natalie, 148n27
Johnson, Lynn Staley, 151n3

Judge, C.B., 159n5
Judson, Alexander, 143n2, 150n53

Kaplan, Lindsay M., 126, 145n10
Kaufman, Peter, 146n10
Keen, Maurice, 148n35, 162n18

Lacey, Robert, 38
laureateship: and autonomy, 4. *See also* Spenser
Leerssen, Joseph, 158n37
Leggatt, Alexander, 157n19
Leicester, 36–7. *See also* Spenser
Leslie, Michael, 147n16, n23
Levin, Carole, 144n6, 158n36, n39
Lewalski, Barbara, 145n8
Lightbrown, Ronald. *See* Corbett, Margery
Lindenbaum, Peter, 145n8
literary transmission: manuscript, 33, 70–1; market, 87; print, 33, 34, 71, 87; reading circles, 35. *See also* print trade
Lobanov-Rostovsky, Sergei, 157n20
Loewenstein, Joseph, 89, 159n5

London, 77, 78, 80, 157n18. *See also* Spenser
Long, Percy, 143n3
Lytle, Guy Fitch, 145n8

MacCaffrey, Isabel, 151n3
MacCaffrey, Wallace, 147n19, n20, 159n16, 160n18, n10
Maccarthy-Morrogh, Michael, 162n19
Maley, Willy, 150n49, 158n31
Manley, Lawrence, 157n19, n22
Manwood, John: on forest law, 18–22. *See also* forests
Marienstras, Richard, 148n35
Marot, Clement, 68, 155n25
Marotti, Arthur, 33, 145n8
Martin, F.X. *See* Moody, T.W.
Marx, Karl: on Spenser, 35, 150n55
Mauss, Katharine, 146n10
Mauss, Marcel, 157n25
May, Steven, 157n16
McCoy, Richard, 147n23, 148n37
McEachern, Claire, 144n3
McKerrow, R.B., 149n46, 149–50n48, 159n5

McKluskie, Kathleen, 145n8
militaristic ethos, 11, 12. *See also* Spenser
Miller, David, 40–1, 73, 125, 150–1n3, 160n1, n2
Miller, Edwin, 144n8
Montrose, Louis, 24, 40–1, 74–5, 150–1n3
Moody, T.W., 160n27
Mulcaster, Richard, 15, 16; *Positions*, 15–18, 147n26
Munster, plantation of, 111, 119

Nashe, Thomas, 75; on the 1590 *Faerie Queene*, 92–3
nationalism, 4, 20, 69, 143n3
Nelson, William, 156n3
Nichols, John, 157n13
noble houses, 4, 14
Norbrook, David, 152n7
Norris family: and Anne Boleyn, 13–14. *See also* Rycote
Norris, John. *See* Spenser
Norris, Thomas: and Ireland, 12–13, 125. *See also* Rycote

O'Connell, Michael, 160n1, 162n1
O'Day, Rosemary, 148n28
Oram, William, 160n28, n1, 162n1

Orgel, Stephen. *See* Lytle, Guy Fitch
O'Rourke, Brian, 86
Owens, Judith, 161n5, 162n17

Pask, Kevin, 149n45
Paster, Gail Kern, 125, 157n19, 162n21
patronage: and literary production, 5, 144n8
Patterson, Annabel, 145n10, 150n2, 155n23
Payne, Deborah, 145n8
Peck, Linda Levy, 73
pedagogy, 6. *See also* Mulcaster, Richard; Clement, Francis
Petrarch: and Wyatt, 26–7, 29; Petrarchism and courtiership, 12, 144n6. *See also* Spenser
Pettit, Philip, 148n30, n34
Plant, Marjorie, 158–9n4, 159n5
poetry and poets: status, 70, 156n3
Ponsonby, William, 30, 149n48, 150n51; on *Complaints*, 30–5; and *The Faerie Queene*, 87, 89. *See also* Spenser
Porter, Roy, 157n18
print trade, 89, 90, 91, 96, 158–9n4,

159n11. *See also* literary transmission
Puttenham, George, 82

Radcliffe, David, 82
Ralegh, Sir Walter: Captain of the Guard, 71, 129–30; and Desmond rebellion, 118; and Elizabeth I, 113; on *The Faerie Queene*, 70–5, 79, 80, 81, 83, 84, 116; in Hooker's *Chronicles*, 118, 119–20, 130–1; "Like to a Hermit Poore," 139; marriage to Elizabeth Throckmorton, 9, 133, 137, 138, 146n15; *The Ocean to Cynthia*, 140; at Smerwick, Ireland, 126, 162n22; on Spenser, 39, 71–2, 73–4. *See also* Spenser
Rambuss, Richard, 41, 158n31
Rappaport, Steven, 157n18
Rasmussen, Carl, 150n57, 160n22
Reeves-Smyth, Terence, 119
Rix, Herbert, 153n13
Roche, Thomas, 162n1
Rosenberg, Eleanor, 144n8
Ross, Charles, 118, 121
Rowse, A.L., 147n17, n20, 161n6, n10
royal entertainments, 6, 77, 157n13. *See also* Bisham and Rycote
R.S.: commendatory poem, 79–83, 85, 87, 157n23. *See also* Spenser
Russell, Lady Elizabeth, 10–11, 147n17. *See also* Bisham
Rycote: royal entertainment at, 11–14, 146n11. *See also* Norris

Saunders, J.W., 156n4
Schleiner, Louise, 35
Schoenfeldt, Michael, 146n10
Sedgwick, Eve, 154n18
Shakespeare, William: and forests, 23–6; *As You Like It*, 7, 24–6; *Henry IV, Part 1*, 7, 23–4
Sheavyn, Phoebe, 144n8
Shore, David, 153n13, 155–6n25
Shuger, Debora, 161n9
Sidney, Philip, 4, 37, 46, 120; and Ponsonby, 149n48. *See also* Spenser
Simon, Joan, 148n28
Smith, Thomas, 50, 152n10
socio-cultural centredness, 30–2
Spencer sisters, 150n53. *See also* Lady Carew and Spenser
Spenser, Edmund: and audience, 81–3, 89, 91; and the court, 6, 34, 35–6, 40, 61–3, 65, 70, 112; and E.K., 40, 41; and Elizabeth I, 45, 71–2; and female patrons, 34–5; feudal values, 4, 36; and Harvey, *see* Letter and *The Shepheardes Calender*; and Ireland, 39, 70–1, 82, 101–9, 110–32, 147n18; and Kilcolman, 82, 117–18; and Lady Carew (Carey), 34–5 (*see also* "To Lady Carew"); and Lady Strange, 34, 35; and laureateship, 4, 40–1, 57, 60 (*see also Shepheardes Calender*); and Leicester, 36, 37, 40, 42, 44; and London, 39, 70–1, 77–8; and militant Protestantism, 97, 101–9; and Mulcaster, 6; and noble houses, 36, 37; on patronage, 40–6, 60, 66, 68 (*see also The Shepheardes*

Calender); and Petrarchism, 4–5, 39, 107–9, 110–32, 133–42; and Ponsonby, 30–5; and print, 94–7; printing of *The Faerie Queene*, 89, 92; and Ralegh, 4–5, 39, 97, 110–32, 133–42; and Sidney, 37–8, 40, 42, 43–5, 48; and Spencer sisters, 33, 36; and title-pages, 31, 92–3, 149n48
WORKS: *Amoretti*, 135; *Colin Clouts Come Home Againe*, 71–2, 112; commendatory poems of the 1590 *Faerie Queene*, 38–9, 69–87; "Epithalamion," 111; Letter to Harvey (1579), 42–3; *Mutabilitie Cantos*, 134–5; *View of the Present State of Ireland*, 104, 121, 147n18
— *Complaints*, 30–8; "The Ruines of Time," 36–8, 131–2
— dedicatory sonnets, 39, 91–109; printing of, 92, 94; "To Buckhurst," 94, 105–6; "To Burghley," 94; "To Lady Carew," 3–6; "To Countess of Pembroke," 101; "To Cumberland," 94; "To Essex," 101; "To Grey," 94, 102–5; "To Hatton," 97–9; "To Howard, Lord Admiral," 94, 95, 96–7; "To Hunsdon," 94, 95, 96–7; "To all the Ladies," 73, 100–1; "To Norris," 105, 107; "To Ormond," 94, 102–5; "To Oxenford," 99–100; "To Ralegh," 97, 105, 107–9, 116; "To Walsingham," 94, 101, 106–7
— *The Faerie Queene*: Book 2 (Bower of Bliss), 127; Book 3 (proem), 39, 110–16, (Timias and Belphoebe), 39, 77–8, 117–32, (Britomart and Paridell), 77–8, (Garden of Adonis), 135; Book 4 (Timias and Belphoebe), 133–42, (Amoret and Amylia), 136–7; Book 6 (dance of graces), 154n19; Letter to Ralegh, 72, 113
— *The Shepheardes Calender*, 38, 40–68, 81–2; "August," 66; "Aprill," 55–61, 154n19; "January," 41, 52–5; "October," 66–7; "June," 50–1, 52, 61–6, 153n12; "December," 67–8, 155n23

Spingarn, Joel, 156n3
Stern, Virginia, 152–3n10, 157n13
Stillman, Carol, 156n6
Stillman, Robert, 162n3
Stone, Jeanne Fawtier and Lawrence, 155n23
Strong, Roy, 147n17
Summerson, John, 155n23

Tennenhouse, Leonard, 145n8
Thomson, Patricia, 144n8
Timias, 39. See also Spenser, Works title-pages, 149–50n48. See also Spenser *Tudor Royal Proclamations*, 161n3
Tylus, Jane, 145n10, 150n2, 155n24

Variorum: Spenser's Works, 77
Virgil. See *Aeneid*

Waldman, Louis, 150n1
Walker, Julia, 158n36
Wall, Wendy, 149n45
Waller, Gary, 77, 144n4
Warnicke, Retha, 149n40

Webbe, William, 82
Wells, Robin Headlam, 158n1
White, Paul Whitfield, 145n8
Wilson, Derek, 150n59
Wilson, Jean, 146n13, n14
Wilson, Richard, 24, 146n12
Wilson, Scott, 147n22
Wilson, Violet, 147n17
Winton, John, 146n15
W.L.: commendatory poem, 84–6, 87. *See also* Spenser, Works
Wolfe, John, 89–92, 158–9n4. *See also* Spenser: printing of *The Faerie Queene*
Wofford, Susanne, 160n2
Wood, Michael, 148n35
Wright, Pam, 73, 156n9
Wyatt, Thomas: "The long love," 26–30; "Whoso list to hunt," 30; and Anne Boleyn, 149n40

Young, Charles. 148n30